Elements of Import Practice

Elements of Import Practice

Alan E. Branch

F.C.I.T., F.I.Ex.

Course Director
International Trade, Basingstoke College of Technology

Consultant to
UNCTAD and the World Bank

CHAPMAN AND HALL

LONDON • NEW YORK • TOKYO • MELBOURNE • MADRAS

UK	Chapman and Hall, 11 New Fetter Lane, London EC4P 4EE
USA	Chapman and Hall, 29 West 35th Street, New York NY10001
JAPAN	Chapman and Hall Japan, Thomson Publishing Japan, Hirakawacho Nemoto Building, 7F, 1-7-11 Hirakawa-cho, Chiyoda-ku, Tokyo 102
AUSTRALIA	Chapman and Hall Australia, Thomas Nelson Australia, 480 La Trobe Street, PO Box 4725, Melbourne 3000
INDIA	Chapman and Hall India, R. Sheshadri, 32 Second Main Road, CIT East, Madras 600 035

First edition 1990

© 1990 Alan E. Branch

Typeset in 10/12pt Bembo by Mayhew Typesetting, Bristol

Printed in Great Britain by St Edmundsbury Press Ltd,
Bury St Edmunds, Suffolk

ISBN 0 412 28480 4

British Library Cataloguing in Publication Data

Branch, Alan E. (Alan Edward) *1933*–
Elements of import practice.
1. Exporting & importing
I. Title
658.848

ISBN 0–412–28480–4

Library of Congress Cataloging-in-Publication Data
Branch, Alan E.
   Elements of import practice / Alan E. Branch. — 1st ed.
     p.   cm.
   Includes bibliographical references.
   ISBN 0–412–28480–4
   1. Imports–Handbooks, manuals, etc. 2. Freight and
freightage–Handbooks, Manuals, etc. 3. Shipping–Handbooks,
manuals, etc. 4. Import credit–Handbooks, manuals, etc.
   I. Title.
  HF1419.B73 1990
  658.7′2–dc20   90–1553
                                                    CIP

To
Joy and Maurice

Contents

Preface

Since the publication of my book *Import/Export Documentation* I have received numerous requests for a companion volume on Import Practice. This book has been written to provide an overall understanding of the theory and techniques of importing goods on a cost-effective basis, involving the complete competitive buyers contract. It is written in simple language and includes information on import buying technique and options; methods of payment and criteria of options available; customs and procedures; import documentation; import office; Incoterms 1990; processing the import order; cargo insurance; exchange rates; import finance; physical distribution and choosing the best transport mode; import facilitation organizations; agents; shipping/international trade terms and abbreviations; visiting the overseas territory to select a product and related criteria; and buying the product and its techniques. In short, it examines the whole area of developing an import-led business on a profitable and professional basis and reflects the author's 30 years' experience in the industry.

Successful importing is only realized through complete professionalism in product selection and in processing the import consignment cost-effectively. This book advises on the development of a profitable import to provide the best quality goods at the lowest possible price for the consumer or industrialist. It is full of useful hints and check lists to help the importer develop the business on a profitable basis. It deals with the subject from the time the business person decides to look overseas for the product until the product arrives at the importer's premises for resale, processing, or assembly, or industrial/consumer use. The appendices include an extensive glossary of relevant terms (Appendix E), although abbreviations are explained in the text to aid the reader.

The book is particularly commended to students taking import, shipping and transport examinations sponsored by Institute of Freight Forwarders Ltd, Institute of Credit Management, Institute of Materials Handling, Institute of Transport Administration, Institute of Bankers, Institute of Road Transport Engineers, Institute of Chartered Shipbrokers, Chartered Institute of Transport, London Chamber of Commerce and

Industry, City University, Leeds University, Bradford University, London School of Economics, UWIST-Cardiff, Plymouth Polytechnic, Kingston on Thames Polytechnic, City of London Polytechnic, Henley Management College, to mention only a few. It is also ideal for the student or executive of importation, shipping or overseas buying taking the short courses currently offered by local Chambers of Commerces and Trade Associations. The publication is also suitable for import and shipping courses in Malaysia, Malta, Jordon, Hong Kong, Thailand, Singapore, Australia, USA, India and Saudia Arabia. In short it is an *aide memoire* to those engaged in the industry and may be regarded as the 'importers' handbook'.

I am greatly indebted to the various organizations listed in the acknowledgements for their enthusiastic assistance; finally, I express my gratitude to my friends Mr and Mrs Splarn for their generous secretarial help, Maurice Hicks with proof-reading, and as always my dear wife Kathleen for her forebearance, encouragement and help in this task, especially with proof-reading.

AEB, April 1990

19 The Ridings   Course Director — International Trade
Emmer Green   Basingstoke College of Technology
Reading   Worting Road
Berkshire   Basingstoke
RG4 8XL   Hampshire
                                          RG21 1TW

Acknowledgements

The author wishes to acknowledge the generous assistance provided by the following companies and institutions.

Baltic and International Maritime Conference
Barclays Bank (International) PLC
British Importers Confederation
British Railways Board
Formecon Services Ltd
HM Customs and Excise
Lufthansa
Maersk Shipping Ltd
Midland Bank International
Morgan Freight Ltd
National Westminster Bank PLC
Ogel Ozalid Group (Export) Ltd
Simpler Trade Procedures Board

1 *International trade*

There are several reasons why nations began to trade with one another. The distribution of natural resources around the world is somewhat haphazard, so nations possess natural ores and chemical deposits in excess of their own requirements while other nations have none. For example, Britain has large reserves of coal but lacks many minerals such as nickel, copper and aluminium, whereas the Arab states have vast oil deposits but little else. In the cultivation of natural products climate plays a decisive role. Some products will only grow in tropical climates whereas others, such as citrus fruits, require a Mediterranean climate. Moreover, some nations are unable to produce sufficient of a particular product to satisfy a large home demand, for example, timber in Britain. These are the fundamental reasons for international trade but, with the development of manufacturing and technology, there arose another incentive for nations to exchange their products. It was found that it made economic sense for a nation to specialize in certain activities, and produce those goods for which it had the most advantages, and to exchange those goods for the products of other nations which had advantages in different fields. This trade is based on the 'law of comparative costs'.

Economists maintain that it will be advantageous for mankind if people specialize in those occupations at which they have the greatest comparative advantage, or the least comparative disadvantage, leaving others to produce the goods and services for which they have little aptitude. This principle is the basis of specialization into trades and occupations. Today it is paramount in the theory of international trade. At the same time, complete specialization may never occur even when it is economically advantageous. For strategic or domestic reasons, a country may continue to produce goods for which it does not have an advantage. The benefits of specialization may also be affected by transport costs: goods and raw materials have to be transported around the world and the cost of the transport narrows the limits between which it will prove profitable to trade. Another impediment to the free flow of goods between nations, in accordance with the principle of comparative advantage, is the possible introduction of artificial barriers to trade, such as tariffs or quotas.

The benefits derived from the development of international trade are: (1) cheaper goods because of the advantages possessed by the supplying country; (2) a greater variety of products available to the consumer; (3) wider markets for the producing country conferring the economies of large-scale production; and (4) the overall growth of trade due to the reciprocal advantages.

One must always bear in mind that in many markets a significant proportion of goods imported are re-exported. Such goods may be subject to processing or assembly techniques and thereby produce a value-added benefit to the product and end-user. Moreover, the development of an import-led economy brings wealth and job opportunities to the importing nation, plus technology and a much wider choice of products. It also raises living standards and in a balanced international economy exploits the law of comparative costs, both for importers and exporters.

1.1 MAJOR TRADING AREAS OF THE WORLD

There are four main types of economy:

1. Free enterprise economies, where government control is at a minimum and trade and industry are largely run by private enterprise; the best example is the USA, but many of the developing countries also have this type of economy.
2. Mixed economies, where some industries are state-owned but many others and most trading activities are in the hands of private firms. The United Kingdom provides a good example of this type, although in fact all advanced nations and many developing countries have at least some state-run industry.
3. Centrally-planned economies, where the state runs all industry and commerce except for tiny pockets of free enterprise such as the small-holdings on which peasants are allowed to grow a few vegetables to sell for cash. This sort of economy is generally communist-controlled and its international trade is conducted by state trading enterprises. In recent years trade has become more liberal. Centrally-planned economies are found particularly in Eastern Europe (COMECON) and in Asia and Latin America. They are managed according to annual and medium-term plans. The state has a monopoly of foreign trade in all these countries and trade must conform to these plans. Imports, exports and the use of foreign exchange are regulated accordingly. Importers deal through foreign trade organizations in such countries. Trade can sometimes involve compensation agreements which link the goods that a country wishes to import to the types of goods it wishes to export (see page 106). In 1990, COMECON trade was being liberalized.
4. State trading economies. Trade in some developing countries such

as Tanzania is conducted through state trading organizations. These organizations operate under the control of government ministries, the degree of control varying from country to country. Trading is linked to development plans and exports are generally connected to export marketing boards by product.

Trading patterns have gradually changed since the end of the Second World War. In the past, Western nations specialized in industrial products to exchange for the raw materials and food they required, whilst primary producers relied upon their sales of natural produce to buy industrial goods. Some countries with a favourable climate were able to combine industrial growth with the production of much of their food requirements. The United Kingdom is probably the best example of a country which relied almost entirely on the export of its manufactures in exchange for raw materials and food. Under the colonial system this was a very satisfactory arrangement for Britain, but with the end of the Empire the newly-independent nations began to cast their net more widely in seeking buyers for their produce and suppliers of their industrial needs. At the same time they sought to diversify their economies and develop some industry.

The basic geographical pattern of produce remains largely unchanged for reasons of climate and the location of raw materials — that is, Western Europe and North America for industrial goods; South America for coffee and rubber (Brazil), wheat and beef (Argentina) and minerals such as copper (Peru); the Near East for rubber and tin; Australasia for wool and mutton; and Africa for timber, cocoa and vegetable oils. However, these divisions are no longer as sharply defined as they were previously. Japan has entered the list of manufacturing countries in a very big way; the Arab nations have developed their oil production; and countries in South America, Africa and the Near East have now established their own industries. At the same time, the Western nations have attempted to come closer to self-sufficiency in food and to intensify the search for minerals at home; examples of this are the encouragement of agriculture and the search for oil in the United Kingdom and the development of fruit and vegetable cultivation in countries bordering the Mediterranean. The interchange of goods between nations is thus expanding, diversifying and moving away from the previously clearly-defined paths. The rate of change is accelerating as more developing nations and less developed/newly-industrial countries develop their industrial base.

1.2 PREFERENTIAL TRADING GROUPS

Since the very beginning of international trade, certain trading groups have felt a desire to join together for mutual protection and assistance.

An early example of this was the Hanseatic League founded in northern Germany during the thirteenth century, an arrangement that came to an end upon the disintegration of Germany as a result of the Thirty Years' War (1618—48). The more important preferential trading groups of modern times may be summarized as follows.

British Commonwealth

This was a free trade area of considerable importance, comprising the members of the British Commonwealth of Nations. As their economies became more highly developed, however, member nations ceased to maintain the system of preferences and sought a wider sphere of trading activity. The vestiges of the Commonwealth preference system disappeared when the United Kingdom joined the European Economic Community (EEC) in 1973.

European Free Trade Association (EFTA)

The United Kingdom was disinclined to join the EC at its inception in 1957, as the member states wished to go far beyond the removal of customs barriers. Accordingly, the United Kingdom, Norway, Sweden, Denmark, Portugal, Austria and Switzerland signed the Stockholm Convention in 1959 establishing the European Free Trade Association, whereby they agreed to reduce import duties among themselves and to maintain their individual tariffs towards non-member countries. Finland became an associate member in 1961 and Iceland a full member in 1970. Now that Denmark and the United Kingdom have joined the EEC, the significance of EFTA has declined considerably.

European Economic Community (EEC)

As the reconstruction of Europe was beginning after the end of the Second World War, there emerged the idea of a supernational European community based initially on economic union but developing towards political union. It evolved through the following stages:

1. Belgium, the Netherlands and Luxembourg formed the Benelux Customs Union in 1948.
2. The European Payments Union was set up in 1950 to help solve the balance-of-payments' problems of individual countries.
3. In 1952 six countries — Belgium, France, West Germany, Italy, Luxembourg and the Netherlands — joined together to form the European Coal and Steel Community.
4. In 1957 these six nations signed the Treaty of Rome by which they agreed to form the EEC, which came into existence on 1 January 1958. The Treaty provided for the removal of customs barriers and other obstacles to trade between member states, the introduction of a

common external tariff towards third countries and common policies for agriculture and transport. Plans were also made for the harmonization of taxation; for example, the French VAT system was to be adopted by the other members.

5. On 1 January 1973 the United Kingdom, Denmark and Ireland became full members of the EEC. By 1987 three more countries had joined — Greece, Spain and Portugal.

By 1992 the Single Market Entity will emerge involving 12 nations with no restrictions on trade permitting free movement of goods and services involving 320 million people.

Council for Mutual Economic Aid
Set up in 1949, the Council for Mutual Economic Aid (CMEA or Comecon) groups together the USSR, Poland, Romania, the German Democratic Republic, Czechoslovakia, Hungary, Bulgaria, Mongolia, Cuba and Vietnam. Although not a member, Yugoslavia enjoys special status that enables it to participate in certain spheres of Comecon's activities. The Council aims to attain self-sufficiency through the complementary development of member countries' economies on the basis of central planning. In its early years it contented itself with co-ordinating the foreign trade of member countries, many of which have been reluctant to agree to further proposals for integration.

Association of South East Asian Nations (ASEAN)
In 1967, Indonesia, Malaysia, the Philippines, Singapore and Thailand signed the Bangkok Declaration, formally recognizing the need for increased regional economic and political co-operation. The sixth member, Brunei, joined in 1984. The subsequent 1976 Declaration of ASEAN Concord provided for four instruments aimed at generating a more rapid pace of economic integration: preferential tariff arrangements (PTA); ASEAN industrial project (AIP); ASEAN industrial complementation (AIC); ASEAN industrial joint venture (AIJV). While the PTA seeks to facilitate increased intra-ASEAN trade, mainly through tariff reductions, the essential objective of the AIP, AIC and AIJV is to harmonize the economic structures of the member states by pooling their economic and financial resources and/or sharing markets. A secretariat was also set up to co-ordinate the operations of ASEAN.

Although ASEAN has deliberately adopted a cautious approach, progress towards faster economic integration has nevertheless been frustrated to a large extent by the difficulty in reconciling the principles of efficiency and equity when pooling resources and sharing markets. What may be considered efficient on economic grounds at the regional level may not necessarily be politically or socially equitable or desirable for an individual country, particularly if the loss of sovereignty, government revenue or employment is involved, even though this may be short term. By 1987 only four AIPS (area projects in Indonesia and Malaysia, a rock-salt/soda-ash project in Thailand and a copper fabrication project in the Philippines) and one AIC in the automotive sector have been identified and are at various stages of implementation, while the effectiveness of the PTA has been reduced by a lengthy exclusion list of sensitive items. Nevertheless ASEAN has shown solidarity in its joint approach to a number of sensitive international political and economic issues at the various international forums. This is best exemplified in ASEAN's collective attitude towards stabilizing export commodity earnings and in seeking to reduce the protectionist trade barriers in the OECD countries.

The benefits to be derived from free trade areas stem from the increased market opened to members, especially where the area has an affluent population. Their advantages are soon appreciated, and free trade areas have been set up in various parts of the world; it is estimated that about two-thirds of world trade is already conducted between such groups. Other free trade organizations include:

1. Latin American Free Trade Association (LAFTA), comprising Brazil, Bolivia, Mexico, Argentina, Colombia, Peru, Venezuela, Chile, Ecuador, Uruguay and Paraguay; in 1983 LAFTA was replaced by the Latin American Integration Association (ALADI), a less ambitious and more flexible form of co-operation.
2. Central American Common Market (CACM), whose members are Guatemala, El Salvador, Honduras, Nicaragua and Costa Rica.
3. Caribbean Free Trade Association (CARIFTA), the forerunner of the present Caribbean Community and Common Market (CARICOM), which comprises Antigua, Barbados, Belize, Dominica, Grenada, Guyana, Jamaica, Montserrat, St Christopher-Nevis-Anguilla, St Lucia, St Vincent and the Grenadines, and Trinidad and Tobago.
4. Andean Common Market (ANCOM) whose members are Bolivia, Colombia, Ecuador, Peru and Venezuela. It was formed in 1967.
5. The Nordic Council, formed in 1953 and comprising Denmark, Finland, Iceland, Norway and Sweden.
6. The Organization Commune Africaine et Malgache was formed in 1965 and comprises the Central African Republic, Dahomey, Gabon, Ivory Coast, Mauritius, Niger, Rwanda, Senegal, Togo and Upper Volta.

The activities of these various trading groups (with the exception of Comecon) have to conform to the principles laid down in the General Agreement on Tariffs and Trade (GATT), which requires its signatories:

1. to concert together to achieve a mutual reduction of tariff barriers and preferences;
2. to avoid discrimination by means of tariffs against foreign products which compete with home products;
3. to abolish quantitative controls; and
4. to remove existing restrictions imposed by exchange control.

Although several of these rules have been given practical application as trade has been liberalized, it is unlikely that the general requirements of GATT will be implemented in the present state of world trade.

An importer must take a close look at the foregoing preferential trading groups and identify those which best suit with regard to product quality, competitive pricing, ongoing commitment/relationships between buyer and seller, market profile, political situation and so on. Full use should be made of the National Chambers of Commerce (see Appendix B) and commercial attachés to obtain more data. At the same time advice should be sought from the relevant trading association and the Department of Trade and Industry. See also Chapter 12 and pages 247-50.

Particular attention should be given to the changing economic and political situation which will emerge as we progress through the 1990's in USSR, COMECON, China, EC, and Latin America.

2 *Import and shipping office*

Importing is a highly skilled and professional operation. To be successful an adequate and cost-effective organization designed to develop the company's business performance on a profitable basis is required. The size and structure of the company, its products and scale of import business will largely influence the form of import organization. The industrial company has three main functions: production, finance and sales. Additionally there are subsidiary activities which contribute significantly to the running of the company, including personnel, administration, research and development, training and purchasing.

If the company is rather small with only an element of import business, an import manager with a secretary and a clerk is probably adequate, but as the import trade grows, it soon becomes necessary to have a properly structured import organization with qualified, specialist staff. One can no longer rely on inexperienced, unqualified personnel in the import field (whether it be the overseas buyer, import manager/supervisor, or shipping clerk) as standards will tend to be low, and the overall financial results probably very indifferent.

The organizational structure of the import department differs widely by company, and many companies have a combined export and import office. It reflects the large number of importers who buy goods overseas and re-export them in a value-added form after processing, assembly or modification. This structure proves very cost-effective and often involves the use of common resources for both the export and import activities such as banks, freight forwarders and carriers. Much depends, of course, on the nature of the business, the products and the overseas territories involved.

The overall function of the import department is to ensure that the most satisfactory importation arrangements are undertaken and concluded. This will include documentation, finance, insurance, customs, distribution, and all the elements involved in the processing of an import consignment from the time the sale has been agreed until the goods arrive and financial settlement has been made. There must be close liaison at all times with the accounts department, and the retail, stock control

and marketing departments, as appropriate. The importer may be a distributor, in which case the import volume will be related to the sales
performance through the retail network. Alternatively the importer may
be receiving component parts for assembly into the finished product for
sale at home and overseas. At all times the import office must maintain
close liaison with the overseas buyer to ensure the best deal is concluded
relative to the import arrangements, especially in the areas of finance,
customs, physical distribution, volume and terms of sale (Incoterms
1990).

2.1   IMPORT OFFICE ORGANIZATION AND STRUCTURE

The smallest import department may consist of an import manager,
documentation clerk and account clerk. At first the department may be
engaged merely in processing orders secured under CIF (cost insurance
freight) (see page 185) but as the business grows the company may feel
cost advantages are obtained when the goods are bought under Ex
Works whereby the buyer undertakes all the arrangements for transportation, customs, insurance, cargo reservation and documentation. This
involves an evaluation of the most suitable method of despatch, and
requires knowledge of rates, services, routes, terminal charges, insurance,
documentation and so on; this is known as transport distribution analysis
(see Chapter 14).

The import department could have an input into the organization
responsible for buying the goods. Such an advisory role would include:
market profile; political situation; exchange rates trend; channel of
distribution options; packaging, cost and options; physical distribution
options, their cost and future developments. Such an input would be an
overview of the various overseas markets currently used and those
considered suitable for further evaluation. Close liaison would be maintained with carriers, freight forwarders, government departments,
customs, trade associations and underwriters to take full advantage of
new opportunities and efficiency initiatives. A continuing dialogue with
carriers and freight forwarders will also ensure that physical distribution
arrangements are satisfactory. These include transit test, claims investigation, customs clearance, documentation, total distribution costs, new
services/facilities such as LCL (less than container load), road transport
developments or air-freight consolidation. The opportunity should be
taken to establish which services the importer's competitors use, and
why.

Payment for the goods is a critical area which requires continuous
review to ensure the most appropriate terms are being used. Close liaison
should be maintained with the buyer's bank and regular reviews

undertaken to resolve any shortcomings and devise alternative arrangements. Such discussions could involve both the import manager and the overseas buyer.

A further area is the enforcement of rights in foreign courts of law. The import manager and overseas buyer must give special attention to the legal areas of their business and have special regard to the International Chamber of Commerce (ICC) regulations found in the ICC publications on Incoterms 1990 and Documentary Credits (see Appendix A).

2.1.1   Staff (see Figure 2.1)

Given below is a brief overview of the responsibilities of key import office staff, all of whom should be multilingual. It is likely, in moderate-sized companies, there would be up to ten import documentation clerks and a similar number of shipping personnel. A critical factor would be the overall work-load and the degree of computerization. With the development of EDI (electronic data interchange) and on-line computers to customs and carriers, the work-load can be much reduced (see pages 116-18 and *Elements of Shipping* pages 428-433 and 334-6).

Import manager
This senior manager is responsible for the efficient running of the import office and executing company policy. This involves formulation of and consultation about overall import strategy; preparation and adherence to budgets; input to the company business plan; liaison with freight forwarders, carriers, trade associations, customs, agents, banks, airports and seaports to obtain the most favourable terms; liaison with the overseas buyer, and other departments relative to import policy, terms of sale, buying policy overseas, production, assembly and distribution departments, and finance department regarding payment terms and strategy; training; monitoring as required the cost-effectiveness of import strategy in all the areas on a joint basis with the overseas buyer and other departments; appointing personnel within the import office; and liaison with senior management to develop the company's business on a viable basis through an import-led policy. The import manager is likely to be responsible to the production director, marketing director or purchasing officer and will probably undertake overseas visits to resolve problems. If the goods are re-exported the import and export offices would be a single unit under an international manager, with some degree of common resource integration such as the use of the computers and shipping office.

Import supervisor
This middle manager is responsible to the import manager for the

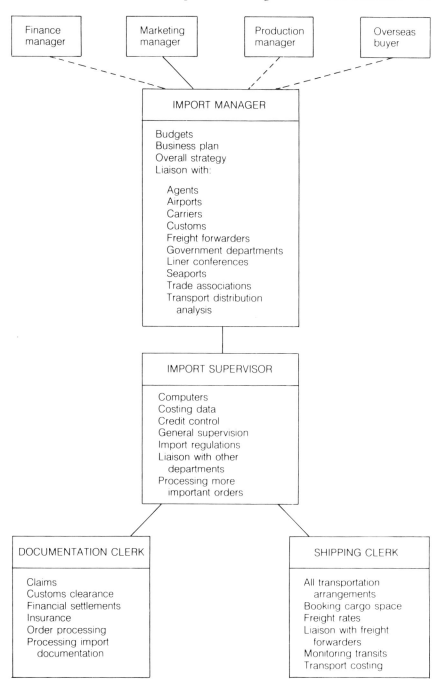

Figure 2.1 Import office organization

efficient running of the import office and deputizes for the import manager. The post also covers monitoring and interpreting import regulations; processing more important import orders, liaising with other departments regarding the interpretation and execution of import orders; credit control; monitoring budget data; liaison with overseas buyers; and contributing to strategy formulation within the import office and overseas buying policy. This involves regular reviews of overseas market profile and suppliers' portfolios. Most import offices use computers, responsibility for the efficient employment of which usually resting with the import supervisor.

Shipping clerk
The shipping clerk or shipping officer is responsible for all aspects of the transportation arrangements relative to the imported product. The post can be a busy one when goods are bought under the Ex Works Incoterm compared with CIF. It embraces the following responsibilities: freight rates; booking cargo space; monitoring transits; liaison with agents, freight forwarders and carriers; liaison with liner conferences.

Documentation clerk
The documentation clerk processes all the papers which ensure the goods arrive at the specified time and place. This involves liaison with the seller; order processing; customs clearance; liaison with customs clearance agent. This post also entails responsibility for payment of the goods in accord with the Incoterms 1990 and liaison with banks. The documentation clerk also effects insurance of the goods. The job can include claims and claims prevention. The position involves close liaison with the overseas buyers and the seller.

2.1.2   Order processing

Given below is a list of order processing activities; full use should be made of the import data folder found on pages 205-8.

1. Orders from the overseas supplier (consignor), to be acknowledged ensuring that no amendments are contained therein and that the delivery time-scale remains unchanged. Cargo delivery terms to be noted and responsibilities of buyer/seller identified. Each order to have a file number. Full details of overseas supplier to be established including name and address, contact name, telephone, fax and telex numbers. Supplier reference order number to be ascertained and time difference noted.
2. If relevant, the details of the representatives or agents (or confirming houses) of the overseas suppliers should be recorded, including name

and address, telephone, fax and telex numbers.

3. The buyer's details should be recorded, including name and address, contact name, telephone, fax and telex numbers.

4. Consignee and delivery address (if different to that of buyer) should be recorded, featuring contact name, telephone, fax and telex numbers. Action to be taken where appropriate on import licence number, payment terms and Letters of Credit — number and dates.

5. To check with the overseas buyer that the order complies with import controls and establish the method of payment, such as Letters of Credit, which have to be reconciled with the forwarding arrangements.

6. Transportation arrangements to be identified and task assigned to the buyer under Incoterms 1990. This involves documentation, rates, booking cargo space, customs clearance, loading point, vessel/flight number details, container number, Bill of Lading, Air Waybill, CMR or CIM number (see Appendix E), estimated arrival date, funding of transportation arrangements (including freight, customs clearance, customs duty, VAT and onward transportation from the seaport, airport, inland clearance depot (ICD), container freight station (CFS). The latter requires liaison with the credit controller. Freight may be prepaid or collect (payment by the buyer); insurance may be for the seller or buyer and related to the insured value (see page 125). It is also desirable to establish the details of clearing agent at the arrival seaport or airport — address, contact name and telephone, telex and fax numbers.

7. Compiling and maintaining the import order processing folder. This is likely to contain supplier's quotation, costing record, official order to supplier (copy), Letter of Credit details, import licence details, supplier order acknowledgement, supplier's despatch advice, instructions to import clearing agent, supplier's invoice (copy), Bill of Lading/Air Waybill/CMR/CIA (duplicate), SAD (Single Administrative Document) copy, insurance certificate, health certificate, supplier's Certificate of Origin and supplier's packing specification note.

8. Payment of the goods which may be by Documentary Letter of Credit, Foreign Bill of Exchange — documents against acceptance, or open account (see Chapter 7). This requires liaison with the credit controller and the buyer's international bank and the drawing up of an action plan regarding presentation of documents and payment of goods.

9. Progress chasing and liaison with the production, distribution and marketing departments regarding the estimated arrival date.

10. Recording any transit delays and cargo damage to ensure any claim can be effected and remedial measures instituted.

11. Maintenance of records of supplier's portfolios and other relevant data.

It will be appreciated the list is not exhaustive and each situation will vary. For example differing circumstances arise with dangerous classified cargo, livestock, chartered tonnage involving bulk shipment, household effects, and so on.

2.2 IMPORT POLICY AND RECORDS

The proportion of a manufacturer's business which is import-led is very much influenced by national policy. The chief concern of a company will be to combine stability with the highest financial return on capital obtainable. In some industries this is achieved by having more than one overseas supplier to counter any unpredicted situation which may arise. This is important where:

1. an overseas supplier may be cut off by changes in the export licensing laws or the political situation;
2. a sharp variation in the buyer's exchange rate in particular overseas markets may jeopardize the economics of dealing with the overseas supplier in the long term;
3. new import licensing laws may be introduced in the buyer's country;
4. a deterioration in the political situation may limit trade and cause a quota system to be introduced;
5. the legislation in the buyer's country regarding product specification may change and the overseas supplier may not want to continue business; perhaps the revised price will be uneconomic;
6. the end-user may be found, using market research, to require a different design which the overseas supplier is unable to meet.

Some businesses exist almost solely for import, with no significant home-based production unit. In such a situation it is prudent, where possible, to have the import markets broadly based to lessen the impact of any change of import circumstances such as detailed above. Unfortunately, with many products this is not practicable, especially in the consumer field when the commodity has a national identity and correlated strong market appeal.

2.3 IMPORT MANAGEMENT

It is important when examining the import office that we consider the import management structure and its constituents. It is desirable that it fulfils the needs of the overall company policy and objectives as contained in the company business plan. Overall, it involves the efficient use of resources. The following points are relevant:

Planning
This involves the identification of problems, opportunities, and formulation and realization of objectives within a time-scale and financial structure. For example, with the importation of component parts or raw materials this would involve finance, production and engineering departments. Special attention should be given to the attainment of objectives and performance monitoring to ensure delivery target dates are met on a cost-effective basis.

Organizing resources
This embraces the identification and selection of possible solutions to problems arising. The delivery schedule may have to be modified to meet an urgent home order, or the factory may change from one shift to a two-shift system, with ramifications on labour resources, availability of raw materials and components, transport, warehouse provision, and so on. Import volume might then have to be increased, possibly by obtaining supplies from another source.

Co-ordinating activities
This embraces effecting the decision and co-ordinating all the activities involved on a cost-effective basis within the objective and strategy laid down. An example is the execution of a major home market contract and the formulation of an overall plan, usually undertaken on a critical path analysis technique basis. This involves the import manager co-ordinating with other senior managers to devise and realize a cost-effective action plan.

Directing towards the objectives
This can arise in the research and development department whereby the sales director, through his management team and market research findings can provide guidance to the research and development department, for example. The overseas supplier is kept informed by the buyer of any likely change in the specification to meet end-user needs or to respond to competition.

Controlling activities
Realization of plans must be monitored and their performance and effectiveness measured; remedial measures should be taken if objectives are not being achieved. This requires effective chairmanship of the team of corporate managers.

Full use should be made of computer technology in all areas of import management. This includes developing adequate management information with continuous feedback systems.

Management policy is ultimately motivated by profit and this must feature uppermost in management strategy and execution. An adequate return on capital must be realized.

An increasing number of importers re-export their products. This may involve processing the raw material or assembling a component part with a home-produced item to make the complete product. Obviously adequate management control is essential if the importing process is to be successfully integrated within the company's production and sales strategy.

3 *Import buying*

3.1 EVALUATION OF METHODS OF BUYING PRODUCTS OVERSEAS

Buying an overseas product or service involves many considerations which will differ according to individual company and nature of product or service. The decision-making process will vary by company. Given below are the various factors to consider when deciding the most suitable method of an overseas purchase:

1. The type of product(s) involved and the product quantity. It may be a one-off purchase or a supply of component parts which is likely to feature in the 3- to 5-year company business plan.
2. The total cost. This will include the product selling price, distribution (freight), insurance, customs duty, VAT, and other charges. Contact HM Customs for the rate of customs duty and Inland Revenue for VAT.
3. The degree of competitiveness of the product compared with those in other overseas markets and the home market source. This embraces total cost, quality, design, warranty, spares availability and their cost; the product life cycle; operational life of the product; training needs and cost; degree of technology; profile of company and position in the market; prospect of repeat/replacement order (a company vulnerable to a takeover within 2 to 3 years may not manufacture the required product thereafter); and purchase options including outright purchase, leasing, hiring and so on.
4. The political and market profile of the overseas territory. This includes constraints on product availability due to trade quota limitations; trading relations between buyers' and sellers' countries; implications of any regulatory controls imposed through export and import licensing; and ease of access to the overseas territory. The more distant the seller's overseas territory the less convenient and more costly to maintain regular contact. For example, to the UK buyer, it is easier to purchase a piece of machinery in West Germany than in the distant market of Taiwan or South Korea. The latter two are distant markets

and present costly communication and visit problems on a reciprocal basis. Moreover, the two Far Eastern markets present a different profile in language, experience and their overseas selling infrastructure.

5. The compatibility of the selling and buying companies. Does the buyer feel comfortable about making the purchase from the prospective seller? This involves screening the seller's company, especially in the areas of product quality, ability to deliver the goods, design, technology, calibre of staff, commitment to the buyer, previous experience in overseas markets, analysis of other overseas buyers or customers in the buyer's country or elsewhere, product research and development programme, and financial position of the company including the seller's market share.

6. Any statutory regulations. This not only includes the need to ensure the goods comply with the standards of the British Standards Institute or of any other approved body, but also other import regulations on which the HM Customs and Excise can give advice. The UK regulations apply particularly to standards, health, safety, agriculture and defence.

7. The overall distribution cost. This requires careful evaluation in consultation with a freight forwarder. Full use should be made of groupage or consolidation services.

8. Packaging cost. It is usual, depending on the cargo delivery Incoterm used, for the overall packaging cost of the transit to be borne by the seller and included in the price. However, on arrival at the importer's premises, additional cost can be incurred in packaging the product for the consumer. As an alternative, skilful negotiations could make such packaging more cost-effective if done by the exporter to the buyers' specification.

9. The resources available in the buyer's company. It may prove advantageous to buy component parts rather than the finished product and undertake the assembly in the importer's warehouse, thereby having lower customs duty and freight distribution costs.

10. A wide range of buying option sources exists and these are examined on pages 21-7. The criteria of their selection must depend on individual needs.

11. Circumstances do sometimes arise whereby two importers work together to buy under joint arrangements, thereby obtaining a volume discount in the goods purchased and yield savings per unit product in distribution costs.

12. An increasing number of overseas territories conduct their sales through their export council or marketing boards. Hence the buyer deals with a corporate body and the negotiations can prove lengthy and tedious.

13. To avoid an unnecessary purchasing trip overseas it is important to assess prices both in the home market and other overseas market sources before making arrangements.

14. A sudden change in the exchange rate can jeopardize an order and future purchases. The buyer's bank can give guidance on exchange rate trends.

15. The buyer must, through adequate research, evaluate the product demand and devise the import strategy accordingly. Surplus stock through attractive bulk purchase can adversely affect the importing company's profitability.

16. Many importers are also exporters. Much benefit will accrue through cross-fertilization of experiences, contacts, and rationalization of resources within a company including, if practicable, using the same bank, freight forwarder, etc. This is particularly advantageous where the trade is undertaken in the same countries.

17. It is often wise for the first-time importer to buy from an overseas territory which the company knows well in market profile, and therefore presents few problems and offers low risk. A good starting point is to establish a suitable seller or commercial representative through the country's Chamber of Commerce or trade attaché at the Embassy. Usually the Chamber of Commerce has a trade directory and useful contacts can be made through telephone or telex to determine prices and obtain literature. A Market Research Agency can be engaged to produce a report on suitable markets to purchase a particular product. Further advice is available from British Importers Confederation, British Overseas Trade Board (BOTB), international banks, British Standards Institution, Department of Trade and Industry, the Chamber of Commerce or commercial/trade attaché attached to the country's embassy, the importers trade association, local Chambers of Commerce, and business reference libraries.

18. The financial status of the supplier. This can be checked out with the help of the importer's international bank who could have a branch office in the overseas territory.

19. Import credit needs are available from major international banks. Details are available on request.

To conclude our analysis, one must stress each item will vary in importance in individual circumstances. The list should not be regarded as exhaustive.

3.2 SELECTION OF A SUITABLE SUPPLIER

Having decided on the best method of making an overseas purchase it is necessary to select a suitable supplier:

1. Conduct desk research involving trade directories, the country's Chamber of Commerce, the commercial attaché to the embassy, the importer's trade association and other sources to identify potential suppliers.
2. Obtain from BOTB the country's Chamber of Commerce the commercial attaché to the embassy a profile of the overseas territories which manufacture the products required at the right price for the buyer.
3. Data obtained from items (1) and (2) must be pooled, discussed 'in house' and a shortlist of potential suppliers drawn up with the name of the director to whom an enquiry should be addressed. In the event of no suitable supplier being identified an advert could appear in the trade magazine or other media in the overseas territory. Advice is available from the country's Chamber of Commerce on this point.
4. The product specification should be despatched to the shortlisted suppliers and tenders/quotations invited. A preliminary telex, fax, telephone call, or letter could outline briefly the nature of the product required and suppliers who are interested could then be sent a more detailed specification. Telephone calls should be conducted in the language of the supplier to obtain maximum benefit from such an enquiry.
5. Depending on the product specification and quantity required, it is possible that the supplier will arrange a visit to the buyer's premises to discuss the matter and provide samples.
6. On receipt of all the quotations, the buyer must decide which to select and this will depend on total costs, quality, time-scale, etc. Prior to making a final decision a visit to several of the suppliers' factories may be desirable to meet the company's executives and workforce and thereby assess at first hand the profile of the company and the possibility of developing a good working relationship.
7. A decision could be taken at the conclusion of the overseas visit, although such visits are not usually undertaken for smaller orders. The supplier may however, visit the buyer to conclude the terms of sale. In making a decision from the responses to direct mail enquiries, little negotiation is conducted between the parties and agreements are concluded after careful scrutiny of the quotation and checking the profile of the supplier.

It will be appreciated each importer will conduct the supplier selection process according to the company's needs. Many small importers never see their seller or visit the overseas territory. Furthermore, a lot of business is done through mail order. However, personal visits and negotiations are most desirable for major contracts.

We will now examine the various buying options available to the importer.

3.3 AGENTS AND DISTRIBUTORS

An agent is a party (be it a person or a company) who acts for an exporter, the latter being the principal. The agent does not make a profit, but is paid commission at an agreed level on all orders secured for which his principal obtains eventual payment by the buyer. Usually the agent works for a number of principals which offer a cohesive group of products. The following kinds of agents are available:

Fee or retainer agent. An exporter setting up in the market will grant the agent in the initial stages an annual fee in the first one to three years to develop product awareness and build up a customer portfolio. Ultimately as the business develops the agent will operate on a commission-only basis.

Stockist agent. Under this arrangement, the agent buys from the principal for his own account and fixes the selling price. Hence the agent carries a stock of the principal's products and sells direct to the buyer on local terms. The agent's cost and profit is earned on the product 'mark-up'.

Consignment stock agent. Such an agent retains a nucleus of stock to meet buyer's immediate needs and exists in markets where the product is required quickly by the buyer. The agent operates on a commission basis.

Salaried agent. The agent is paid a salary with or without expenses or fringe benefit. This exists primarily for capital or industrial products where the agent would respond to a tender for a major project or contract emerging from a government's 5-year economic plan.

Del credere agent. This involves an agent selling on a commission basis (whatever the other terms of reference) and undertakes that orders passed to the principal will be paid for in due course by the buyer, thereby involving the principal in a credit risk.

Commission agent. An agent which sells on behalf of a commission, the salient features of whom is found in Table 3.1. This is the most common form of agency.

A distributor buys direct from the supplier and sells at his own price direct to the buyer on local conditions (see Table 3.1).

It is the practice amongst many suppliers, particularly from the Eastern Bloc countries, to have their representative in selected overseas territories. The countries targetted are those which enjoy a bilateral trade agreement.

Table 3.1 Comparison of the roles of agents and distributors

Agent	Distributor
1. Represents seller (principal) and does not usually carry stock.	Buys from seller and carries stock for sale to the buyer.
2. Leaves importation to the buyer; passes the buyer's order to the principal.	Imports the product — buyer purchases product on local terms.
3. Buyer negotiates price and terms of sale through the agent. Buyer arranges importation from the supplier. Product price will include in overseas territory plus distribution and insurance cost to the buyer's address usually under Incoterms 1990.	Distributor decides price level and terms of sale in negotiation with the buyer. Price will include product price plus any delivery charges to buyer's premises.
4. Agent paid commission at an agreed percentage by the principal on orders secured. Accordingly, principal fixes the price.	Distributor fixes the price and the mark-up represents distributors profit margin.
5. Agent carries no stock other than for showroom purposes.	Distributor carries stock.
6. Agent unlikely to be involved in publicity except when required to give advice.	Distributor devises own publicity and funds it out of the product sales.
7. Agent deals with buyer and passes details onto his principal the supplier. Hence supplier and buyer maintain close contact and supplier is able to establish consumer profile.	Distributor develops good relations with the buyer/end-user through customer liaison service, but the manufacturer/supplier is not aware of the end-user and is unlikely to have any direct contact with the buyer to establish consumer profile.
8. Agent may be authorized to engage sub-agents.	Distributor may appoint sub-distributors.
9. Agent has no control of resale prices.	Distributor controls selling prices in countries where retail price maintenance is possible.
10. All distribution arrangements are the responsibility of the buyer, who may buy under Ex Works, CIF, CFR, CPT, FCA or other Incoterms 1990.	Distributor imports the goods and the buyer purchases on local terms.
11. After-sales arrangements by various types of agents differ. Usually the agent and principal come to an arrangement for the agent to provide an after-sales service (particularly with industrial goods including spares) the cost of which is borne by the agent.	The distributor undertakes the after-sales service.

The agent represents the government and conducts business with local buyers.

To conclude our analysis of the agent and distributor, the buyer must decide the most effective method of purchase. Buying through an agent enables contact to be established with the supplier and some freedom of price manoeuvre may be possible coupled with other advantages. To buy from a distributor is primarily to conduct a local purchase with no supplier contact. Hence there is little likelihood of product development.

3.4 IMPORT MERCHANTS

The basic function of an import merchant is to buy goods in volume from an overseas source and sell them to the wholesaler or retailer in the home market. In reality the import merchant is the middleman conducting business from a warehouse and buying in bulk; a favourable price is therefore obtained which the small importer alone could not secure due to the low volume of business involved. Conversely the retailer or wholesaler buying from the import merchant has no direct contact with the exporter and thereby is unable to develop any business relationship in terms of product development and the exporting company's profile. Nevertheless, there do exist distinct advantages from buying from the import merchant:

1. there is no need to have an import section to handle the processing of the goods bought overseas;
2. a purchase from the import merchant yields quicker delivery time as it is a local delivery without any customs documentation and procedures or overseas freight distribution cost. This can be advantageous when goods are required quickly to meet an unexpected seasonal demand;
3. there are no hidden charges, merely the price of the goods plus transportation cost from the import merchant warehouse to the buyer's premises;
4. all queries are dealt with by the import merchant and not by the overseas supplier. Likewise all negotiations are conducted with the import merchant on the basis that it is a local sale;
5. all the financial risks of overseas purchase and holding stock rest with the import merchant.

Import merchants tend to specialize in their commodities which may limit the buyer's choice. Moreover, the pricing differential between the import merchant compared to the negotiated price between the importer and the overseas seller, supplier or exporter may be marginal. Details of various import merchants are usually available from the relevant trade association. Products from the Far East are frequently sold through import merchants.

3.5 INTERNATIONAL TRADE FAIRS AND EXHIBITIONS

International trade fairs and exhibitions are very much on the increase worldwide. They provide excellent opportunities for suppliers, large or small, to display a company's product(s) to would-be clients. The exhibit can be products such as cars, electrical machinery, computers and foodstuffs, or services such as travel, finance and insurance. Each year the trade fair/exhibition list grows and thereby aids the development of the exhibitors' client base. The trade fair or exhibition may be held annually or biannually and key exhibition stand sites are much sought after by the exhibitors; the exhibition is regarded by the trade as a major event in the calendar.

To the importer the international trade fair and exhibition offers much benefit in the search for quality products at a competitive price. The following points are relevant:

1. The importer can see at first hand the range of products available and evaluate them. A visit to an exhibition may identify more attractive suppliers in terms of price, design, quality, and so on. It may even point the way to developing component supply products rather than the finished product and assembling in the importer's factory. This may produce a better and cheaper product using more than one supplier and also yield savings on customs duty (see pages 27-9).
2. The first-time importer has an excellent opportunity to see at first hand the products on offer and negotiate with the supplier the best deal.
3. The cost of such a trade fair visit is relatively inexpensive, bearing in mind the concentration of suppliers at one centre and relatively large number of exhibitors which can be visited in a short period of time.
4. It develops the personal contact approach and tends to overcome the language barrier problem as most personnel at the exhibition stands are multilingual. Such personal contacts are very useful: often the first-time importer receives an invitation to the manufacturing plant which is a good business omen, showing commitment and interest on behalf of the supplier.
5. A large number of importers are keen to develop their business in related areas, such as the garden tools' importer looking for a supplier of garden furniture. Exhibitions provide the opportunity for such ideas to be explored and developed cost-effectively.

International trade exhibitions and fairs are well publicized. They feature in trade association journals, trade directories, and the trade press. The Department of Trade and Industry, the British Overseas Trade Board and Chambers of Commerce have up-to-date lists.

It is important to plan a visit to an overseas exhibition or fair carefully. Ideally, the buyer should identify the names of the exhibitors and their products and formulate a strategy regarding possible selection choice and their product costings. Over-priced goods will not sell in the importer's market. Such an analysis should take account of what is available in the home market and other supply sources. Long-term commitment by the supplier is an important consideration, especially in the area of after-sales.

3.6 OVERSEAS GROUP SELLING

Overseas group selling is the system employed when two or more manufacturers market their products jointly. Each principal retains its own individual activity as a manufacturer of the same merchandise or range of products, except that the goods maybe modified or the range extended to the overseas requirements.

The products dealt with form a cohesive group of manufactured goods normally handled by a specialist type of marketing channel or they represent a number of different types of similar merchandise of varying quality. Alternatively the goods must be produced under competitive conditions, but marketed by the group selling organization on a basis which eliminates such competition. The buyer has the advantage of dealing with the seller in his home country, enabling a good relationship to be built up quickly.

3.7 OVERSEAS SALES SUBSIDIARIES

An increasing number of major freight firms, especially multinational industries, have a sales subsidiary operating in the buyer's country. This enables the seller or importer to deal direct with the consumer, and thereby develop a good business relationship especially in the area of gearing the product specification to consumer requirements.

The sales subsidiary deals with the order and is responsible for the distribution, pricing and promotion of the product in the buyer's country. Hence, in reality the buyer is dealing with a local purchase and has no responsibility in regard to the importation and distribution arrangements, costs and risks. Moreover, there is no middleman as the buyer is dealing direct with the manufacturer's sales subsidiary. All queries are dealt with by the sales subsidiary and the conditions of sale reflect those operating in the buyer's country. Hence the purchase price of the product will be based on local conditions and the only likely additional charge is the delivery cost from the sales subsidiary's warehouse to the buyer's premises. In some cases the price will be inclusive of delivery. Some sales subsidiaries distribute direct from their warehouse whilst others tend to call forward stock from their overseas manufacturer and have only limited stock supplies.

3.8   TRADE JOURNALS AND DIRECTORIES

Numerous exporters obtain much of their business through advertising in overseas markets and given below is the broad selection of the data sources targeted to the potential importer.

1. Trade directories. A useful source, updated annually. Usually available in business reference libraries.
2. International trade journals issued monthly, or bimonthly. An example is the *Railway Gazette (International)*.
3. Importer association's year books and supporting magazines. An example is the bimonthly *Importing Today* magazine and the *British Importers Confederation Annual Year Book*.
4. Publications produced by the various importers' trade associations such as the Fruit Importers' Association, the Basketware Importers' Association, etc. Such associations can help the buyer find a suitable overseas supplier.
5. Journals/monthly newsletters/annual year books published by the Chambers of Commerce of various countries. These include the Italian, Japanese, New Zealand and Brazilian Chambers of Commerce (see Appendix D).
6. International banks produce trade bulletins at regular intervals and detail suppliers' products.
7. Trade exhibition directories feature all their exhibitors and their products.
8. Major national newspapers feature from time to time a survey commentary on a particular country. Such a survey will give a profile of the country and contain numerous manufacturers' advertisements.

3.9   TRADE MISSIONS

The British Importers' Confederations arrange trade missions to overseas markets, often in association with the import trade association. Usually they are supported by the host country's government. A full programme is devised and geared to meet individual importers' needs. The trade mission programme would include: air travel and hotel accommodation; attendance at all functions including travel, entertainment and leisure activities; attendance at trade exhibitions, seminars, and visits to manufacturing companies and their plants; and advice on trade procedures and regulations.

Trade missions are one way to find a suitable supplier and develop an ongoing business relationship. The number of participants is usually 20-25; individual needs are assessed before the visit and potential exporters programmed into the visit. The suppliers interested in the trade mission meet the delegation shortly after their arrival at an official reception which is usually hosted by the government or export trade association. Thereafter individual programmes can be progressed to provide opportunities for discussion, evaluation, negotiation and seeing at first hand the manufacturing base and meet the company's executives. Individual exporters plan the arrangements for such trade mission delegates and give presentations of their products in the importer's language and present senior executives to the potential buyers. At the same time they entertain the delegates who may be accompanied by their spouses.

Trade Missions are very much on the increase, particularly between countries which have bilateral trading agreements.

3.10 POTENTIAL SAVINGS IN THE COSTS OF IMPORTING GOODS

Skilful planning, adequate market research and objective evaluation can realize significant cost savings on importation of goods. Opportunities arise in distribution, packaging, customs, currency and so on. The more significant ones are given below.

1. A number of importers may be buying the same or similar product from the same supplier. The importers could all be based in the same country or neighbouring countries. Advantage would be gained if the distribution arrangements were centralized on one route with one carrier, goods being delivered to one destination from which they were despatched to the neighbouring countries or local importers. Hence imported citrus fruit from the Far East such as Malaysia or Thailand could be air-freighted to Brussels, Frankfurt or Paris, and distributed by road to importers in neighbouring countries. This would yield substantial air-freight cost reductions and could offer a more frequent service.

2. The customs tariff classification is based on the imported product description or specification. The duty level can change when it is regarded as a commercial product. Likewise the duty level will vary relative to a component part or finished goods. Over 15 000 items feature in the tariff classification (see page 79). A copy of the classification of goods in the harmonized system featuring the tariff classification and duty rate is available from the HMSO Publications Centre, PO Box 276, London SW8 (telephone 081-873-9090). Accordingly, company strategy should be examined at product design stage and component sourcing. Buying strategy should be similarly evaluated to ensure the goods are imported in such a condition to incur the lowest customs duty; for example, the importation of component parts will generate a lower customs duty than buying the finished product.

3. Currencies which are unstable can quickly jeopardize the economics of importation (see pages 108-15). Advice should be sought regularly from the importer's international bank.

4. Customs tariff suspension should be explored. This can yield cost savings and can be processed with the Department of Trade and Industry (DTI), or the importer's trade association. Full details are available in HM Customs Notices and feature in the weekly DTI publication, *British Business.*

5. Cost savings can be realized by using the same carrier and/or freight forwarder when the importer is also in the export business. It can yield discounts on freight rates and centralizes the administration and documentation arrangements.

6. Substantial custom duty concessions are available for products originating in specific overseas territories. They require a Certificate of Origin or commercial invoice duly authenticated to confirm the goods are manufactured and originate from a particular overseas territory (see pages 88-90). This is supplied by the seller and ideally should be confirmed with the supplier when evaluating the import source options. It may be that the exporter obtained the bulk of the product from another country, thereby removing any prospects of a Certificate of Origin being issued to benefit the importer. The same criteria of analysis enquiry should be obtained from a local purchase import such as an import merchant overseas sales office, to ensure imported goods specify the source of the manufacturing country. Again the importer should contact HM Customs for guidance.

7. The buyer is in a stronger position than the seller in negotiating an overseas sale. In many areas the buyer can dictate the terms but this can only be achieved through skilful negotiation. Moreover, it requires complete professionalism and ideally the ability to negotiate in the seller's language.

8. A number of countries conduct their trade within a bilateral trade agreement, involving a quota system. For example, the UK and USSR may have a trade pact of £3500 million spread over 2 years, with each trading partner buying £3500 million of goods and services during this period. The commodities are usually specified and the trade is developed through trade missions involving interested manufacturers and initiated at government level. The system is regulated by the import licence and the buyer should check out whether the permitted volume of goods to be bought will be within the quota system limitation.

9. The period entry (PE) system offers major benefits to the major importer and HM Customs are keen to see the facility become more popular with traders. It involves the importer supplying brief details to customs of the commodity at the time of importation. Subsequently, full customs and

statistical data are provided by using the trader's own computer system (see pages 88-90). It yields a substantial reduction in documentation costs and freight forwarders charges. Full details are available in a HM Customs Notice.

10. Another customs facility which can help the importer become more competitive is termed local import control (LIC). It is available to importers with ten or more full container or trailer loads per calendar month and enables the goods to be cleared by customs at the importer's premises. This obviates the need to clear the cargo at the ICD or seaport. Again details are available in a HM Customs Notice and importers are urged to discuss the matter with HM Customs.

11. For companies in the export market using imported components or raw materials, it is prudent to obtain written evidence of the supply source in order to obtain or claim any duty relief. The exporter may be using a home-based company to source the manufacturer and it is from the latter the documentary evidence should be produced regarding the importation source.

The foregoing list should not be regarded as exhaustive. Importers in their business plan must consider their import strategy and only resort to importation when the home market source is inadequate. It requires careful planning and much benefit can accrue to the larger importer by engaging a consultant to look at the current import policy and its competitiveness.

3.11 TRAINING THE OVERSEAS BUYER

In the past, company policy has unfortunately tended to ignore this area to the detriment of the company's results. The training of the overseas buyer involves a certain amount of theory and a great deal of practice, controlled by the guiding hand of experience. The successful trainee will learn how to identify the overseas seller, comprehend the criteria of selection, and conduct the successful purchase. One must bear in mind that every overseas contract involves the execution of four contracts: the contract of finance; the contract of insurance; the contract of carriage and the overseas sales contract.

Too many companies take the view that the successful home buyer can operate successfully in overseas markets. This is unlikely to be so and the competent overseas buyer must ideally have the following qualities:

1. Professional or technical qualifications in the area of the product or service.
2. Fluency in the seller's language.
3. Knowledge of Incoterms 1990 and the roles of buyer, seller, carrier, international bank and insurance broker.

4. Knowledge of the constituents of total price including product, insurance, packaging, transport, exchange rates, customs dues, import/export tariffs and VAT.

5. Knowledge of legal environment overseas.

6. Familiarity with import/export documentation.

7. Commitment, ability, and enthusiasm in the post with complete professionalism.

(Details of training courses available to the overseas buyer are available from the author.)

4 *Physical distribution*

Physical distribution involves the movement of goods from point A to point B by air, sea, road, rail, or a combination of these. An international road haulier carrying machinery from Munich to Birmingham will cross from Zeebrugge to Dover by ferry and use the motorway networks from Munich to Zeebrugge and Dover to Birmingham. Moving a furniture container from Bangkok to Manchester might involve a sea transit from Bangkok to Felixstowe and a rail journey from Felixstowe to Manchester.

Physical distribution is becoming more important to the importer as an increasing number tend to conduct the transportation arrangements from the seller's warehouse as found in Ex Works, or the departure port as under FOB (free on board). This places the onus of arranging all the transportation schedules, choice of transportation cargo reservation documentation, customs clearance, etc., on the importer. In most situations the importer appoints a freight forwarder in the seller's country to undertake all the distribution arrangements. The freight forwarder will work in close liaison not only with the importer/buyer but also with the seller/exporter and liaise with the correspondent agent, in charge of customs clearance and distribution, in the buyer's country. Hence, under an Ex Works contract, the seller would hand over the goods to the freight forwarder in the seller's country who in turn would arrange for the merchandise to be despatched to the buyer's address. On arrival in the buyer's country the correspondent agent would arrange customs clearance, and despatch of the goods to the buyer's premises as prescribed on the Bill of Lading/Air Waybill, etc.

The importer exercising the choice of transport mode(s) will be influenced by many factors and these are fully described on pages 238-43. However, two important determinants of such a judgement are the despatch of goods in the most economical way practical, and the physical characteristics of the transport mode, especially from the shipper's/importer's standpoint.

During the past decade the international physical distribution network has radically changed. Overall it has greatly facilitated the development of trade bringing markets closer together and opening up new markets. The following features are relevant.

1. Containerization is now operative in some 95% of deep-sea liner cargo trades. It offers a wide range of container types, quicker transits and provides a door to door service under LCL/FCL (less than container load/full container load) conditions, thereby favouring both the small and large importer.
2. Packing techniques have improved providing better protection, ease of handling, improved stowage, and often lower cost.
3. The development of the wide-bodied and combi types of aircraft have improved the economics of airline operation favouring the expansion of the air-freight market. In particular larger payloads and better deployment of the unit load concept.
4. The International Air Transport Association (IATA)-accredited agent has opened up the air-freight market by offering competitive rates and frequency of service under freight consolidation between key airports on an international scale. In so doing the agent guarantees to the airline, on specific flights, a cargo volume for which the airline provides a discounted overall rate. This allows the agent to offer inclusive rates to the shipper at a very competitive level, embracing not only the air-freight, but also collection, customs clearance, and documentation cost. Hence, on one flight the agent may despatch some 60 consignments under one consolidated shipment.
5. Documentation has been rationalized, the best example being the introduction of the Single Administrative Document (SAD) (see pages 77-9).
6. Combined transport operation has been developed thereby lowering distribution cost, yielding quicker transits, and achieving high utilization of the transport infrastructure on the most viable basis practicable.
7. Numerous seaports and airports have been modernized worldwide to improve cargo handling techniques and cater for the modern transport unit on a viable basis.
8. Governments worldwide are increasing their interest and commitment towards developing their nation's external trade performance. Many countries with hard currency and debt repayment problems are exercising stringent control over the level of imports. Moreover, many such countries insist on such import cargoes being conveyed on their national shipping line or airline to save hard currency. Such a policy in shipping is called 'flag discrimination'.

It is against this background that the importer must conduct his business on a competitive basis, exercising prudence, diligence and sound judgement on the best method(s) of physical distribution. The following considerations apply:

1. To the importer dealing with small consignments the consolidated shipment by air-freight, container or road trailer should be used. Such consolidation is organized by an IATA agent for air-freight; the freight forwarder or shipowner for the LCL container movement; or the freight forwarder or international road haulier for the trailer or truck movement. Details of such consolidated services are found in the shipping press and air-freight publications.

2. A number of importers in some trades actually collect the goods from the seller's warehouse using the importer's transport. This can be advantageous especially where purpose-built vehicles are concerned and regular shipments are involved. It does ensure all the movement arrangements and cost are under the control of the importer, but usually involves the importer's transport incurring an empty leg for the outward journey which can prove uneconomical.

3. Importers frequently enquire whether it is best to use an agent for all their business in a particular trade or to have one for air-freight and one for surface distribution. The latter is usually preferable but in large-volume, regular shipments it maybe prudent in surface transport to use two different shipowners which will lessen the impact of any industrial dispute affecting one shipowner but not the other.

4. Importers are encouraged to ship their goods on an indivisible load basis rather than CKD (completely knocked down) requiring the merchandise to be assembled on the site at the importer's premises. This produces less commissioning problems and ensures the merchandise is operational immediately on arrival. Guidance in this area can be sought from the importer's agent, shipper's Council or trade association.

5. Importers fresh to the business and uncertain of the best method of distribution can often obtain useful information and guidance by studying the methods of their competitors.

6. Many importers opt for the shortest route but this does not necessarily result in the shortest transit time and can be the most costly method. A tortuous route with a high trade volume can prove to be cheapest and quickest.

7. In some trade markets there may exist a dispersed distribution network, as with goods from the Far East or Africa. A cluster of departure and arrival ports may be involved, centralized with substantial cost savings due to consolidated consignment and feeder services developed from and to the central departure and destination seaports or airports. Again a study of the distribution network requires to be made by all concerned including airlines, shipowners, shippers, trade associations and freight forwarders.

8. Packing cost can represent a formidable expense in the distribution expenditure. Such cost can be reduced significantly by using the

correct packing technique, or by despatching the goods by air or container. Proper guidance should be sought from the shipowner or airline.

9. The stowage arrangements for FCL traffic should be studied regularly. The importer, by skilfully varying the product specification and/or packing design, may be able to adopt modifications which increase the utilization of the container's or trailer's cubic capacity, thereby reducing the cost per unit conveyed.

10. The importer should study closely the airports and seaports through which his goods can be routed. Establish their charges, clearance efficiency, industrial relations record, users of the airport or seaport, convenience of the airport or seaport to both the seller and buyer, and so on. Again, establish which airports or seaports the competitors are using and for what reasons.

The foregoing considerations should be reviewed in the light of any Transport Distribution Analysis undertaken as explained in Chapter 14.

Given below is a checklist the importer may chose to use when reviewing or selecting a suitable freight forwarder or carrier to undertake the conveyance and importation arrangements.

1. Establish the freight rate and the nature of the tariff structure offered by the freight forwarder or carrier, in particular the nature of the W/M ships option (see pages 66-7) and the criteria of its application. For example the W/M ships option may be based on the FAK (freight all kinds) basis involving a common rate for all commodities. Alternatively it may be a commodity-based tariff involving a group of six commodity classifications.

2. The currency on which the tariff is based — sterling, US dollars, French francs, etc.

3. Documentation and customs' clearance — import or export charges.

4. Routeing of the cargo. Establish the charges at the relevant airports or seaports and their overall efficiency, especially in the area of customs' clearance and handling charges.

5. Transit time, overall schedule, involving departure and arrival time and general reliability of the service including its industrial relations record. This should include general 'loadability' of the transport units and packing cost.

6. The trading conditions of the freight forwarder, carrier, etc. and credit terms such as payment of billed invoice within one calendar month of postal date.

7. Scale of rebate or discount on the freight tariff relative to volume shipments for specific period (usually one year).

8. Location of the warehouse or distribution centre relative to the location of the seller's and buyer's premises — convenience, scale of charges and transport costs.

9. The CAF (currency adjustment factor) and BAF (Bunker adjustment factor) and the basis of its calculation.
10. Experience of other shippers using the service. Contact a couple of regular users of the service and evaluate their views of the service especially in the areas of cost, reliability, market profile and quality of management.
11. Nature of the service and quality of management. In particular the level of technology and service infrastructure.
12. An evaluation of the service's main competitors.
13. The track record of the service during past 3 years and its plans for the future.
14. The prospects of a test transit of the new service.

The foregoing analysis should be undertaken regularly by the importer, especially when the market situation changes.

We will now examine the various types of transport modes and how they favour the importer.

4.1 CONTAINERIZATION

Containerization is a method of distributing merchandise in a unitized form, thereby permitting an intermodal transport system to be evolved. The system is long established and today some 90% of major deep-sea trades conveying general merchandise are containerized. It is the most modern form of physical international distribution and overall is highly efficient in terms of reliability, cost, quality of service, advanced technology and so on. It enables the importer to receive the goods in a quality condition and opens up new markets continuously as new services are introduced and the range of container types continues to grow. Countries featuring on the container network are able to develop their market either as an importer or exporter. It has brought markets closer together and thereby improved the prosperity of many nations.

The International Air Transport Association has also encouraged the development of its own type of container to facilitate air-freight distribution. It is ideal to the importer and offers concessionary rates (see pages 60-5).

The container has brought a new era in international trade distribution to both the small and large importer. The importer may use a complete ISO (International Standards Organization) container (FCL) or, if LCL, despatch his merchandise to a container base, freight station or inland clearance depot for it to be consolidated with other compatible cargo to a similar destination country or area for despatch.

Features of containerization can conveniently be summarized as follows:

1. It permits a door-to-door service which, with the ISO or IATA container, may be a distance of several thousand kilometres from the factory production site to the retail distributors store. It must be appreciated that many airline operators today convey cargo on the air-freighter under the unit load device (ULD). This permits concessionary rates being given to shippers.

2. There is no intermediate handling at terminal transhipment points, i.e. the seaport or airport.

3. The low risk of cargo damage and pilferage enables more favourable cargo premiums to be obtained, compared with break-bulk cargo shipments and individual air-freight consignments.

4. Elimination of intermediate handling at seaports permits substantial dock labour savings, particularly in industrial countries where there is a high income per capita.

5. Less packing is required for containerized consignments. In some cases, particularly with specialized ISO containers such as refrigerated ones or tanks (liquid or powder), no packing is required. This produces substantial cost savings in the international transit and raises service quality.

6. The elimination of intermediate handling, coupled with the other inherent advantages of containerized shipments, tends to permit the cargo to arrive in a better condition thereby aiding quality of service and market development.

7. Emerging from the inherent advantages of containerization, rates are likely to remain more competitive. A significant reason is that containerization is, in the main, a capital-intensive transport network, compared with the individual consignment distribution system which tends to be more labour intensive. This is particularly so with maritime container distribution which has produced substantial labour cost savings.

8. Maritime container transits are much quicker compared with break-bulk cargo. This is usually achieved through a combination of circumstances — faster vessels, rationalization of ports of call, substantially quicker transhipments. For example, on the UK—Australia service the schedule has been reduced by half to less than 4 weeks.

9. Faster transits and the advantages under items (6) and (7) encourages trade development and permits quicker payment of export invoices.

10. Maritime containerization has permitted maritime fleet rationalization, producing substantial capital cost replacement savings as fewer ships are needed. However, these ships must be more intensely operated and of overall larger capacity. On average, one container ship (usually of much increased capacity and/or faster speed) has displaced up to seven 'tween deck vessels on deep-sea services. This development has been facilitated by the rationalization of ports of call.

11. Container vessels attain much improved utilization and generally are very much more productive than the 'tween deck tonnage.

12. Faster transits usually coupled with more reliable maritime schedules, and ultimately increased service frequency is tending to encourage many importers in selective shipping trades to hold reduced stocks and spares. This produces savings in warehouse accommodation needs, lessens risks of obsolescent stock and reduces importers' working capital. These are good selling points to bear in mind by the shipper when deciding the mode of transport to be used.

13. Containerization produces quicker transits and encourages rationalization of ports of call. This in many trades is tending to stimulate trade expansion through much improved service standards. This is resulting in increased service frequency which will aid trade development.

14. There is provision of through documentation (consignment note), e.g. Air Waybill or Combined Transport Bill of Lading.

15. A through rate can be obtained, for example, embracing both the maritime and surface transport cost of the ISO container. Again, this aids marketing the container concept.

16. Transits are more reliable, particularly disciplined controlled transit arrangements in maritime schedules. Most major container ship operators have computer equipment to facilitate the booking, stowage and control of containers.

17. New markets have emerged through container development and its inherent advantages.

18. Maritime containerization is a capital-intensive project and as such is beyond the financial limit of many shipowners.

19. Not all merchandise can be conveniently containerized. The percentage of such traffic falls annually as new types of maritime containers are introduced.

20. Maritime containerization has greatly facilitated the development of consolidated or break-bulk consignments. This particularly favours the small importer with LCL which can be consolidated through a container base.

21. Containerization facilitates the maximum use of computerization in many areas, especially container control, customer billing, container stowage on the vessel and documentation processing.

A wide range of container types exist and these are detailed in Table 4.1 which deserves close study. A selection of container types is detailed below.

General purpose.   This closed container is suitable for the carriage of all types of general cargo and with suitable temporary modification for

Table 4.1 ISO container dimensions by type

Container type	Overall dimensions – ft (m) Length Breadth Height	Minimum interior dimensions (mm) Length Breadth Height	Door dimensions (mm) Breadth Height	Minimum cubic capacity (m³)	Maximum tare weight (kg)	Maximum gross weight (kg)
General purpose	20 × 8 × 8.5 (6.1 × 2.4 × 2.6)	5 890 2 345 2 400	2 335 2 290	32.7	2 450	24 000
General purpose	40 × 8 × 8.5 (12.2 × 2.4 × 2.6)	12 015 2 345 2 362	2 335 2 260	66.3	3 700 – 4 380	30 480
Insulated	20 × 8 × 8.5 (6.1 × 2.4 × 2.6)	5 760 2 260 2 235	2 260 2 215	29.0	2 413	24 000
Fruit	20 × 8 × 8.5 (6.1 × 2.4 × 2.6)	5 770 2 300 2 275	2 300 2 215	30.2	2 362 – 2 732	24 000
Refrigerated	20 × 8 × 8.5 (6.1 × 2.4 × 2.6)	5 450 2 260 2 247	2 260 2 247	27.7	3 460	24 000
Refrigerated	40 × 8 × 8.5 (12.2 × 2.4 × 2.6)	11 550 2 270 2 200	2 270 2 170	57.8	4 670 – 4 940	30 480
Bulk	20 × 8 × 8.5 (6.1 × 2.4 × 2.6)	5 892 2 347 2 379	2 335 2 285	33.1	2 730	24 000
Ventilated	20 × 8 × 8.5 (6.1 × 2.4 × 2.6)	5 892 2 303 2 380	2 305 2 273	32.3	2 720	24 000

Side openings (mm) Length Height

Container type	Overall dimensions – ft (m) Length Breadth Height	Side openings (mm) Length Height	Minimum cubic capacity (m³)	Maximum tare weight (kg)	Maximum gross weight (kg)
Flat-rack	20 × 8 × 8.5 (6.1 × 2.4 × 2.6)	5 576 2 310	31.9	2 610 – 2 810	30 480
Flat-rack	40 × 8 × 8.5 (12.2 × 2.4 × 2.6)	11 662 2 134	58.6	5 960 – 6 100	40 640

Table 4.1 contd.

Container type	Overall dimensions – ft (m)			Overall interior dimensions (mm)			Door dimensions (mm)		Roof aperture (mm)		Minimum cubic capacity (m³)	Maximum tare weight (kg)	Maximum gross weight (kg)
	Length	Breadth	Height	Length	Breadth	Height	Breadth	Height	Length	Breadth			
Open-top	20 × 8 × 8.5 (6.1 × 2.4 × 2.6)			5 890	2 345	2 340	2 335	2 260	5 712	2 175	32.4	2 093 – 2 513	24 000 – 30 480
Open-top Tarpaulin top-sliding roofs bows	40 × 8 × 8.5 (12.2 × 2.4 × 2.6)			12 025	2 247	2 305	2 235	2 200	11 832	2 150	63.47	3 949 – 4 650	30 480
Half-height	20 × 8 × 4.25 (6.1 × 2.4 × 1.3)			5 906	2 313	1 075	2 280	1 003	5 775	2 224	14.3	1 724	24 000
Half-height	40 × 8 × 4.25 (12.2 × 2.4 × 1.3)			12 010	2 235	940	2 284	980	11 900	2 073	25.2	3 656	30 480

Container type	Overall dimensions	Total water capacity (l)	Tare weight (kg)	Tank material	Gross weight (kg)
Tank	20 × 8 × 8.5 (6.1 × 2.4 × 2.6)	24 000	3 150	Stainless steel	30 480

Table 4.1 contd.

Container type	Overall dimensions - ft (m) Length Breadth Height	Minimum interior dimensions (mm) – gates in position Length Breadth Height	Minimum door dimensions (mm) Breadth Height / Door dimensions (mm)	Minimum side dimensions (mm) Length Height	Minimum cubic capacity (m³)	Maximum tare weight (kg)	Gross weight (kg)
Open-sided	20 × 8 × 8.5 (6.1 × 2.4 × 2.4)	5 895 2 310 2 300	2 335 2 180	5 602 2 235	31.1	3 365	24 000 – 30 480
Bulk	20 × 8 × 8.5 (6.1 × 2.4 × 2.6)	5 892 2 347 2 379	2 335 2 285		33.1	2 730	

the carriage of bulk cargoes, both solid and liquid. The containers are basically a steel framework with steel, glass reinforced plastic or aluminium alloy used for cladding; the floors are either hardwood timber planked or plywood sheeted. Access for loading and unloading is through full-width doors. Aluminium cladded containers have plywood lined interior walls. Cargo securing and lashing points are located at floor level at the base of the side walls.

With suitable temporary modifications solid bulk commodities, granular or powder, may be loaded into general purpose containers. These modifications, depending on the nature of the cargo to be loaded, usually involve the location of a bulkhead at the door end of the container and in most, but not all, instances the fitting of a polythene liner.

This method of transport has proved successful in reducing costs to both shipper and consignee due to the reduction of manpower involved in both loading sacks or bags and the stuffing and/or stripping of same into and out of the container. The cost of packaging e.g. polybags, is of course eliminated. The commodity payload may also be increased thus allowing an increased cargo-to-freight margin.

Before implementing a bulk movement system it is necessary to ensure that:

1. the loading point is capable of loading bulk, i.e. that throwers, blowers, etc. capable of end-loading are available;
2. suitable receiving facilities are available, e.g. bulk silos, receiving hoppers, etc., and that premises (if under-cover) are high enough to accept a container when in the tipping position;
3. tipping trailers are available at the final destination.

It is also possible to transport certain non-hazardous bulk liquids in general purpose containers which have been fitted with special flexible tanks. These tanks are laid out in the container and a securing harness attached. A bulkhead is then positioned at the door end of the container and the left-hand door closed. The tank is then ready for fitting.

Insulated. These containers are insulated against heat loss or gain and are used in conjunction with a blown-air refrigeration system to convey perishable or other cargo which needs to be carried under temperature control. Internally the container is equipped with an aluminium T-section floor and the inside face of the doors are fitted with moulded vertical battens to permit air-flow around the cargo. It is important when cargo requiring temperature control is loaded in this type of container that an air space of approximately 7.5 mm is left over the top of the cargo to allow free air circulation. Securing points are positioned along each side of the floor, and lashing points are sited at the door end of the container by the corner posts to prevent cargo falling out.

The fruit container. This has been developed to carry fresh, deciduous and citrus fruits, the internal dimensions being slightly larger than the standard insulated container to accommodate the packing of standard fruit pallets and cases. The internal structure of the fruit container is basically the same as the insulated container.

Refrigerated. These containers are designed to operate independently of a blown-air refrigerated system and are fitted with their own refrigeration units which require an electrical power supply for operation. Each container is capable of being set at its own individual carriage temperature. The internal structure of these containers is similar to that of the 'port hole' insulated container with alloy T-section floor and securing points each side at the base of the side walls and fall-out lashing points at corner posts. The container is of steel construction with the cladding of stainless steel lined or aluminium alloy. The electrical supply will usually operate on either 200-220 volts, single phase or 380 to 440 volts three phase at 32 amps both at 50/60 Hz.

Bulk. These containers are designed for the carriage of dry powders and granular substances in bulk. To facilitate top loading three circular hatches (500 mm in diameter) are fitted in some containers in the roof structure. For discharge a hatch is fitted in the right-hand door of the container. Full-width doors are fitted to allow loading of conventional cargo. Constructed of steel framework with steel cladding, the containers are usually equipped with mild steel floors for ease of cleaning. Lashing points are fitted at the base of the side wall and at the top of the container along the top side rails to enable the securing of polythene liners (if required).

Ventilated. These containers are of steel construction. They are broadly similar to the general purpose container specification, except for the inclusion of full-length ventilation galleries sited along the top and bottom side rails, allowing the passive ventilation of the cargo, but preventing the ingress of water. They are ideal for such products as coffee.

Flat-rack. This type of container is designed to facilitate the carriage of cargo in excess of the dimensions available in either general purpose or open-top containers. They consist of a flat bed with fixed ends, the external dimensions conforming in all respects to the ISO requirements. Suitable lashing points are fitted to the floor and/or side rails of the container with in some cases, four corner rings. A combination of two or more flat-rack containers can be used to form a temporary 'tween deck space for uncontainerable cargo moved on a 'port-to-port' basis, provided the total weight and point loading the cargo does not exceed the static capabilities of the flat racks.

Open-top. This container, with its top-loading facility, is designed for the carriage of heavy and awkward shaped cargoes and those cargoes whose height is in excess of that which can be stowed in a standard general purpose container. The floor of the container is of hardwood timber plank or plywood, and there are a number of cargo securing points in the floor or along the bottom side rail at the base of the side walls. The container has a removable door header either removable or sliding roof bows to allow loading to be effected either directly through the roof aperture or through the door using overhead lifting equipment. Tarpaulin tilts are available to protect the cargo. There are also containers with overheight tilt for use with overheight cargo which can be described as an open-sided/open-top type.

Half-height. The half-height version of the open-top container is designed for the carriage of heavy, dense cargoes such as steel, pipes and tubes. It is ideal for shippers whose premises have a restricted height for loading or discharge. The steel containers have a tarpaulin top, a removable door header bar and securing points set into the floor.

Tank. Tank containers are generally constructed with the carriage of a specific product or range of products in mind. It is usual for shippers to provide their own tanks. Such containers are owned or leased by the shipper. They are usually constructed of stainless steel and for liquid cargoes may be used for either dangerous goods or non-hazardous cargo. A wide variety of products are shipped in tank containers ranging from the wet to dry bulk cargoes. Many are dedicated to one product.

Open-sided. This type of container is designed to accommodate specific commodities such as plywood, perishable commodities and livestock. These steel containers have a fixed roof, open sides and end-opening doors, the sides being closed by full height gates in 1.37 m wide sections, and nylon reinforced. PVC curtains (the curtains maybe rolled up to the top side rail when not in use) which meet TIR (Transport International Routier) requirements. There are eight lashing points each side affixed to the bottom side rail (outside) below floor level, nine rings located in the floor and five rings vertically up each corner post.

High cube reefer. These containers are 12.2 m long, 2.4 m wide and 3.0 m high. They are equipped as the refrigerated containers.

Artificial 'tween deck. This type of container is without end walls, side walls or a roof and also known as a platform carrier. It is 6.1 m long and 2.4 m wide or 12.2 m long and 2.4 m wide. These units are used for oversized and overweight cargo which cannot otherwise be containerized. By combining several artificial 'tween decks on board a vessel it is possible to obtain a very high payload (see also flat-rack containers).

Hanger.   This type of container is used for dry cargo and is equipped with removable beams in the upper part. It is used for the shipment of garments on hangers. It is 12.2 m long, 2.4 m wide and 3. 0 m high, or 6.1 m long, 2.4 m wide and 3.0 m high. A container has been developed and operated by Maersk which has a 27% larger cubic capacity than the general purpose container. It is termed a 'super high cube' and is 13.7 m long, 2.4 m wide and 3.0 m high.

Bin.   This type of container has a cargo capacity of 21 600 kg and a tare weight of 2400 kg. Its length is 6.06 m, width 2.44 m and height 1.30 m. It is ideal for heavy dense cargoes such as steel, pipes, etc. It has no doors.

Bolster flat.   This type of container has a cargo capacity of 23 000 kg and a tare weight of 1940 kg. Its length overall is 6.06 m, width 2.44 m and height 0.23 m. It is ideal for a variety of heavy cargoes.

The average operational life of a container is 12 years. As we enter the 1990s, the fourth generation of container vessel will be operative. It has a capacity of 4000 TEU (see glossary in Appendix E) and will further reduce the cost in real terms of distributing goods. Such vessels are likely to rely more on feeder container services. Moreover, the fourth generation container vessel will have fewer ports of call and rely on major ports. The importer is strongly advised to contact his freight forwarder or shipowner to determine what is available and how best the container network can help develop the importer's business profitability.

4.2   INLAND WATERWAYS

It is desirable the importer recognizes the importance of inland waterways as a method of distribution on an increasing scale in many markets. This applies especially in the Netherlands, West Germany and France, where between 10 and 40% of freight is conveyed by inland waterway.

The inland waterway system is linked to the seaport and thereby acts as a distributor and feeder to the shipping services. In some countries, especially underdeveloped ones, inland waterways are a major form of distribution as the road and rail systems are unable to cope or are non-existent in many areas. The following features are relevant:

1. The transits are slow compared with road or rail.
2. Many of the inland waterway users, especially in overseas territories, have warehouses on the network.
3. The rates are low and very competitive.
4. It relieves port congestion through overside loading and discharge and eliminates the cargoes passing through the port warehouse which can prove costly in tariffs and time-consuming through customs processing and tallying.
5. It is ideal for loose cargo.
6. It is suitable for a range of commodities extending from general cargoes to bulk shipment of timber, coal, oil, chemicals and so on.
7. It speeds up the turn-round of vessels.
8. The capacity of the barges and lighters using the inland waterway system varies enormously. In the European market with its modern system and well organized distribution network, the craft can be up to 5000 tonnes capacity, rising to 10 000 tonnes when the pusher technique on the River Rhine is used. In areas such as the Far East, Africa, and South America the systems are more primitive but nevertheless effective and long established.

The UK canal network has less than 1% of the market share and therefore plays a very insignificant role in the UK distribution network. It is primarily confined to bulk cargoes such as oil and coal.

Coastal shipping services convey a substantial volume of business in many countries. They tend to be reserved to the national flag and convey both bulk and general cargo. Rates are competitive and likewise transits in many markets. They act as feeders to the major ports and compete with inland distribution methods such as rail and road for the internal distribution market.

4.3 INTERNATIONAL POSTAL SERVICES

A large number of importers use the international postal and courier network for letters, packages and parcels. The documentation is simple and the tariff system and transit times are very competitive. Overall, the international postal network is becoming more popular and improvements in the quality and range of services are constantly being realized. It is ideal especially for despatching samples and small packages. A comprehensive commentary on the rates and range of services available is found on pages 55-71; importers are urged to contact their nearest main post office to obtain up-to-date details.

4.4 INTERNATIONAL RAIL TRANSPORT

International rail transport is not a very popular form of distribution to the small importer as road and air-freight tend to be more favourable. This is particularly so of road transport which provides a very competitive service on a door-to-door basis for such a market.

The modern railway system is most economical when it provides the complete train load for a shipper on a regular basis. It is termed the block train load system and operates from private sidings or terminals of customer built requirements. Examples include the importation of cars, oil, timber, coal and ore from the ports to the importer's premises.

A market which is growing is the distribution of containers by rail from the port to the inland rail terminal. It is called the Freight Liner system and major container ports such as Felixstowe and Southampton rely on this method of distribution. Some 35 terminals exist in the UK and the system operates on the basis of fixed formation trains to provide fast and reliable services. Road transport distributes the FCL container to the importer's premises from the inland terminal. The great majority of the rail terminals are inland clearance depots thereby permitting goods to be cleared locally by customs and not at the port of entry. The importer is advised to use this method of distribution for container shipments as it is very cost-effective and ideal for both FCL and LCL cargoes.

A limited market exists in the movement of goods by train ferry. This involves the wagons travelling on a vessel termed a train ferry as found on the Dunkerque—Dover route. It has the following features:

1. Simplified documentation involving the CIM consignment note (see Appendix E).
2. No intermediate handling at the ports or in the transit countries as the consignment is under customs bond throughout.
3. Wagon types range from those for general merchandise to those purpose-built for conveying chemicals, cars, transporters, etc.
4. Packing costs are low and insurance rates are competitive reflecting the low risk of damage and pilferage.
5. Customs clearance maybe undertaken at the port or at the inland clearance depots.
6. The modern train ferry wagon is the bogie bolster with a payload of 60-80 tonnes. It may be purpose-built for one particular commodity such as a liquid tank or poly-bulk hopper wagon, of the covered type for general cargo in unitized, or break-bulk form.
7. A major disadvantage of the train ferry is the inflexibility, poor transit times when compared with road; reliance of road as a distributor from the rail terminal which increases cost; and absence of multiplicity of routes and services from the Continent to the UK, as found in the international road transport market.

Overall the popularity of the train ferry may change when the Channel Tunnel is opened in May 1993.

4.4.1 Eurotunnel

Construction is underway of a 31 mile-long tunnel between Folkestone and Frethun (Calais) called the Eurotunnel. Each terminal will have road and rail access. It will be comprised of three tunnels, two of which will carry trains and one a service tunnel which will be linked to the two rail tunnels. Two types of trains will operate through the tunnel; cars, lorries and coaches at Folkestone and Calais will drive onto special shuttle trains operated by Eurotunnel; through passenger and freight trains will operate through the tunnel linking the European rail network with British Rail. This is likely to involve the development of Freight Liner container services from Rotterdam, Hamburg, Dunkerque, Antwerp, and the expansion of the train ferry business.

The provision of the Eurotunnel is likely to change the pattern of international physical distribution between Europe and the UK and the importer must review the situation as the scheme unfolds and plan accordingly.

4.5 INTERNATIONAL ROAD HAULAGE

The road vehicle is a low capacity but very versatile unit of transport, very flexible in its operation. It is a very popular method of distribution over the UK/Continent routes where over 80% of all consumer goods are trailer movements. Some of these services extend to Asia and the Middle East. The road vehicle has a maximum gross weight of 38 tonnes and overall length of 15.5 m. The driver usually accompanies the vehicle on the ship, but an increasing number of the larger road hauliers allow the trailers to travel unaccompanied. There is a large range of road vehicle types but the majority of the trade operates under consolidated arrangements. This involves forwarding agents or road hauliers providing regular services between industrial and commercial centres. Depots would be situated in both centres where goods from the exporter are assembled for shipment and distributed to the importer. The forwarding agent or road haulier would be responsible for marketing the business in both centres. The road vehicle is often called a juggernaut and operates on the 'Ro/Ro' (roll on — roll off ferry) market.

Another example of the trailer market is the MAFI trailer. This equipment is used in deep-sea services where the load, which may be a piece of machinery, agricultural equipment, or indivisible load, is conveyed throughout the transit on the MAFI trailer. The trailer is driven on and off the vessel by a tug master and via the ship's ramp. The deep-sea

Ro/Ro vessel also conveys other wheeled cargo such as trade cars and industrial equipment.

Features of international road transport are given below:

1. It has a high distributive ability offering a door-to-door service with no intermediate handling.
2. No customs examination arises in transit countries provided the haulier is affiliated to TIR as the cargo passes under bond.
3. It is very flexible in operation which is particularly useful when circumstances demand a change in routeing, because of road works or disrupted shipping services, for example.
4. Documentation is simple: under CMR a through consignment note is operative with a common code of liability and conditions.
5. It is very competitive within certain distance bands compared with air-freight and train ferry, both in terms of transit times and rates.
6. The service tends to be reliable and to a high standard. Delays usually only occur when bad weather prevails or for some other exceptional circumstances.
7. Packing costs are less when compared with conventional shipping.
8. The driver accompanies the vehicle throughout the road transit thereby exercising personal supervision and reducing risk of damage and pilferage. Accordingly the operator can control his vehicle at all times as the driver usually 'reports in' to his company control office at staged points *en route*.
9. The trailer or vehicle has limited capacity which imposes certain weight and dimensional restrictions on the traffic which can be carried.

To conclude, the Ro/Ro unit is ideal for the importer shipping general merchandise and selective bulk cargoes in small quantities conveyed in a specialized vehicle — liquid cargoes, livestock, dry bulk merchandise such as fertilizer and cement, for example. It is renowned for its scheduled groupage services between the UK and the Continent, involving the UK freight forwarder working with a counterpart on the Continent.

4.6 INTERNATIONAL AIR TRANSPORT

Air transport is one of the youngest forms of distribution and undoubtedly continues to make a major contribution to the exploitation of world resources. The bulk of international passenger travel is now by air and a significant proportion of freight; at present the latter constitutes 1% in volume and 20% in value terms of total world trade.

The number of importers using air-freight services is increasing and the market is expanding. Given below are the features of international air transport:

1. Quick transits and high speeds.
2. Reliable transit times.
3. Low risk of damage and pilferage, with consequent very competitive insurance premium.
4. Simplified documentation system — one document an Air Waybill for the through air-freight transit, interchangeable between IATA-accredited airlines.
5. Common code of liability conditions to all IATA-accredited airlines.
6. Virtually eliminates packing cost — an important advantage.
7. Ideal for palletized consignments (see pages 51-3).
8. Quick journeys reduce the amount of capital tied up in transit.
9. Quick, reliable transits eliminate need for extensive warehouse accommodation and reduces the risk of stockpiling, obsolescence, deterioration and capital tied up in warehouse and stock provision. Moreover it enables the importer to replenish his stock quickly, when demand is greater than forecast.
10. Ideal for a wide variety of consumer-type cargoes, particularly consignments up to 2000 kg.
11. The IATA air-freight network is very extensive worldwide, offering frequent flights between major commercial and industrial centres worldwide. Such frequency does not exist with shipping services. Moreover the airport tends to be closer to the commercial and industrial centres than the seaport which has a competitive advantage in terms of lower collection and distribution costs.
12. On IATA-scheduled international services there is parity of rates and competition only on quality.
13. Services are reliable and high quality.
14. The IATA agent air-freight consolidation services has developed a market especially for the small shipper or importer (see pages 63-5).
15. Air-freight services are vulnerable to disruption when fog prevails, particularly in airports with less modern traffic control equipment.
16. Air-freight relies on road primarily as a feeder and distribution service.
17. Air transport is subject to a high operating cost and initial cost of aircraft when compared to overall capacity; average aircraft capacity 2000–25 000 kg. It is for the latter reason that many air-freighters are converted passenger aircraft.

An increasing volume of cargo is now conveyed on air-freight charter flights. Air-freight is ideal for merchandise of high value to low weight ratio. This includes a wide range of goods including computers, photographic material, electronic equipment, perishable cargoes, fashionable garments, samples, spares, and so on. The importer involved in products falling within this criteria is strongly advised to consider air-freight, especially through an IATA agent offering consolidation. Use the transport distribution analysis evaluation as described in Chapter 14.

4.7 SEA TRANSPORT

As we enter the 1990s, the pattern of international sea transport will continue to change. During the past decade the oil market has fallen by 35% whilst the range of ship types continue to expand to meet the needs of a changing international market. Flags of convenience fleets have increased and likewise flag discrimination. Moreover, governments are tending to take a keener interest in their maritime fleets and this has changed the national pattern of the disposition of the world mercantile fleet.

There are three main sea transport divisions: liners, tramps and specialized vessels such as tankers.

The liner vessel operates on a scheduled service between a group of ports. Such services offer cargo space or passenger accommodation to all shippers and passengers who require them. The ships sail on scheduled dates and times irrespective of whether they are full or not. Container vessels in deep-sea trades and Ro/Ro vessels in the short sea trades feature prominently in this field. The passenger market is now only relevant to the UK—Continent trade and similar short sea trades in other parts of the world. The deep-sea liner services often operate under the aegis of the liner conference system. The Bill of Lading features very prominently as the consignment note used in the liner cargo service with the exception of the international road haulage shipment which involves the CMR document and rail which involves the CIM consignment note.

The tramp or general trader does not operate on a fixed sailing schedule, but merely trades in all parts of the world in search of cargo, primarily bulk shipments. Such cargoes include coal, grain, timber, sugar, ores, fertilizers and copra, which are carried in complete shiploads. Many of the cargoes are seasonal. Tramp vessels are engaged under a document called a Charter Party on a time or voyage basis. Such negotiations usually are conducted by shipbrokers on behalf of their principals. The fixture rate is determined by the economic forces of supply and demand with respect to cargoes seeking shipping space and the availability of vessels. Such vessels occasionally are chartered to supplement existing liner services to meet peak cargo-shipment demands, or by the shipper with a substantial shipment of cargo, that is, trade cars/chassis.

The specialized vessel such as the oil tanker, ore carrier, timber carrier, may be under charter or operated by an industrial company that is oil company, motor manufacturer etc., to suit their own individual needs or that of the market.

A selection of the more important vessels is given below:

Oil tankers. Responsible for the movement of the world's oil, these may be VLCC (very large crude carriers, exceeding 200 000 dwt) or ULCC (ultra large crude carriers exceeding 350 000 dwt), although a large number of oil tankers come within the 100 000-200 000 dwt range which are very flexible in their operation.

Coasters. These are all-purpose cargo carriers operating in coastal waters.

Pure car and truck carriers (PCTC). Designed for the conveyance of cars, lorries and other wheeled units, these vessels have a capacity of up to 5800 cars, or permutations of up to 600 lorries and 3200 cars.

Liquefied natural gas carriers (LNG). Designed to convey gas.

Container vessels. (See pages 35-44).

Oil/bulk ore (OBO) vessels. Multi-purpose ships designed for switching between bulk shipments of oil and bulk grain, fertilizer and ore.

Ro/Ro vessels. These are designed to convey private cars with passengers, coaches, road haulage vehicles, etc.

SD14 and Freedom type vessels. Both vessels are multi-purpose, dry cargo carriers designed to convey traditional bulk cargoes such as grain, timber, ore and coal.

'Tween-deck vessel. This is a general cargo vessel engaged primarily on deep-sea liner cargo services. It has other decks below the main deck called 'tween decks and all run the full length of the vessel. This type of vessel has been displaced in many trades by the container ship and the combi carrier.

The combi carrier. This is a unitized cargo carrier combining container and vehicle shipments, including Ro/Ro. It is tending to displace 'tween-deck tonnage and is particularly suitable for trading in third world countries where port transhipment facilities are rather inadequate.

4.8 PACKING CONSIDERATIONS

4.8.1 Palletization

Palletization is the process of placing or anchoring the consignment to a

DG
DANGEROUS GOODS DECLARATION, SHIPPING NOTE
& CONTAINER/VEHICLE PACKING CERTIFICATE
© SITPRO 1985

DANGEROUS GOODS NOTE

Special
Information
is required
for (a)
Dangerous
Goods in
Limited
Quantities
(b)
Radioactive
Substances
(class 7)
(c) Tank
Containers
and
(d) In certain
circumstances
a weathering
certificate
is required

SHADED
AREAS
NEED NOT
BE SHIPPER
COMPLETED
FOR SHORT
SEA, RO. RO,
RAIL

This is DRG TRANSCRIPT carbonless copy paper

MUST BE
COMPLETED
FOR FULL
CONTAINER/
VEHICLE
LOADS:—

Exporter	1
Veh. Bkg. Ref.	2
Customs Reference Status	3
Exporter's Reference	4
Exporter Freight Forwarder / Port Charges Payable by*	5
Fwdr's Ref	6
SS Co Bkg No.	7
Consignee	8A
Other (Name & Address)	
Name of Shipping Line or CTO	8
Port Account No.	
Freight Forwarder	9
For Use of Receiving Authority Only	
Receiving Date(s)	Berth/Dock/Containerbase etc	10
Consecutive no. or DG reference allocated by shipping line or C.T.O. (if any)	10A
Vessel	Port of Loading	11
Port of Discharge	Destination Depot	12
Name of Receiving Authority	13

TO THE RECEIVING AUTHORITY
Please receive for shipment the goods described below subject to your
published regulations & conditions (including those as to liability)

Marks & Numbers; No. & Kind of Packages; Description of goods.†
INDICATE: HAZARD CLASS, UN NUMBER, FLASHPOINT °C. — 14

Receiving Authority Use	Gross Wt(kg) of goods	15	Cube (m³) of goods	16
	Net Wt(kg) of goods	16A		

†CORRECT TECHNICAL NAME, PROPRIETARY NAMES ALONE ARE NOT SUFFICIENT

CONTAINER/VEHICLE PACKING CERTIFICATE — 17
It is declared that the packing of the container has been carried out
in accordance with the provisions shown overleaf —

Name of Company

Signature   Date
of person responsible for packing container

DANGEROUS GOODS DECLARATION
I hereby declare that the contents of this consignment are fully and accurately
described above by the correct technical name(s) (proper shipping name(s))
that the shipment is packaged in such a manner as to withstand the ordinary
risks of handling and transport by sea, having regard to the properties of the
goods to be carried, and that the goods are classified, packaged, marked and
labelled in accordance with the requirements of the Merchant Shipping
(Dangerous Goods) Regulations 1981 as currently amended. I further declare
that if appropriate the goods are classified, packaged and marked to comply
with the requirements of the European Agreement concerning the International Carriage of Dangerous Goods by Road (ADR) and of Annex 1 (RID) to
the International Convention concerning the Carriage of Goods by Rail (CIM)
or special arrangements made between the contracting parties to these
Agreements

The shipper must complete and sign box 19

Total Gross weight of goods

Total Cube of goods

Prefix & Container/Vehicle Number	18	Seal Number(s)	18A	Container/Vehicle Size & Type	18B	Tare wt (kg) as marked on CSC plate	18C	Total of boxes 15 and 18C	18D

DOCK/TERMINAL RECEIPT
Received the above number of packages/containers/trailers in apparent good order and condition unless stated hereon.
RECEIVING AUTHORITY REMARKS

Haulier's Name

Vehicle Reg No.

DRIVER'S SIGNATURE   SIGNATURE & DATE

Name of Shipper preparing this note & tel. no — 19

NAME/STATUS OF DECLARANT

DATE

Signature of Declarant

890   *Mark X as appropriate. If box 5 is not completed the company preparing this note may be held liable for payment of port charges
Non-completion of any boxes is a subject for resolution by the contracting parties

LONSDALE BUSINESS FORMS LTD 0933 228855

Figure 4.1 Dangerous Goods Note, reproduced by kind permission of SITPRO pallet, or base, made of wood or metal. It is a very common technique in air-freight where the pallet accompanies the consignment throughout the transit from the factory premises to the retailer. The shrink-wrap technique is frequently used. It may be a stillage involving base plates, the box pallets where one side can be dropped, or the skeleton pallet for light-weight cargoes.

Palletization is also used in container shipment in the process of general freight forwarding on surface transport. Basically, palletization aids cargo handling, reduces packing, facilitates stowage, and mechanizes the technique of cargo handling involving the pallet truck and fork-lift truck. To the shipper involved in general merchandise distribution, an enquiry into the possible use of pallets may prove worthwhile. Some shipowners and port operators offer rates' concessions on palletized cargo.

4.8.2 Dangerous Goods

The subject of conveyance of dangerous classified goods is an extensive one; the following points are made as guidelines:

1. The rates are 50% above the normal tariff. Dangerous classified cargo must be stowed in isolation from other incompatible cargoes.
2. The description of the cargo must be a technical and not a commercial one. This will determine the dangerous cargo classification of which there are nine for each transport mode — sea, international rail, air and international road. The nine classifications are broadly the same and determine the packaging specification, maximum quantity per package, labelling to identify the classification, documentation requirements, operational emergency arrangements, handling and stowage needs, and the specification of the transport permitted to convey the goods.
3. The shipper (person/company) sending the goods is responsible for providing an intrinsic technical description of the goods and any false data given is subject to severe litigation penalties involving a heavy fine or imprisonment. Hence, the cargo description provided for example by sea is found on a Dangerous Goods Note (Figure 4.1) which is signed by an executive of the company despatching the goods. Similar documentation is required by other transport modes.
4. A ship's master and airline pilot have the power to refuse to accept any dangerous classified cargo.
5. The organizations responsible for the determination of the code of practice relating to the conveyance of dangerous classified cargo are the International Maritime Organization (sea transport), IATA for air-freight, ADR for international road transport and RID for international rail. All involve international conventions which over 130 countries have adopted.

6. The usual forwarding procedure is for the shipper to call the freight forwarder or carrier, giving the full details of consignment and technical specification of the cargo to establish whether it is acceptable to the carrier. This will be checked out and on acceptance the type of packaging will be specified, the maximum quantity per package, the classification code and appropriate pictogram label given; dangerous goods declaration completed by the shipper, and records made of forward dates and details of flights or sailings.

7. On arrival at destination — the airport or seaport — these cargoes are given priority in customs clearance and onward despatch.

Dangerous classified cargo is a growth market and demands special arrangements (*Elements of Shipping* (Appendix E), pages 305-313).

4.8.3 Cargo packing

Circumstances may arise when the importer has, under the cargo delivery terms, to undertake the cargo packing for an international consignment. The factors involved will vary by circumstances but the two prime considerations are the nature of the cargo and transit. Other factors include cost of packing, aid to handling and stowage, packing material available, security aspects, prospects of its being palletized, climatic conditions, weight/size limitations on any transhipment arrangements, and onward despatch.

Improved stowage performance and risk of damage in transit can be much reduced through skilful packing. The Research Association for the Paper and Board, Printing and Packaging Industries (PIRA) can provide good advice and the optimum of packing specifications (see page 226).

5 *Freight tariff*

Distribution costs represent a significant element in the pricing structure of the importer's product in the competitive market place. It is an area which too few importers challenge, mainly because of the complexity of the tariffs. The discerning importer obtains the best deal possible through his forwarding agent but this requires to be evaluated regularly. Attention should focus on competitive distribution services not only in terms of tariff structure, but also in overall quality of service. It is particularly important to conduct the analysis in situations where the shipment volumes vary monthly or on a seasonal basis, to ensure the best deal is concluded. Areas to scrutinize include the following: tariff structure; currency; payment terms and period of credit; level of rebate; additional charges including customs clearance, documentation, collection and delivery (an advantage of the consolidated rate is that many of such charges are included in the overall rate); comparison with competitive rates and services in the market place including other transport modes; quality of the transport service in terms of reliability, frequency, customer care; claims; and finally the quality of the management and degree of modernization of technology and the transport infrastructure.

The demand for sea or air transport is affected both by direct competition between carriers and by the competition of substitutes or alternatives of the commodity carried (derived demand). The elasticity of demand for sea or air transport varies from one commodity to another. In normal times, an important factor affecting elasticity of demand for sea or air transport is the cost of transport in relation to the market price of the goods carried.

The price eventually fixed for a chartered vessel or aircraft depends largely on the relationship between buyers and sellers. Where both groups are numerous and have equal bargaining power, and where demand is fairly elastic, relatively perfect competition prevails. Under these conditions for chartered tonnage, prices are fixed by the 'haggling of the market' and are known as contract prices. The tramp charter market operates under such conditions and the contract is drawn up as an agreement known as a charter party. Hence the rates structure for tramps is a very simple product and emerges from the competitive interplay of supply and demand. A similar criteria applies to air-freight charters. It must be borne in mind, however, that the air charter market extends both to the very large shipment offering, for example, an indivisible load urgently required such as a ship's propeller, and the smaller split charter involving consignments of 500-2500 kg. Many air-freight forwarders have access to air-charter subsidiaries and the importer is advised to examine the market.

The importer must critically examine the total freight cost of the transit and reconcile it with the distance. Generally, the shorter the total journey distance, the greater the need to ensure the cost is proportionate to the distance, otherwise it could quickly price the goods out of the importer's market. Generally, documentation and customs entry costs do not vary greatly.

In liner conferences, which include container trades, the shipowners control fairly large concerns, and although some of their shippers may be large companies, the bulk of their traffic comes from the numerous small shippers. In these conditions it is more convenient for the shipowner to estimate how much his customers are prepared to pay and fix his own rate. Such prices are known as tariff prices which the liner conference issues. It should be stressed that a significant volume of the liner cargo trade operates outside the liner conference system. The same cargo mix obtains but the pricing structure is determined by the individual or group of shipowners. In such situations the rates may be more competitive but no loyalty rebate exists as found in the liner conference system under the immediate or deferred rebate. Moreover, non-conference liner cargo operators have greater flexibility in terms of rate manipulation and operation, as the individual shipowners make the decisions and are not obliged to confer with other shipowners within the trade as found in the liner conference situation. Evergreen, the round the world container operator, is a good example. The importer should bear the foregoing in mind when evaluating the merits of conference and non-conference shipping services (see also page 224).

Air-freight tariffs operative on regular scheduled international services are decided by member airlines at their IATA traffic conferences, usually held biannually. IATA adopts a policy of parity on rates for any particular route and allows competition to play its part on service quality. The rates reflect market conditions and airline service cost. The level of air-freight consolidation rates is outside the influence of IATA and this is set by the IATA forwarding agent. It would take account of the contracted rate negotiated with the airline for the volume shipment guarantee on specific flight(s) on a regular basis.

One cannot stress too strongly the importance of rates negotiation and regular evaluation by the importer to obtain the best deal for his/her merchandise.

5.1 CONSTITUENTS OF THE FREIGHT TARIFF

The rate is formulated from the following constituents, as found in the published public tariff:

1. The cost of transportation to the carrier. This includes a proportion of fixed cost such as asset depreciation, interest on loans, mortgages or leasing expenses, maintenance costs and administration. The direct cost element includes fuel, airport or seaport dues, crew expenses, and costs to load or discharge the cargo. The more intensely the transport unit is used the lower the cost per ton conveyed in so far as fixed costs are concerned.
2. The level of competition. Strong competition tends to depress the freight rate as carriers offer high discounts or rebates to retain the business.
3. The profit margin. Transport has tended to be a market with a low investment return and a level of 3% on the capital is typical in many shipping companies. Hence profit margins tend to be low and in some trades companies run at a loss through a government subsidy intervention. Moreover, in situations where trade imbalances occur, significant profit margins are recorded on fully loaded sailings and a loss recorded on the return leg with a poor load factor.
4. The nature of the cargo and packaging; its volume, its weight/volumetric rates; its handling characteristics and period of shipment. Generally the larger the volume, the lower the cost per tonne conveyed. Cargo which requires special facilities because it is awkward to handle usually attracts high rates. Regular shipments usually attract discounted rates.
5. The existence of any statutory rates' control, subsidies, or intervention by government. This tends to operate where the airline or shipping line is state-owned. Rate levels are influenced or controlled by the government but, more significantly to the free market carrier, the state-owned carrier is subsidized. Such governments tend to direct imported cargoes and where possible exported shipments to their own national shipping line or airline to save hard currency and build up a favourable level of trade. Government intervention is also found in flag discrimination. The importer can do little to counter such practices (the subject is fully examined in *Economics of Shipping Practice and Management*, Chapter 18 — see Appendix A).
6. The origin and destination of the cargo and routeing of the consignment. Obviously, the long-distance cargo generates a higher overall rate. Terminal cost at the seaport or airport tends to represent a higher percentage of the transportation cost on the shorter transit compared to the longer haul.
7. Liner conferences exist in many deep-sea cargo liner trades (see page

224). Such organizations operate a rates parity amongst their ship-owner members and offer rebates on customer loyalty. The services are reliable and of a high quality, but the importer is given little room to manoeuvre in terms of rate manipulation either through the forwarding agent or direct with the shipping company.

8. The level of commission earned by the freight forwarder. The importer has the choice of dealing direct with the carrier or operating through an agent. Both will deal with all the documentation needs. The agent may offer a groupage or consolidated service which is ideal for the importer of small-volume shipments and offers favourable rates. Alternatively the agent may quote from the carrier public tariff and in so doing earns a commission on cargo originated from the carrier.

9. The inclusion or not in the rate of the costs of documentation, customs clearance and handling. Some agents quote an inclusive charge. The importer should check out this point and involve the seaport or airport of destination.

10. The imposition of any currency adjustment factor (CAF) and bunker adjustment factor (BAF) The former represents the payment to the carrier relative to loss of earnings consequent on the variation in the exchange rate of the currency of the published tariff. Hence, a falling French franc against sterling will result in the carrier requiring more francs to maintain the sterling equivalent in the freight rate quotation. Likewise an increase cost in the price of bunker fuel will result in the carrier requesting more monies from the shipper to meet the increased fuel cost. The freight forwarder or international bank can advise the importer of the most favourable freight rate currency to use and likewise effect payments in that currency. It may be beneficial to have a sterling-based freight rate.

11. The mode of transport. Air-freight rates are high whilst those by sea are very much lower. Combined transport operation involving the ISO container and road trailer is very competitive.

12. The level of rates are not usually identical in both directions on one route. A major factor is the volume of trade. Where transport capacity is fully utilized in one direction, i.e. east—west the rate would tend to be higher compared with the direction west—east which has a lower load factor. The importer should determine prospects of any rates reduction in this area.

The importer must strive for 'value for money' in his choice of transport mode and carrier(s), keeping the situation constantly under review with full liaison with the exporter. Tariffs which are cheap tend to offer less reliable transits and do not offer the most modern transport infrastructure.

5.2 FACTORS AFFECTING CONTROL OF INTERNATIONAL TRANSPORT ARRANGEMENTS

The options confronting the buyer in regard to whether or not to proceed with undertaking the transportation arrangements are very varied by country, trading customs and legislation, relationship between buyer and seller, and so on. We will examine a number of the more salient factors.

1. The country of the buyer or importer. Buyers in countries with currency problems in which all or many imported products are subject to government control, tend to be very stringent on saving hard currency by undertaking all the transportation arrangements. This requires the buyer to appoint an agent in the seller's country who accepts the goods from the seller on an Ex Works basis. In so doing the goods are transported by the buyer's national airline or shipping line. At the same time the agent arranges the insurance in the buyer's country.

   Such countries practice 'flag discrimination' whereby through the issue of export/import licences or other documentation they direct cargoes to their national shipping line. The rates are usually lower as the vessels have a state subsidy and enjoy preferential port charges and the most favoured treatment at the ports of the buyer's country. Hence, foreign flag vessels using such ports are subject to higher charges and less favoured treatment.

2. The buyer is usually the stronger party in the sale negotiations which places him or her in a good position to negotiate the transportation arrangements. Generally, the nearer the market the easier it becomes for the importer to arrange the transportation.

3. An increasing number of importers are also engaged in the export business. In consequence, the company has experience in international trade and is usually in close liaison with freight forwarders and transport operators. Such experience and contacts can be used to develop the transportation arrangements.

4. Trade associations, the British Importers Association, Chambers of Commerce and competitors all provide a source of information of the terms of sale under which their members purchase their imported goods and the agents or transport operators used.

5. A further source of help is the British International Freight Association who are happy to give details of their members who are available to help. Freight forwarders tend to deal with particular markets and trades and have offices, or work in collaboration, with agents based in the exporter's country.

6. Airlines and shipping companies have a network of offices and routes worldwide. Again the importer can contact the UK office of the

airline or shipping company they are interested in to obtain service and rate details.

5.3   AIR-FREIGHT RATES

The formulation of air-freight rates is controlled by the International Air Transport Association (IATA); most of the major world airlines are affiliated to it, representing about 98% of international air-freight services. The significant aspect of the IATA-affiliated airlines is that no competition is permitted on air-freight rates and competition is permitted only on service quality, frequency, etc.

Basically, there are six types of air-freight rates each in its own way designed to stimulate traffic. Individual rates are not necessarily the same in both directions — they reflect the differing market situations. Thus, routeing of cargo is significant both in terms of transit time and tariff. If two routes are available, the shorter route could be cheaper, but the transit time might be greater due to the less frequent and slower schedules and connections.

Air cargo is charged by weight except where the volume is more than 366 in^3 kg^{-1}. In such cases, volumetric charges apply and each unit of 366 in^3 is charged as 1 kg. To calculate this, the maximum dimensions of the piece should be multiplied together to give a volume in cubic inches. This volume must be divided by 366 and the result will be the volumetric weight. If this is more than the actual weight, then the volumetric weight will be the chargeable weight. Where the consignment consists of pieces varying in density, the volumetric calculation will be based on the whole consignment. For metric measurements, 6000 cm^3 = 1 kg (see page 66). Exceptions to the rates per kilogram (gross weight or volume equivalent) are specific commodity rates to certain European countries and Ireland which are quoted per 100 kg. The 100 kg rates apply from airport of departure to airport of destination and do not include charges for cartage, customs entry and clearance, etc.

A brief examination of each air-freight rate classification now follows:

Specific commodity rates.   These reduced rates apply to a wide range of commodities and to qualify the shipper must comply precisely with the commodity specifications as found in the tariff. For example, the specified airports of departure and arrival must be used — it is not possible to send goods at these preferential rates to alternative destinations even where the alternative airport is on the same route and nearer to the airport of origin. The minimum quantity at each rate is 100, 300, 500 and 1000 kg (shipping above the limit is allowed but not below it). Hence a consignment of 85 kg would be charged at the minimum kilogram rate, that is, 100kg at 65p, which is £65.00. This type of rate has done much to stimulate air-freight development and by encouraging quantity shipments has produced cost savings in documentation, handling and packaging. In the event of the merchandise not qualifying for the reduced commodity rate, the shipper is advised to contact the agent or airline who may be able to introduce a special rate when regular and substantial shipments are involved.

Classification rates (surcharges and rebates).   Classification rates apply to the following commodities where no specific commodity rate is available.

1. Consignments of newspapers, periodicals, magazines, books, catalogues, talking books for the blind and Braille-type equipment are carried at reduced rates. Special rates are available on application to the airline.
2. The regulations governing the carriage of human remains vary from route to route. Prior application is necessary to the airline.
3. Certain types of gold and platinum, diamonds (including industrial), rubies, emeralds, sapphires and pearls (including cultured pearls), legal bank notes, travellers cheques, securities, shares and share coupons are charged at the 'under 100 kg' air cargo rate plus a 100% surcharge. The minimum charge for valuable cargo is the normal applicable minimum charge plus a surcharge of 100%, but not less than US $50 (operative rate October 1990). Quantity rates are not applicable.
4. Collection charges are not normally available for the carriage of live animals except under special circumstances. Prior arrangements must be made for the carriage of animals. Stringent regulations apply regarding documentation and travel facilities. Every consideration will be given to flight conditions such as altitude and temperature, but no responsibility can be accepted by the airline in the event of death or injury to the live animals due to atmospheric or climate conditions, or natural causes. A shipper's certificate for live animals is required.

Valuation charge.   Where consignments are offered for international carriage, a declaration of value must be made. It is permissible to make the statement, 'no value declared'. Where goods for carriage have a declared value per kilogram higher than a certain level, a valuation charge will apply in addition to the freight charges. Details of the current valuation can be obtained from the local National Airline Cargo Offices. The scale of such charges will be based on the weight or volumetric basis plus a valuation charge.

General cargo rates.   These are the basic rates and fall into three categories: minimum charges; normal rate — the 'up to 100 kg' rate; quantity rate — applicable on the various minimum quantities shipped, called break-points. It is permissible to charge a consignment at a higher weight rate if a lower charge results overall.

Unit load device (ULD) rates.   These apply to any type of container, a container with an integral pallet, or an aircraft pallet whether or not owned by an IATA member, and whether or not considered to be aircraft equipment.

5.3.1   Charges

Charges can be paid at the time of despatch by cash, cheque or credit card (most major credit cards are accepted). However, regular shippers and importers make use of credit facilities available from most major airlines. This enables their air-freight charges to be billed for settlement on a monthly basis. No cash on delivery consignments can be accepted on most airline Air Waybills or services.

Goods despatched to most countries may be sent 'charges forward', i.e. cartage, export fees and freightage payable by the consignee importer. Consignments cannot be sent with carriage and valuation charges partly prepaid and partly forward. 'Charges forward' facilities are not available on domestic routes, when all charges must be prepaid. This service is not normally available for perishable goods or live animals.

Most airlines will charge 10% with a basic minimum fee for collection from a consignee of any disbursement shown on the Air Waybill. This charge will be made when collection is on behalf of any shipper or agent. Disbursements will not usually exceed the freight charges shown on the Air Waybill. When the issuing carrier cannot collect the amount from the consignee for any reason, the amount will be charged to the shipper or agent.

Air-freight charges for perishable cargo must normally be prepaid. If required, a deposit to cover surface reforwarding charges from the airport of arrival will be collected from the consignor. Cargo subject to regulations relating to the carriage of dangerous goods must be offered separately, and clearly indicated in the Shipper's Declaration (see page 69).

A mixed consignment is one which contains a number of different commodities which do not qualify for the same rate and conditions. Charges for mixed consignments are based on the applicable general cargo rate. Where the shipper declares separately the weight, or volume and contents of each package in the consignment, charges are based on either the appropriate commodity rate or the general cargo rate for each package. Packaging of the consignment will be charged on the basis of the highest rated article in the consignment. Articles which cannot be included in mixed consignment are: live animals, perishable goods, human remains, diplomatic bags, baggage shipped as cargo, and valuable cargo which includes articles with an actual value of US$ 1000 or equivalent, or more per gross kilogram.

Valuation charges are based on the total declared value for carriage of the entire consignment.

Aircraft can be chartered for special consignments. Rates vary according to market conditions and other factors. The shipper conducts his negotiations through an air charter broker found on the Baltic Exchange or direct with an airline or air-freight forwarder (see page 213). As indicated earlier, a certain degree of bargaining can emerge to settle the ultimate charter rate for the larger air-freighter. Much depends whether prospects exist for the aircraft to be chartered on the next flight otherwise the operator will be faced with an empty aircraft to fly to the next assignment. Little room exists for bargaining for split charters for small consignments varying between 500 kg and 3 tonnes. The charterer may need to wait a few days in such circumstances to combine with other cargo thereby obtaining a favourable rate based on a full aircraft.

All these air-freight rates exclude customs clearance charges and duty, road or rail collection and distribution, warehousing, demurrage, etc.

5.3.2   Air-freight consolidation

During the past 10 years there has been a substantial development in air-freight consolidation. This involves the freight forwarder (usually referred to as the agent) who has a contract with an airline on specified flights to provide consolidated cargo for allocated cargo hold space which the agent undertakes to fill. The consolidated consignment is under agent sponsorship and may involve up to 30 consignments including differing consignees and consignors. Each consignment tends to be destined for the same destination or those close together which enables the shipper to take advantage of the favourable competitive rate and convenient regular quality service. The cargoes are mixed subject to their compatibility; dangerous cargo is exempt from such a facility; limitations are imposed on weight and general dimensions of the cargo.

The agent prepares a cargo manifest to accompany the Master Air Waybill throughout the flight and issues House Air Waybills to individual shippers. The agent's responsibility includes cargo collection and/or delivery; payment of all reasonable costs throughout the transit including collection and delivery charges (usually involving the agent's own vehicles); air-freight; airport or airline disbursements; documentation; customs and so on. The agent is able to charge an inclusive rate throughout which is usually much lower than those for individual packages or consignments. The agent usually works in close liaison with a counterpart in the destination area and the two agents work on a reciprocal basis, developing the consolidated air-freight business in both directions.

Features of the scheme are given below:

1. It is particularly attractive to the importer or shipper engaged in receiving small consignment(s) which can be conveniently accommodated into a ULD subject to its compatibility with other cargo shipped. Any queries on weight or dimension limitations should be directed to the agent.

2. Documentation is simplified and all the documentation needs relative to the transit are usually taken care of by the agent. The agent issues a 'House Air Waybill' at the time of flight departure to the shipper.

3. The promotion of the consolidated service is undertaken by the agent who takes care of all the transit needs of the consignment, including documentation. This enables the airline to concentrate on providing a quality air-freight flight service.

4. The rate is calculated on a W/M basis (see page 60).

5. It is a competitive, inclusive rate structure compared with an individual package despatched under IATA freight rate structure arrangements (see pages 60-2).

6. Airlines can obtain the maximum income from the allocated aircraft hold accommodation earmarked for the agents; i.e. airline profitability is improved through good utilization of capacity.

7. The airline can plan ahead with confidence in the knowledge that airfreight consolidated consignments are being developed by the agent, virtually guaranteeing traffic to the airline.

8. The agreement between the airline and the agent usually permits the latter to vary or cancel his pre-booked cargo hold space up to 36 hours before flight departure time. The airline can then use the cargo space for other shippers.

9. The consolidation facility does not exist on every air-freight service, which tends to restrict its user. However, it is a fast-growing market and the initiative for its expansion in terms of extending the range of flights and services on which it is available rests with the agent in consultation with the airline.

10. The rates structure is inclusive of collection and/or delivery charges, documentation, customs clearance, airline disbursements and so on, which is a good selling point of the service. It permits the shipper to avoid the minimum freight rate regulations found in the airline (IATA)-approved rate structure (see pages 60-1).

11. Packing costs are substantially reduced and risk of cargo loss and/or damage is minimized, thereby lowering insurance premiums.

12. Consolidated consignments tend to be cleared quicker through customs.

13. The freight forwarder is encouraged to maximize profitability through an equal mix of high-and low-density cargoes.
14. The use of the ULDs is encouraged, with all its attendant advantages.
15. The agent can offer guaranteed services, thereby aiding quality of service and development of the market.
16. The general competitiveness and favourable quality of service facilitates the development of international trade.
17. Quicker and reliable transit times are offered which is a good selling point of the service.

Air-freight consolidation services exist worldwide and there is every evidence to suggest its growth will continue. It is especially suitable for the smaller importer and through its competitiveness and quality of service is aiding the development of international trade by air.

5.3.3 Courier rates

An expanding courier service exists today in many markets. It is basically air transport orientated and provides a door-to-door service worldwide for a wide variety of items from letters and documents to packages and heavy cargo. Major operators include TNT, DHL and Emery. Both commercial value and non-commercial value shipments are accepted.

The rate for envelopes is based on a maximum weight of 250 g and rated by zone for various parts of the world. For parcels and documents the rate is based on weight up to a maximum of 100 kg, above which the rate virtually doubles. The transit time for a parcel is about twice that for an envelope. All rates include customs clearance and include delivery within prescribed zones. It is an ideal service for urgent documents, samples and other packaged goods.

5.4 MARITIME CONTAINER RATES

A substantial volume of world trade is moved in maritime ISO containers. The range of container types continues to increase and this is aiding the expansion of the business. Furthermore as port modernization proceeds in many countries the size of container vessels capable of being handled at container berths is on the increase. New ports are also being developed by some countries to facilitate the development of their trade. An example is Bangkok where a new port offering deep sea berths will permit direct container services to be provided and eliminate the need for feeder services which are costly and extend the transit time. These on-going developments lower transportation costs and permit more competitive rates.

Rates are generally formulated by container capacity and the origin and destination of the merchandise. This is called 'box rate' and is irrespective of the commodity inside the container. The through rate will embrace the inland transportation cost known at the time of despatch, including collection and terminal expenses. It will also include: the collection of the goods from the exporter's premises to the local CFS/ICD/warehouse; conveying them to the port; customs processing and loading them onto the vessel, plus the sea freight. It is likely to include the port handling charges of unloading the cargo at the destination, but customs clearance, demurrage and import duty together with delivery charges is for the importer's account.

This practice applies to full container load (FCL) traffic. An ideal cargo delivery term for the importer wishing to undertake all the transportation arrangements is Ex Works or FOB (see Appendix E and pages 181-2). A further type of container rate is called a commodity box rate (CBR) which is based on the commodity inside the container. Hence the rate will vary by the commodity in the container (FCL). Some large multinational companies own or lease ISO containers. They are usually of a specialized type, offering a two-way traffic, and subject to specially negotiated contract rates.

A very substantial volume of traffic which is conveyed in containers is less than container load (LCL). A consignment comprising various LCL cargo is assembled and loaded into a container at a container base or inland clearance depot, with each individual LCL attracting a separate rate. Such rates are calculated on a weight per 1000 kg or per cubic metre basis, whichever produces the greater revenue. An example is given below:

> Two cases machinery for shipment from Singapore to Felixstowe. Each case measures 1.5 × 0.5 × 0.6 m; case A weighs 600 kg, case B weighs 550 kg W/M $900
>
> *Weight calculation*
> Total weight of consignment = 1150 kgs
> Freight rate per metric tonne = $900
>
> Total freight rate of 1150 kg $= \dfrac{1150}{1000} \times \$900 = \$1035$
>
> *Volume calculations*
> Total cube measurement of consignment = 1.5 × 0.5 × 0.6 × 2
> $\qquad\qquad\qquad\qquad\qquad\qquad\qquad\qquad\quad = 0.9 \ \mathrm{m}^3$
>
> Total freight rate of 0.9 m³ $= \dfrac{0.9}{1.0} \times \$900 = \$810$

As the rate will be higher by weight rather than by volume calculation the $1035 rate for weight will prevail.

When calculating the W/M ship option rate, the volumetric rate (per m³) will apply when the goods are of a low weight but high volume such as clothing, furniture etc. Conversely the actual weight rate (per 1000 kg) will prevail when the goods have a high weight but low density ratio, as in machinery, bulk paper, etc. The small importer is urged to use the LCL container service when possible as it offers regularity of service coupled with competitive rates and reliable transits. Separate container rates exist for livestock, trade vehicles, indivisible loads requiring heavy lifts, etc. In some trades a commodity rates' scale exists which may have broad divisions based on commodity category, stowage factor, value etc.

5.5 INLAND WATERWAYS' FREIGHT RATES

A significant proportion of European cargo is imported using the inland waterway system. The cargo may commence its journey by canal and then be transshipped to a vessel. Alternatively it may arrive at a UK port and be off-loaded onto a barge. A further option is to convey the goods in a coaster with limited draught, permitting the cargo to be loaded at an inland wharf and discharged on a UK canal, thereby providing a warehouse-to-warehouse transit between Europe and the UK.

Goods conveyed by canal are subject to a tariff based on distance, commodity type, transhipment cost, handling charges and other miscellaneous charges. If it is an indivisible load, special heavy lifting equipment may be required for example. Rates are available for containers, palletized cargoes, and special contract tariffs are provided for regular shipments. The tariffs vary by individual country and inland waterway authority. They exclude customs clearance charges. The rates for general cargo are usually based on the W/M ships option concept (see page 66).

5.6 FIXTURE RATES

A substantial volume of world trade moves in chartered tonnage under Charter Party terms (see pages 159–61). The rate of hire for a vessel is called a fixture rate and is dependent on market conditions: rates are low when vessels are plentiful and high when tonnage is scarce. It may be for a particular voyage or period of time. The process is called chartering and is explained fully in *Elements of Shipping*, Chapter 15 (see Appendix A).

The importer who is interested in chartering a vessel or aircraft should conduct the negotiations through a shipbroker (see page 221). Factors influencing the formulation of a fixture rate are: ship specification; type(s) of traffic involved; general market conditions; daily cost to be borne by the charterer; duration of the charter; terms of Charter Party; identity of cost to be borne by the shipowner; survey cost responsibility; urgency of charter; convenience of the charter to the shipowner.

5.7 PALLET RATES

Pallet rates exist in some trades when goods are conveyed on a pallet throughout the transit. The rate is usually on the W/M ships option basis (see page 66). Palletization aids stowage, cargo handling and stacking, and reduces damage and pilferage. The rates apply to break-bulk cargoes and include both ocean-going ships and lighterage. Special pallet rates also exist for port handling.

5.8 INTERNATIONAL ROAD HAULAGE FREIGHT RATES

The development of the international road haulage market between Europe, Asia and the Middle East has been outstanding in recent years, particularly the Continent—UK traffic under CMR conditions. It will be further accelerated with the Single Market Entity in 1992.

The rates charged on a Ro/Ro ferry to the international road freight forwarder or importer operating his own account vehicle are based on the vehicle length, whether it is empty or loaded, accompanied or unaccompanied. Hence an importer with an articulated vehicle of 15.5 m length loaded and accompanied may be charged £20 per metre (£310) on a sailing from Calais to Dover. This would be subject to any rebate based on a guaranteed annual volume of business. Additional charges are raised for excessive width and/or height. Special rates exist for declared valuable cargoes and dangerous classified commodities. These rates are exclusive of any customs clearance charges, etc.

To the importer using the international road freight forwarders door-to-door service (much of which is groupage traffic) the actual rate is based on the W/M ships option concept as explained in the example on page 66. It is a very popular service amongst importers. The importer wishing to arrange his own transportation arrangements by road throughout is advised to contact a UK international road haulier. Details are available in *Lloyds List*, *International Freighting Weekly* or the *Importer's Handbook*.

5.9 INTERNATIONAL TRAIN FERRY RATES

British Rail under COTIF/CIM conditions (see Appendix E) operate Continent—UK freight rail services. The COTIF Convention came into force on 1 May 1985 for the 34 (mainly European) ratifying states. An ideal cargo delivery term for the importer wishing to undertake and bear all the combined transportation costs is 'FCA' (see page 191). The rates are based on the origin and destination of the consignment and a per wagon charge to encourage good loadability. Special rates exist for particular streams of imported traffic and between selective countries or centres. There is an increasing number of privately owned or leased wagons of high capacity ranging from 70 to 90 tonnes, such as VTG, and special rates apply in such cases.

A significant volume of cargo passes in groupage wagon consignments under forwarding agent sponsorship. To the agent the rate is based on the wagon unit; to the importer, it is based on weight or volume of the consignment, whichever produces the higher revenue.

The popularity of international rail transit will increase with the opening of the Channel Tunnel, both for full wagon load and groupage imported consignments. The importer should consult the British International Freight Association to obtain a suitable freight forwarder.

5.10 BUNKER AND CURRENCY ADJUSTMENT FACTORS

The bunker adjustment factor (BAF) is a surcharge expressed either as a percentage of the freight or a price per tonne W/M added when fuel prices increase above the level allowed for by air or shipping lines in their freight rates. Overall it is a surcharge on the freight rate.

The currency adjustment factor (CAF) is a technique whereby a surcharge is raised by the shipowner on the basic freight rate to reflect a variation on the currency exchange rate. This helps to minimize the shipowner's losses through variations in the exchange rates. The currency adjustment factor is usually consolidated with the basic freight rate.

5.11 SUMMARY OF TYPES OF RATES

An alphabetical list of some salient rates is given below:

Ad valorem. This is based on the declared value of the cargo whereby merchandise declared at £1000 with 2.5% *ad valorem* rate would be charged £25 (see also page 61).

Antiques. Antiques including art treasures require special packaging by an accredited company and special freight rates apply. Freight forwarders tend to specialize in this business.

Bloodstock. This involves the movement of race horses. Special arrangements and rates apply by air and Ro/Ro ferry. All must be accompanied by a groom.

Box. A container rate (see pages 65-7).

Commodity. (See pages 60-1.)

Commodity box. A container rate (see pages 65-7).

Consolidated. The rate is for consolidated consignments, usually based on W/M option. Also termed the groupage rate (see pages 63-7).

Dangerous cargo. This would be conveyed under ADR, RID, IMO and

IATA regulations (see Appendix E) involving a rate about 50% above the general cargo rate (see also pages 62-4).

Dead freight. This usually arises when a charterer fails to provide a full cargo for a ship.

FAK (freight all kinds). This rate applies to all types of cargo irrespective of commodity type.

Fixture. Chartering a vessel (page 67).

Groupage. (See Consolidated entry.)

Household effects. Removal of household furniture. Special packaging applies and rates. Some agents specialize in this business.

Indivisible loads. Such consignments are of excessive weight or dimensions and require special handling equipment and arrangements.

Livestock. Special rates and arrangements apply.

Lump-sum freight. This is the amount payable for the use of the whole or portion of a ship.

Pallets. Rates applicable to palletized cargo (page 68).

Postal. There is a wide variety of postal services ideal for documents, small packages and samples. Contact the nearest main Post Office for details (page 172).

Project forwarding. This involves the co-ordination, through a freight forwarder, of all the international transportation arrangements of all the imported products relative to a major capital project such as a new airport terminal, power station, etc.

Rebate. A discount on a published rate attained through negotiation, guaranteed volume, etc. (page 224)

Ro/Ro rates. Applicable to road haulage movement (page 64).

Trade vehicles. Rates involving the movement of imported trade cars, buses, lorries, etc.

W/M option. Weight/measurement ship option based on weight or volumetric evaluation (see pages 64-6).

6 *Import customs practice*

6.1 ORGANIZATION AND WORKINGS OF THE HM CUSTOMS AND EXCISE

Her Majesty's Customs and Excise is one of the two main tax-collecting departments in the United Kingdom. It has origins in one of the oldest departments of state, the Board of Customs, which was appointed in 1671. The Department of Customs and Excise was established in 1909. The Board of Customs and Excise, composed of commissioners individually appointed by the sovereign under the Great Seal of the United Kingdom, is responsible to Treasury ministers for the work of the department.

The work of HM Customs and Excise may be divided into two broad areas:

1. The control of imported and exported goods for the purpose of duties, statistics, and the prevention of importation of prohibited goods.
2. The administration and collection of most of the taxes on consumer expenditure (indirect taxes) levied in the United Kingdom. In 1985-86, Customs and Excise receipts were just under £37.4 billion and represented 39.2% of the total revenue from central government taxation. Most Customs and Excise revenue is derived from value added tax (VAT), duties on hydrocarbon oils, tobacco products, alcoholic drinks and car tax. Other indirect taxes collected by Customs and Excise are betting and gaming duties, and duties on matches and lighters.

Like most Government departments, HM Customs and Excise has been affected by United Kingdom membership of the European Community (EC). All EC member states use a common customs tariff to charge the same rates of duty on imported goods from outside the Community. Goods from within the EC generally move free of customs duties between the member states (Belgium, Denmark, France, Greece, Ireland, Italy, Luxembourg, the Netherlands, Portugal, Spain, the United Kingdom and West Germany) but are subject to physical examination at the frontier points such as the airports, seaports and inland clearance depots (ICDs). This will cease under the 1992 Single Market Entity as the trading barriers of the EC are removed.

The principal functions of the customs side of the Department have traditionally been the assessment and collection of customs duties on imported goods and the control of smuggling. The Department collects customs duties on goods coming from countries outside the EC which do not qualify for relief under any preferential trade agreements made with the EC. In addition, customs collect and control the other charges which may be levied at import and remitted at export, such as excise duties and VAT, and the levies payable on agricultural products under the EC Common Agricultural Policy (CAP).

6.2 IMPORT PROCEDURES AND CUSTOMS TARIFFS

Prior to 1988 a separate customs declaration was required for all goods imported into or exported from the United Kingdom to control the payment of duties and taxes, to enforce prohibitions and restrictions and to collect trade statistics. Traditionally these declarations were provided at ports and airports in the UK and on the Irish Land Boundary, but over recent years a number of options were developed, including the creation of ICDs and facilities to clear goods at traders' own premises.

Declarations are increasingly provided by computer input from forwarding agents' offices to customs computers, via a direct trader input (DTI). Today 90% of import declarations are made this way. Facilities also exist for large importers to provide data periodically on magnetic tape, using simplified documentation at the ports for customs clearance purposes.

Goods frequently have to cross several national frontiers to reach their destination and customs transit systems have consequently been developed; the TIR system (see Appendix E) has existed for this purpose for many years. In the EC, Community Transit serves the same need and provides evidence that the goods are (or are not) in free circulation within the EC.

6.2.1 Customs 1988

Customs procedures in the United Kingdom have been subject to a number of important changes since we joined the Common Market in 1973. None have been as significant as two which occurred throughout Europe on 1 January 1988. On that date a new customs tariff required traders to reclassify all their imported and exported goods. Simultaneously the Single Administrative Document (SAD) was introduced to replace over 100 customs import, export and transit declaration forms previously used. A new valuation system for goods in Customs warehouses was implemented and the origin rules were suitably transposed for the EC's various preferential trade agreements.

6.2.2   Harmonized system

Over the years a number of goods' classification systems have been developed to meet a variety of different needs. For example transport operators have devised their own systems for the purpose of collecting freight charges, governments use different systems to collect revenue and compile production statistics and manufacturers have developed them as a means of identifying their products internally. Some customs administrations, notably the US, used their own systems rather than adopt the CCCN (Customs Co-operation Council Nomenclature).

In the early 1970s the need to develop a single goods' description system to satisfy all the requirements of international trade was recognized. The increasing use of computers meant that a common coding system was also necessary. As a result, customs and statistical administrations came together with several international trade and transport bodies to develop a Harmonized Commodity Description and Coding System (HS for short) which was finally adopted on 14 June 1983.

The HS incorporates many features of the CCCN. Its structure is broadly the same, but it is much more up-to-date, including many products which did not exist when the CCCN was developed some 40 years ago. It also meets the needs of many more countries and for this reason is more detailed. The CCCN's four-digit code is replaced by six digits in the HS, although some countries, notably in the developing world, will only apply it at four-digit level. Even so, it still does not meet all EC and UK needs and further subdivisions are added for duty or statistical purposes.

6.2.3   TARIC

The EC has a Common Customs Tariff but its nomenclature for statistical purposes, though related, is separate. Whilst they have for some years been brought together in the UK tariff, a host of other tariff-related measures (including many that flow from application of the Common Agricultural Policy) still stand apart and require a much finer level of detail than the basic tariff provides. The EC decided to bring all of these together into an integrated tariff (TARIC) for implementation with the HS on 1 January 1988. The result was a tariff considerably more convenient to use than is presently the case; furthermore, the allocation of unique codes to these measures will allow information relating to them (e.g. rates of duty) to be transmitted from the Commissioner's computer to member states' computers. This, in turn, will facilitate speedy and more accurate handling of customs declarations.

6.2.4 The new tariff (HS/TARIC)

The practical effects of the HS and TARIC are best illustrated by explaining how the UK printed tariff changed on 1 January 1988 to cope with them. All goods imported or exported were classified under an eight-digit Tariff Trade Code Number made up as follows:

Digits 1–4	The CCCN description for the goods
Digits 5–6	Additional breakdowns for the Community's Common Customs Tariff (CCCT) and statistical nomenclature (NIMEXE)
Digits 7–8	Further breakdowns for UK statistical purposes

The layout and content of the tariff adopted on 1 January 1988 differs markedly from the previous version in that much information that was shown in 'annexes' was incorporated into the main body of the tariff. As a result it is much easier to see whether goods are subject to quota, duty suspensions, tariff preferences, etc. and what the special rates are. VAT information is also shown. The incorporation of additional detail into the coding structure has resulted in more (and longer) code numbers.

Overall TARIC has 15 000 eleven-digit headings. The function of those digits is as follows:

Digits 1–6	HS code to be used internationally
Digits 7–8	EC breakdown for the CCT and NIMEXE

These descriptions and codes at the eight-digit level constitute the combined nomenclature of the European Community.

Digit 9	For use by the individual member state (or other community intra member states) to provide a more detailed national breakdown for trade or statistical purposes
Digits 10–11	Additional (TARIC) subdivisions to identify Community tariff measures applied to imports from non-EC countries

The Community measures incorporated in TARIC are:

Accession compensatory amounts (ACAs)
Anti-dumping duties

Countervailing duties
EC import licensing
Monetary compensatory amounts (MCAs)
Preferences
Quantitative restrictions and limits
Simplified procedures for value (fruit and vegetables)
Surveillance
Tariff quotas
Tariff suspensions
Textile categories
Variable charges for CAP
Wine preference prices

However, some of these special measures require such a detailed breakdown of the basic nine-digit code that the two further TARIC digits are insufficient and a separate additional code of four digits will be used in these circumstances, which include: variable charges, some MCAs and ACAs, some anti-dumping duties and wine preference prices.

The new tariff operates at two levels — one for imports from EC member states and all exports, to which a nine-digit code will generally apply; the second for imports from non-EC countries, which will require an eleven-digit code. Although the eleven-digit TARIC code will be used for all non-EC imports, the additional code will only be needed when goods are subject to one of the special measures.

It is important to understand that the TARIC code identifies goods, not the measures to which they may be subject. Thus goods which qualify for a preferential duty rate when originating in Sweden will have the same code as identical goods imported at the full rate from the US.

There is no obligation on Member States to present the printed tariff in any particular way but in the UK a landscape format will be adopted, with HS headings (first four digits) in bold block capitals and sub-headings in bold lower case (coded at the fifth and sixth digits). Nomenclature in medium lower case will represent either a Community subdivision for duty or statistical purposes (coded at the seventh and eighth digits) or a UK subdivision for statistical purposes (coded at the ninth digit).

Additional nomenclature text introduced for TARIC purposes will be shown in italics. TARIC subdivisions will often apply to a block of nine-digit headings. To repeat them after each nine-digit heading would have resulted in a UK tariff of vast proportions. This problem is avoided by printing the TARIC information after the block of headings to which it applies, and is required of tariff users to link correctly the two-digit TARIC level code with the appropriate preceding nine-digit code.

The new tariff comprises three volumes: Volume 1: General information;

EUROPEAN COMMUNITY

1 | 2 Consignor/*Exporter*   No

1 DECLARATION   A OFFICE OF DISPATCH/EXPORT

3 Forms | 4 Loading lists

5 Items | 6 Total packages | 7 Reference number

Copy for the country of dispatch/export

8 Consignee   No

9 Person responsible for financial settlement   No

10 *Country first destin* | 11 *Trading country* | 13 *CAP*

14 Declarant/Representative   No

15 Country of dispatch/*export* | 15 C disp/*exp* Code a| b| | 17 Country destin Code a| b|

16 Country of origin | 17 Country of destination

18 Identity and nationality of means of transport at departure | 19 Ctr | 20 Delivery terms

21 Identity and nationality of active means of transport crossing the border | 22 Currency and total amount invoiced | 23 Exchange rate | 24 Nature of transaction

25 Mode of transport at the border | 26 Inland mode of transport | 27 Place of loading | 28 Financial and banking data

1 | 29 Office of exit | 30 Location of goods

31 Packages and description of goods | Marks and numbers — Container No(s) — Number and kind

32 Item No | 33 Commodity Code

34 Country origin Code a| b| | 35 Gross mass (kg)

37 PROCEDURE | 38 Net mass (kg) | 39 *Quota*

40 Summary declaration/Previous document

41 Supplementary units

44 Additional information/ Documents produced/ Certificates and authorisations

A I Code

46 Statistical value

47 Calculation of taxes | Type | Tax base | Rate | Amount | MP

48 Deferred payment | 49 Identification of warehouse

B ACCOUNTING DETAILS

Total

50 Principal   No   Signature

C OFFICE OF DEPARTURE

51 Intended offices of transit (and country) | represented by   Place and date

52 Guarantee not valid for | Code | 53 Office of destination (and country)

D CONTROL BY OFFICE OF DEPARTURE   Stamp

Result

Seals affixed Number

identity

Time limit (date)

Signature

54 Place and date

Signature and name of declarant/representative

C88 (1-8)   Printed in the UK for HMSO 8055017 8 87 G H B 15822 (SEP)

Figure 6.1 Single Administrative Document, reproduced by kind permission of HM Customs and Excise.

Volume 2: Nomenclature and codes; Volume 3: Customs freight procedures (including information on the Single Administrative Document) replacing the Yellow Pages of the tariff. It is available from HMSO bookshops. The tariff is also available on electronic media. This will be of particular interest to software houses marketing entry preparation systems and to electronic publishing companies.

6.3   THE SINGLE ADMINISTRATIVE DOCUMENT (SAD)

The Single Administrative Document (Figure 6.1) was conceived as a replacement within the EC for existing export, community transit (CT)-movement and import forms, with the intention that a single set of forms made out at export would serve all these purposes. It has been developed as an 8-copy set, copies 1-3 for export, 4-5 for CT and 6-8 for import, although in practice some copies have dual functions.

Unfortunately the practical realities of moving goods between EC countries do not always fit such neat theories and the original concept has been adapted in a number of ways. Although the goods themselves may not change between departure and destination, information (notably that relating to their transport) often does. Data needed at import may well not be known at the time of departure. The needs of commercial confidentiality also prevent certain details being included on documents travelling with goods. Consequently the forms are printed so that some information on the export copies does not carry through to the import parts of the set.

In addition, the provision of all this information at the time of export is inconsistent with current simplified procedures which allow much of the data to be provided later. Withdrawal of these facilities would not be regarded as a simplification by the many companies currently using them and they will therefore be allowed to continue, with the result that even less information will travel with the goods in those instances. It follows that the document will almost always arrive at its destination still requiring further data to be added.

In order to minimize clearance delays many forwarding agents currently prepare import declarations before the goods arrive. To wait for an arriving document and add information to it before presentation to customs would increase rather than reduce delays. The option of 'splitting' the SAD and using relevant copies for their individual functions separately has therefore been introduced. In practice it will be possible, for example, to complete a fresh import SAD before the goods have arrived and input the data in advance at the increasing number of locations where customs clearance is computerized (DTI). Split use of the SAD will also be available at export (customs declaration/clearance), where, for sound commercial reasons different traders deal with export and transit (movement) formalities — although the benefits of combining these functions are likely to be sufficient to outweigh in most cases the advantages of export split use.

Whilst the concept of a single customs form for use in trade through-out the EC is appealing there would be disadvantages if declarations for trade with non-EC countries continued unchanged. They will therefore also use the SAD, although they will have to supply additional import value information because of the application of customs duty. In prac-tice the same form will be used in all circumstances, since even imports from Spain and Portugal will be subject to duty for several years and EFTA countries use the SAD for trade and CT-movement certificate purposes.

Although the SAD has created a need to harmonize customs infor-mation requirements throughout the EC, no country needs all the information which the SAD could contain and there are several boxes on the form which will not be completed in the UK. Also, exporters and their forwarding agents increasingly produce customs documents by computer and many computer printers will not print 8-copy sets of documents. For them there will be a 4-copy alternative, each copy having a dual function and two sets being printed when a full 8-copy SAD is needed. Because of these variations in the way the SAD can be used a number of different sets with copies appropriate to the various situations have been made available by customs.

6.4 CHANGES IN INFORMATION REQUIREMENTS

In addition to the new Commodity Code resulting from the HS and TARIC a number of other changes to the way information is declared on customs forms was introduced as a result of adopting the SAD. In particular new transport codes will be used and at export it will be necessary to identify the actual exporter of the goods, by means of his VAT number. The way in which duty and tax calculations are presented on import declaration will be significantly different and some information currently allocated its own space will be provided in a general 'additional information' area. The need to declare how the import values have been calculated for dutiable goods will remain, DTI agents will still, of course, have access to the screen format and calculation facilities on the customs computer ('DEPS' see Appendix E), but because the SAD has no space for manual calculations, a separate value build-up sheet will be used at non-DTI computer locations.

Perhaps the most significant change, however, will be the introduction of customs procedure codes to identify the customs regime (e.g. IPR, warehousing — see page 80) to and from which the goods are moving.

6.5 CUSTOMS PROCEDURE CODES

The SAD replaced over 100 customs forms by the use of six-digit customs procedure codes (CPCs), which give the form a considerable degree of versatility. These CPCs are designed to identify the purpose or customs regime for which goods are being imported, or in the case of exports, whether they have been subject to customs control whilst they were in the UK. The CPC replaced the customs transaction code (CTC) that was used for imports.

The CPC is built into a six-digit code based on three pairs of digits as follows:

1st pair	Community code for the procedure being applied for, i.e. regime to which the goods are being entered
2nd pair	Community code for previous customs regime, if there is none '00' is used.
3rd pair	National coding to analyse community headings in more detail

In general terms, the first digit of the community code gives an indication of the nature of the import or export as follows:

0	Entry to free circulation only (i.e. outright payment of duty only)
1	Permanent despatch/export
2	Temporary despatch/export
3	Re-despatch/re-export
4	Entry to home use with simultaneous entry to free circulation (i.e. outright payment of duty and/or VAT)
5	Temporary importation
6	Re-importation
7	Entry to warehouse or free zone
8	National transit/transhipment (not used in the UK)
9	Other

It is essential for importers to use the correct CPC, since failure to do so could mean the loss of entitlement to some special customs facility or duty refund that might be applicable. To conclude our explanation of import customs tarriffs, the present tarriff based on the Harmonized System (HS) was developed following over 10 years of detailed discussion amongst the major trading nations and is used by some 85% of the world's trading nations. It is a major aid to international trade. The tarriff embraces the European Community's Integrated Customs Tarriff (TARIC) and also includes the UK statistical requirement. Every different item at import has its own Commodity Code and this must be correctly declared. It is the legal responsibility of the importer to declare correctly the Commodity Code but many smaller importers especially rely on the

Freight Forwarder to do so. Commodity Codes for goods either originating within the European Community, or being in free circulation within it, comprise a minimum of nine digits, or up to thirteen according to the item involved. The latter is for special traffic. Commodity Codes for imports from other places, or goods which are not in free circulation, comprise eleven digits, or in the case of that same special traffic (CAP goods, etc.) up to fifteen digits.

6.6   IMPORTATION OF GOODS

Most imports are cleared under the 'split-use' option. For importers and agents who decide to use incoming SADs as the basis of their import declarations it is important to understand that they are required to sign the document and accept legal responsibility for everything contained on the document, including information entered at export. If any of that data is wrong it is their responsibility to change it before presentation. In deciding whether to use this option, however, it is worth bearing in mind that only about one-third of the information needed at import will copy through from export copies.

For DTI users the facility to present plain paper entries is available but the data have to be in the same location as they would appear on a pre-printed SAD. Customs have available a plain paper entry sample design for importers preferring their own keying document.

6.7   WAREHOUSED GOODS: VALUATION AND DOCUMENTATION

The system for establishing the sterling value for duty of warehoused goods subject to 'ad valorem' charges is based on the exchange rates current at the time of removal from customs warehouse into free circulation.

The proprietor is able to use any sale for export to the UK or to any other member of the Community up until the time of removal from warehouse to establish the value by reference to the price paid or payable. Where more than one sale takes place before entry of the goods into free circulation, the proprietor is free to choose any one of these sales. The owner, however, must be in possession of all relevant facts regarding the chosen sale and be able to attest documentary evidence to them.

Where any of the elements (price of the goods, transport, insurance, ancillary charges, etc.) making up the customs value are charged in a foreign currency, conversion to sterling must be carried out by reference to the customs weekly period rate of exchange appropriate at the time of removal. This currency conversion rule will also have to be followed in the case of *ad valorem* goods liable also to VAT at the time of removal.

Although the customs value will have to be established at the time of despatch, for the purposes of UK trade statistics a sterling CIF UK port value will continue to be required at the time of importation or entry to warehouse. The value established at the time of removal will also be used to meet EC statistical requirements.

It is the responsibility of the proprietor of warehoused goods to declare their value for duty. Where the owner relies on the warehouse-keeper's records for the necessary information those records will need to be adapted so that foreign currency elements can be retained for conversion to sterling at the time of removal. Where import consignments are removed from warehouse in small lots it will be necessary not only for the price of the goods to be apportioned but also for the additional charges (transport, insurance, etc.) to be appropriately allocated according to the quantity being removed.

Goods imported to and exported from a warehouse will be declared on a SAD. This involves form C259, based on the SAD, for all removals into free circulation and other customs regimes.

6.8 CUSTOMS COMPUTERIZATION

From a customs point of view direct trader input (DTI) is the most efficient method of obtaining information from carriers and forwarding agents. The DTI trader, has on-line communication with the customs computer, submits the data relevant to his customs declaration in advance of the actual paper document and all validation queries, etc., are sorted out before any customs personnel become involved. Customs receive clean and complete information and the customs computer will already have carried out all necessary accounting functions, checks, etc. before the documentation is lodged with them. The computer will also give a preliminary indication to the import carrier and the importer's agent of how the consignment is likely to be dealt with by customs, whether a documentary check only or full examination (turn out) of the goods.

From the trade point of view the main advantage of DTI is speed of clearance. Instead of there being lengthy manual processing every time errors are detected, the majority are sorted out immediately without customs being directly involved. When DTI is linked with inventory control within each port complex both official and commercial clearance can be given in an efficient and effective manner.

After the initial introduction of DTI at London Airport it took a long time for it to be introduced elsewhere. When ACP80 was extended to Manchester Airport in 1983 over 95% of air cargo imports were covered by DTI. Progress in the maritime sector has been slower but in the early

1980s the Port of Felixstowe was suffering from the same problems as London Airport had faced in the late 1960s. The growth of traffic had outstripped the port's ability to cope with manual processing. DTI was introduced at Felixstowe in 1985. The improvement in customs clearance times was dramatic, from days to hours from the moment FCP80 was introduced. Later, inventory facilities were added and FCP80 was extended to Harwich, Ipswich and other ports between 1986 and 1988.

Today most of the other major maritime ports have introduced or plan to introduce DTI. At the end of 1989 over 90% of import entry information was being given to customs electronically. A significant proportion of postshipment export statistical information is also being input by export agents at DTI locations.

Imports have continued to increase in volume, and some 5.5 million import entries are handled by customs staff annually. This represents information exchange on a massive scale and the only way HM Customs and Excise has been able to carry out controls and at the same time not impose unacceptable burdens on the trading community is by the continuing use of data-processing techniques.

The Departmental Entry Processing System (DEPS) has worked well, but is due to be replaced by CHIEF (Customs Handling of Import and Export Freight). Following a review of the implementation plan and development timetable for the Customs '88 Project, HM Customs and Excise have decided that it would not be practicable to introduce the new entry processing system at the same time as a new tariff and the SAD. It was considered that the best way forward for both customs and the trade was to use the existing DEPS to cope with the new tariff and SAD procedures from 1 January 1988, allowing a suitable period for familiarization with the new procedures before implementating the proposed CHIEF system by 1992–93.

A number of enhancements to CHIEF are likely to be introduced after the initial implementation. These include removals from warehouse, reduced manual intervention in the entry process, and electronic writing-off of import licences and tariff quotas. These facilities will require all clearance locations to have access to the network. This will be particularly necessary when the control of claims to tariff quota is included in the system, in order to ensure that all traders receive equitable treatment. CHIEF should also bring computerized entry processing and DTI to all locations handling more than 500 entries per year. Those locations handling less than 500 entries per year will be linked to an EPU.

A particularly valuable feature of CHIEF will be the comprehensive export processing system. This will allow exporters and their forwarding agents to input export declarations to the system before goods arrive at the export location. The computerized export procedure will not be available in its entirety until the latter stages of CHIEF's implementation;

until then the present arrangements which allow DTI traders to input export details postshipment under the simplified clearance procedures (SCP) will continue.

Importers will need to keep a close eye on the systems and developments outlined above, in order to maximize the efficiency of their operations. Speed, reliability and cost of customs processes are of major importance, but companies should be looking at other aspects of their organization to ensure that improvements at ports are not cancelled out by inefficient procedures elsewhere.

6.9 SIMPLIFIED PROCEDURE FOR IMPORT CLEARANCE (SPIC)

The above procedure was also introduced on 1 January 1988. Most consignments with a value of less than £475 will be eligible for SPIC but the eligibility criteria also specified that no data other than those which appear on the SPIC format are required for control or statistical purposes. The consignments which will be entered on SPIC are mainly those of the type which have in the past been entered on a Transit Shed Register or an Abbreviated Entry (the C15). As with those procedures SPIC requires a minimum of data, and up to six items may be entered on each page. There is no pre-lodgement facility.

6.10 COMMERCIAL IMPORTATIONS

6.10.1 General principles

Customs procedures for commercial importation vary according to the type of traffic involved but the principles remain broadly the same as follows:

1. Goods may be imported legally only through places approved by customs (e.g. wharves, airports, and approved routes across the land boundary with the Irish Republic).
2. Ships and aircraft must lodge a report, including a cargo list with customs on arrival (usually before unloading begins).
3. All goods must be properly 'entered' and any duty (or levies on goods subject to the Common Agricultural Policy (CAP)) and other charges due must normally be paid before they are released from customs control; this usually takes place at a wharf or airport of importation but the requirements can be completed at inland clearance depots or, under a special scheme, at the importer's premises.
4. Customs officers have the right to examine all goods to confirm that they correspond with the 'entry' made for them.

6.10.2   Import entry procedure

The importer is responsible for preparing an 'entry' for all the goods he is importing. The 'entry' is a document (SAD) on which he declares the description, value, quantity, rate of duty and various other details about the goods. When presented to customs it is normally accompanied by supporting documents such as copies of commercial invoices and packing lists to provide evidence of the nature and value of the goods, but frequently also by an official document to prove their status for duty purposes. The usual procedure is to complete the SAD and process it through the DEPS (see pages 78–80).

Information about the supplier of goods, the importer, the goods, shipment details, duty, VAT, etc., are required on the form which must be completed by the importer or his authorized agent. Normally, completed entry forms must be presented at the appropriate customs office within 14 working days (7 days if by air) of the arrival of the importing ship, aircraft or vehicle. Customs entries can usually be presented before the expected arrival of the ship or aircraft although they should not be earlier than 4 working days. However, certain classes of goods are not accepted for entry prior to importation, e.g. goods affected by the announcement of an increase in duty.

Formal entry is not normally required for postal consignments. However, such imports must comply with post office and customs requirements.

The following are the main documents required:

Commercial invoice.   The original invoice and a copy for retention by customs must be submitted. If the invoice is in a foreign language a translation may be required. If the invoice does not give details of the contents of individual packages a separate packing list, weight note or similar advice will also be required.

Import Licence.   Required for goods which are not covered by an Open General Licence.

Certificate of Origin.   If required.

Community Transit Document.   For goods imported from another member of the EC.

Single Administrative Document.   Customs entry.

Evidence of freight charges.   For goods bought on FOB terms.

Out of Charge note (Form C130). Gives details of the goods imported, shipping marks, etc. When the entry has been processed and examination of the goods completed, it will be returned to the importer as an authority that the goods may be released from customs.

Other documents may be required depending on the type and value of the goods. For full details of the import entry procedure contact any HM Customs and Excise office.

Payment of duty

Customs import duty and any additional charges must be paid before the goods are released from customs. In certain cases payment of customs duties and other charges may be deferred for a period, subject to adequate security and other conditions.

Examination of goods

All imported goods are legally liable to be examined by the customs authorities but in practice only a sample are selected. Where examination is required the opening, unpacking and re-packing of the goods must be carried out by the importer or his agent; some port authorities require that the goods must be opened and unpacked by a member of their own staff acting as the importer's agent for the purpose. Customs officers do not open or unpack goods and do not normally accept responsibility for any damage that may occur during examination of the goods. If the customs officer is satisfied that the goods are in order he will certify the entry form, stamp the 'Out of Charge note' and return it to the importer. This authorizes the removal of goods from customs charge.

Payment of dock dues

The charges made by the dock authority for handling the goods must normally be paid before the goods leave the docks. However, regular importers usually arrange for dock dues to be put to an account which is settled on a monthly basis.

Certain ports levy a charge on imported goods in addition to the normal handling charge. The charge is called Port Rates or Dues and must be paid before the goods can be cleared through customs. The rates charged vary according to the type of goods and a complete schedule is issued by the appropriate port authority.

Import licences

The import of goods into the UK is governed by the *Import of Goods (Control) Order 1954*, prohibiting the import of all goods except under a licence issued by the Department of Trade. Import licences are broadly of two kinds:

1. An Open General Import Licence (OGIL) which allows anyone to import any of the goods to which it applies. Most goods can be imported under an OGIL and their importers do not have to present an import licence to customs officials at the port of entry. Goods which are not covered by the licence are listed in its two schedules. Importers requiring details of the Open General Import Licence can obtain copies of it, together with the two accompanying schedules, from HMSO bookshops or through booksellers.
2. Individual import licences which must be obtained for any goods not covered by an Open General Licence. These are issued to a named importer from the Import Licensing Branch, Department of Trade, 375 Kensington High Street, London W14 8QH. There are two types of individual licence:
   (a) An Open Individual Licence which allows the import of a specified commodity without restriction on the quantity or value. This is usually valid for 12 months but can be valid for longer or shorter periods in specific cases.
   (b) A Specific Individual Licence which allows the import of a stated quantity or value of a specified commodity from a specified source. A specific licence is valid only for a specified time.

It should be noted that neither the Open General Import Licence nor any individual licence issued under the *Import of Goods (Control) Order, 1954* exempts importers from compliance with requirements under other legislation, e.g. *Food and Drugs Acts*, *Disease of Animals Act*, *Endangered Species (Import and Export) Act, 1976*. Examples of some of the goods for which importation is prohibited or restricted are given in the section below entitled 'Other prohibitions and restrictions'.

Importers should not arrange to ship goods to the UK until they have ascertained that a licence will be granted or that a separate licence is not required. Penalties can be incurred for attempting to import goods without a licence. Goods must be imported on or before the expiry date of the licence and renewals or extensions of licences will not generally be made.

Details of changes in the licensing arrangements for imports into the UK are given in 'Notices to importers' published in *British Business*, the weekly publication of the Department of Trade and Industry.

Documetary proof of origin for certain textile products
Under the Council Regulation (EEC) 616/78 certain textile products must be accompanied by specified documentary proof of origin when commercially imported into the European Community. Information about the forms of documentary proof required is available from Import Licensing Branch, 375 Kensington High Street, London W14 8QH (telephone 071-603 4644).

Other prohibitions and restrictions
Additional controls governing the importation of a wide range of goods have been introduced for a variety of reasons such as public protection, animal and plant health, conservation, or on moral or humanitarian grounds. Importation may be either completely prohibited or only allowed under the authority of an import licence, issued by the appropriate government department, or a veterinary or plant health certificate issued in the country of origin.

In very general terms, the import of all animals and associated products, most plants and other agricultural produce is subject to some form of import control. Failure to comply with legal requirements will almost certainly result in delayed clearance, with the possibility of forfeiture of the goods and prosecution.

Import quotas
Quotas are established for specified goods from particular sources as the need arises, either by negotiation and agreement between the European Commission and the country concerned or, failing that, by imposition. Generally, where a quota has been agreed with the exporting country it is administered by that country, and the Import Licensing Branch issues import licences against export certificates essentially as a double-check that the quota is not being exceeded. Where, however, a quota is imposed upon an exporting country, that country may not agree or be given the opportunity to export administer, and in such cases it falls to the Import Licensing Branch to allocate the quota amongst importers. Details of licensing arrangements for quota goods and quota levels are also published as 'Notices to importers' in *British Business*.

Trade agreements
The UK, as member of the EC, enjoys duty-free trade with other members of the Community. Trade agreements giving preferential tariffs also exist between the EC and the following:

1. EFTA (European Free Trade Area) countries — Austria, Finland, Iceland, Portugal, Sweden and Switzerland.
2. Algeria, Cyprus, Egypt, Israel, Jordan, Lebanon, Malta, Morocco, Spain, Syria, Tunisia and Yugoslavia.
3. The Faroe Islands.
4. Certain African, Caribbean and Pacific States (ACP) and the Overseas Countries and Territories (OCTs).

In addition preferential tariffs are granted to more than 150 developing countries under the Generalized Scheme of Preference (GSP). This system is designed to help those countries increase their export earnings and promote their industrialization. All enquiries concerning these agreements should be directed to ITP Division, Department of Trade, 1 Victoria Street, London SW1 H0ET.

6.10.3   Variations in procedure

Variations in the import entry procedure include the following:

Suspension of duty and reliefs
There are procedures for suspending the payment of duty or for relieving goods of duty provided that certain conditions are met and, usually, that the goods remain under customs control. One example is where goods are moved to an approved warehouse. An approved warehouse is a secure place approved by HM Customs and Excise for the storage of goods on which the duty has not been paid. Warehouses are not owned by the Crown but are operated mainly by warehousing companies, dock and harbour authorities and similar bodies. In certain circumstances, importers can be approved to operate a warehouse on their own premises. Except for warehouse-keepers of customs warehouses (who enter into an undertaking) each warehouse-keeper must enter into a bond with approved sureties as a guarantee that duty will be paid on any goods not accounted for to the Commissioners' satisfaction.

The level and intensity of official control at each warehouse is determined with regard to the revenue risks involved. Official staff are employed in a flexible manner to monitor traders' physical and documentary control systems. Some large warehouses may have resident official staff, others may be controlled on a visiting basis. The objective in either case is to ensure that, except for those goods which are lawfully entitled to be delivered without payment of duty, the proper amount of duty is paid when the goods leave the warehouse. Natural losses such as evaporation are taken into account, but all losses are subject to close scrutiny by official staff and duty is charged if deficiencies cannot be satisfactorily explained.

Further examples of suspension of duty and reliefs include goods imported under a variety of temporary importation reliefs, goods imported by certain traders to undergo an authorized process before being re-exported, and goods claiming 'end-use' relief from duties under EC regulations which allow free entry only if the goods are used for a specified purpose such as shipbuilding. Goods being transhipped (i.e. imported for re-export either from the port of importation or from another port) are also relieved of duty.

The Department of Trade and Industry is prepared to consider applications for temporary suspensions of import duty where, for the time being, the goods to be imported (which must normally be raw materials or semi-manufactures) are not produced in the European Community.

Duty relief may also be allowed on certain goods in certain circumstances (e.g. scientific instruments imported for scientific research; goods for industrial research; goods for the handicapped, etc.).

Local import control (LIC)
Traders who regularly import repetitive traffic and who can satisfy specific conditions may make entry of their goods locally and have them cleared at their premises.

Period entry (imports)
Traders who use computers for stock control and accounting purposes and whose import trade is repetitive and on a large scale may apply to submit a simplified entry at the time of import supplemented by periodic schedules in a computer medium such as magnetic tape. It includes goods eligible for EC Preference; goods eligible for tariff quota relief; goods subject to CAP charges and to CAP licence; goods requiring a Department of Trade and Industry Individual Import Licence and/or textile goods requiring documentary proof of origin. The benefits of Period Entry can be enhanced for traders who qualify by local import control (LIC), under which clearance takes place at the traders own premises.

Air traffic
The procedure followed at airports lays particular emphasis on speed of turn-round of aircraft and the clearance of cargo. At Heathrow, Gatwick and Manchester airports the procedures have been speeded up by setting up a communual cargo inventory system and this is linked to the customs computer used for entry processing. This enables forwarding agents and airlines to make electronic freight declarations.

Sea traffic
The system of direct trader input (DTI) has also been introduced at over twenty seaports and inland clearance depots (ICDs).

Postal consignments
Goods imported by post are subject to the same duties, taxes, prohibitions and restrictions as other imports. Postal packages enter the country through postal depots where they are subject to customs' scrutiny. In most cases any charges due are assessed on the basis of the customs declaration by the sender and/or examination and are collected by the postman when he delivers the package.

Inward processing relief
Goods imported by authorized traders for process and exportation outside the EC may be relieved of customs duty and other import

charges but not VAT. Officers visit processors for control purposes and ensure that duty is paid on any goods diverted to use within the EC.

Free zones
Free zones have been set up on an experimental basis at a number of ports and airports. A free zone is an enclosed area into which goods may be moved without payment of customs duty and similar import charges, including value added tax (VAT) charged at importation. Such charges become payable only if goods are brought out of the zone into the UK market or are consumed within the zone. In addition, duty (but not VAT) is payable if goods are processed other than for export outside the EC.

6.11 VALUE ADDED TAX

Value added tax (VAT) is a broadly-based tax on the value of most goods and services supplied in the course of business. It also applies to imported goods and to certain imported services. All traders who supply taxable goods and services are required to be registered with HM Customs and Excise if their annual turnover of taxable goods and services exceeds a set figure. This figure is adjusted periodically with the agreement of the EC. There are nearly 1.5 million VAT registered businesses in the UK. The net tax yield from VAT for the year 1985–86 was £19 328 million which represented nearly 52% of the total revenue collected by Customs and Excise.

There are now only two rates of tax, the Standard Rate of 15% which applies to most goods and services and a Zero Rate (0%) which, broadly, applies to food (but not catering), public transport, new buildings, books, young children's clothing, domestic fuel and to most exports. Some services, such as banking, finance, and insurance services are exempt from VAT and traders exclusively engaged in such activities cannot be registered. In a tax with two different rates and a number of exemptions, border-line problems inevitably arise. Where these cannot be resolved through discussions with local VAT staff or the Headquarters office concerned, an appeal can be made first to an independent VAT tribunal and subsequently through the courts.

A registered trader is required to make periodic returns of the tax payable to, or recoverable from, Customs and Excise. This is calculated by deducting the total amount of tax he has paid (or is due to pay) to his suppliers (with certain exceptions, notably VAT paid on motor cars and business entertainment suppliers) from the total of the tax due on the goods and services he has supplied. In certain circumstances (e.g. a trader making only zero-rated suppliers who buys standard-rated equipment for his business), the tax paid to his suppliers may be greater than the tax due and a repayment is made to the trader by Customs and Excise. A central computer record of all VAT traders is kept in the VAT Central Unit at Southend. The computer issues tax returns direct to traders. The returns, along with any payment due, are normally made every 3 months, but traders who usually receive repayment of tax may opt to submit returns every month. Where a return from a trader who usually makes a payment of tax is not received in the time allowed, an assessment of that period's tax is automatically issued by the computer. There is also a financial penalty applied to traders who persistently send their returns in late. Where the department fails to pay an acceptable repayment claim within a reasonable period, it will make an additional compensatory payment.

VAT is controlled by staff based in VAT offices situated in principal towns throughout the United Kingdom. At present there are more than 80 main VAT offices, some with sub-offices in neighbouring towns. VAT staff are responsible for advising registered traders on problems involving VAT and for ensuring that they are fully aware of their obligations to account for tax. Traders range from one-man businesses to large companies with turnovers of many millions of pounds. Periodic 'control visits' are made to check that the correct amount of tax is being paid and that the trader's tax records are adequate. The VAT central computer subjects each tax return to a number of checks and supplies each local VAT office with information about the returns submitted by traders in the area and indicates which traders are due to be visited.

6.12 CONCLUSION

It is important to bear in mind that customs regulations are subject to constant change and the importer is strongly recommended to keep in close touch with the local HM Customs and Excise information officer who can supply Customs Notices free of charge.

The DTI system exists virtually nationwide and is cost-effective to the importer. It is constantly being improved and the next major change will be the abolition of customs examination of goods at frontier points of those commodities originating within the European Community. This will reduce the work-load of HM Customs and Excise. Currently 55% of UK imports originate from EC.

Importers fresh to the business are urged to obtain adequate training or consultancy on how best to conduct their import business or customs processing. Listed alphabetically below are the HM Customs Notices which will help the importer:

Customs Warehousing: No. 232
Delaying Payment of Customs Duty: VAT and other charges: No. 101

European Community Preferences Imports: No. 826
Import duty relief for exports (inward processing relief): No. 221
Imported Goods — End-use relief: No. 770
Inland Clearance Depots: No. 464
Local Import Control: No. 464A
Period Entry — A simplified import entry procedure: No. 480
Tariff quotas — goods originating in a preference country: No. 375
The European Community: Community Carnets — Goods temporarily
    imported by Community Carnet: No. 756
VAT Imports: No. 752.

7 Import finance

Buying products overseas requires a different financial strategy compared with buying in the domestic market. Delivery takes longer, contracts are not as straightforward, and payment for the goods is correspondingly more complex. The prime consideration is to ensure the payments are made on time and financial interests of the importers are safeguarded as much as possible.

The method of payment chosen by the importer, specified in the contract of sale and reflected in the export/commercial invoice will have regard to:

1. available financial options;
2. the usual contract terms adopted in the manufacturer's country;
3. how quickly payment is required;
4. the political situation in the buyer's country;
5. the availability of foreign currency to the buyer;
6. the terms of contract of sale;
7. exchange control regulations, if any;
8. the nature of relationship between buyer and seller;
9. whether the cost of any credit can be borne by the buyer or the supplier;
10. resources of the buyer.

The GATT valuation code has been adopted by the EC and the method of operation in the UK is explained in HM Customs Notice No. 252. Interest payable under a financing arrangement for imported goods may be excluded from the imported value, but interest must be clearly distinguished from the price of the goods. This condition is fulfilled when the financing is provided by a bank or finance company.

7.1 METHODS OF PAYMENT FOR OVERSEAS PURCHASES

7.1.1 Payments on 'open account'

Open account trading is an arrangement whereby the seller sends the goods and shipping documents direct to the buyer, thus enabling him to take delivery and dispose of the goods — payment being made some time later, usually not more than 180 days. If the goods are to be sold on open account terms, it is sensible to have a clear sales contract showing exactly when payment is to be made. It might, for instance, indicate that this should be effected on receipt of the goods, or of the documents, or perhaps 30 days after receipt of the documents by the buyer. Thus, the open account method of payment confers the main advantage with the importer; the exporter has far less security. It is very popular within the EC and US because it is straightforward and saves money. Such is its popularity that it is difficult for an exporter to resist the pressure from the buyer to trade on these terms, other than for the first one or two orders.

The seller must have absolute trust in the integrity of the buyer, which is usually based on an established relationship. In addition, there must be confidence that regulations and availability of foreign exchange in the buyer's country will not prohibit or delay the transfer of payment. It is especially popular between established exporters and importers who have a good and continuous trading relationship.

A cheque is the most advantageous way for an importer to settle since up to a month's extra credit is gained in the time taken in the post for the cheque to reach the seller, to be paid into the seller's bank, and be sent through the international banking system, before ultimately being debited to the importer's account in his own country. Further delays will arise if exchange control authority has first to be obtained in the importer's country. The seller can arrange with his bank to collect the cheque, in which case he does not receive credit to his account until his bankers have received advice of final payment of the cheque in the buyer's country. Alternatively, he may arrange for the cheque to be 'negotiated/purchased with recourse'. The bank will then make the funds available before the cheque has been paid, although retaining the right to charge back the customer's account should the cheque be unpaid.

Another method is the banker's draft where an importer can purchase from his bank a draft in favour of the exporter drawn on a bank in the exporter's country, either in sterling or foreign currency. The importer pays his bank for the draft at the time of issue, but there is still the delay in the post before such a draft reaches the exporter. However, once received, the draft can be cleared quickly if it is payable in the exporter's own country. Overall, the banker's draft avoids exchange control problems but there could still be delays in the post and in clearance between the banks in the chain of remittances. A bank draft is not a guaranteed payment. It is a cheque drawn by one bank on another, with all the characteristics of a normal cheque.

The International Money Transfer and Express International Money Transfer are the quickest means of making payment and result in the exporter receiving cleared funds direct into his bank account. The importer instructs his bank to make payment through the banking system and usually the exporter will indicate on his invoice his account number and the branch of the bank where his account is held. The importer's account is debited by his bankers. This involves the buyer's bank instructing a bank in the seller's country to make the payment. This instruction can be sent by mail, telex or through the Society for Worldwide Interbank Financial Telecommunications (SWIFT). SWIFT is an automated interbank system for transfers and other communications. It offers a secure, standardized and rapid method for members (the banks) to make financial transactions between themselves.

In the case of larger amounts, and where cashflow and interest are factors to be considered, payment may be made by Express International Money Transfer. The buyer's bank then gives instructions to a bank in the exporter's country, either by coded cable or telex, or by a priority SWIFT message. In both cases, bank charges can be met either by buyer or seller, depending on the agreement between them.

Finally the fastest method of making payment, but usually the most expensive, is the telegraphic transfer. In such situations the buyer's bank cables, telephones or telexes the exporter's bank instructing them to pay the seller the agreed amount. Few importers use this system.

7.1.2 Bill of Exchange

The Bill of Exchange has been defined as 'an unconditional order in writing, addressed by one person to another, signed by the person giving it, requiring the person to whom it is addressed to pay on demand or at a fixed or determinable future time a sum certain in money to the order of, a specified person, or to the bearer'. It can be used in international trade involving practically all countries of the world and has numerous advantages as detailed below:

1. It is an instrument long recognized by trade custom and by the law, so that it is governed by an established code of practice (ICC publication No. 322).
2. It is a specific demand on the debtor.
3. It provides a useful mechanism for granting a pre-arranged period of credit to an overseas buyer.

4. It permits the exporter to maintain a degree of control over the shipping documents by making their release subject to payment or acceptance of the Bill. However, it should be noted that the drawing of a Bill of Exchange does not guarantee payment: Bills can be dishonoured.

5. The importer does not have to pay for the goods or raw materials until the supplier has despatched them.

In normal circumstances the exporter draws a Bill of Exchange, attaches the shipping documents to it and lodges the whole with his bank, giving very precise and complete instructions as to the action to be taken in certain circumstances: whether to forward the Bill by airmail and ask for the proceeds to be remitted by cable or airmail; whether the documents are to be released against payment or acceptance of the Bill; whether the Bill is to be 'protested' if dishonoured; whether the goods should be stored and insured if not taken up by the buyer; whether rebate may be given for early payment; the party to whom the collecting bank may refer in case of dispute.

The exporter's bank will forward the Bill and documents to its correspondent bank in the buyer's country, passing on exactly the instructions received from the exporter. Acting as collecting bank the correspondent will present the Bill to the buyer and release the documents in accordance with the instructions received. If the arrangement called for payment to be made immediately, then the Bill of Exchange will be drawn at 'sight' and the instructions will be to release the documents against payment (D/P). If it is payable at a fixed or determinable future time it is called a term draft because the buyer is receiving a period of credit which is identified by the tenor of the Bill. Hence the Bill will be drawn before maturity which calls for the payment after a certain time interval, usually 30, 60, 90 or 180 days. For example it may be '90 days sight' and the instructions will be for the documents to be released against acceptance (D/A) of the Bill by the buyer. In this case, the buyer signs his acceptance across the face of the Bill, which now becomes due for payment in 90 days, and he receives the documents of title to the goods. The collecting bank will advise the remitting bank of the date of acceptance and hold the Bill until maturity, when he will present it to the buyer for payment. In the event of dishonour, the collecting bank will arrange 'protest' by a notary if it has been instructed to do so. This procedure provides legal proof that the Bill was presented to the drawee and was dishonoured, and enables action to be taken in the courts without further preliminaries.

The procedures and responsibilities of the banks and other parties are laid down in the Uniform Rules for the Collection of Commercial Paper issued by the International Chamber of Commerce publication No. 400 and accepted by major banks throughout the world.

The method of collecting payment described above is based on the Documentary Bill, but in certain circumstances use may be made of a 'clean' Bill, that is, a Bill to which no documents are attached. This involves the supplier sending the Bill for the value of the goods through a local bank for payment or acceptance by the buyer or drawee on presentation. The Bill of Exchange would be drawn by the supplier or drawer on the purchase of the goods. Such Bills may be drawn for the collection of monies due for services or for any debt which does not relate to goods. A clean Bill may also be used to obtain payment for goods sent on 'open account', especially where payment is overdue. Clean Bill collection requires no shipping documents to be attached and is particularly popular in European markets where the method is also used in internal trade.

The Bill of Exchange is most likely to be used in a documentary method of payment. This involves the supplier sending the Bill through the international banking system with the shipping documents, including the document of title to the goods i.e. the original Bill of Lading. The bank then releases the document on payment or acceptance of the Bill by the importer.

The supplier can use the banking system for a cash against documents (CAD) collection. In such situations only the shipping documents are sent and the supplier instructs the bank to release them only after payment by the importer. This method is used in some European countries whose buyers often prefer CAD to a sight draft if the supplier insists on a documentary collection for the settlement of the contract.

The alternative to the Bill of Exchange is the use of the promissory note — 'an unconditional promise in writing by one person to another, signed by the importer (the author of the document), agreeing to pay on demand or at a fixed future date, a certain sum in money to a specified person or to the bearer of the note'. It differs from a Bill of Exchange in that it is written by the buyer to the seller rather than being drawn by the seller on the buyer. A promissory note provides a commitment to pay as does the acceptance of a Bill of Exchange.

Whilst a buyer may acknowledge a seller's preference for a documentary collection, he will at the same time bear in mind the voyage duration to determine whether a documentary collection is ideal. All documents must be available and with the importer before the carrying vessel or other means of transport arrives. A clean Bill with documents sent separately by courier may be essential.

7.1.3 Documentary credits and allied documents

A common and secure method of payment is by Documentary Letter of Credit. Basically this is an undertaking by the issuing bank to an exporter (beneficiary) through an advising or confirming bank in the exporter's country, that the issuing bank will pay for the goods provided the exporter complies precisely with all the conditions of the credit. Payment may be in the supplier's own currency or another currency depending on the contract of sale.

The importer is in reality providing the exporter with immediate payment in return for a guaranteed assurance from the issuing bank that the importers terms required have been completed to the bank's satisfaction. The exporter must of course deliver to the advising/confirming bank whatever documents are required by the Documentary Letter of Credit, e.g. Bill of Lading, Air Waybill, invoice, insurance certificate, preshipment certificate and so on. The importer will receive from the issuing bank documents which comply with the Credit terms. The advising/confirming bank will ensure that these documents are correct and comply with the Letter of Credit terms before passing them to the issuing bank which will check them before releasing them to the importer.

Basically, this is an arrangement whereby the buyer requests his bank to establish a Credit in favour of the seller. The buyer's bank (the issuing bank) undertakes, or authorizes its correspondent bank in the exporter's country, to pay the exporter a sum of money (normally the invoice price of the goods) against presentation of specified shipping documents. It is a mandatory contract and completely independent of the sales contract. It is concerned only with documents and not the goods to which the documents refer. Liability for payment now rests with the issuing bank and not the buyer. Such Credits are usually 'irrevocable', which means that they cannot be cancelled or amended without the agreement of the beneficiary (the exporter) and all other parties. The exporter can thus rely on payment being made as soon as he has shipped the goods and produced the necessary documents. The security provided by an irrevocable Credit may be further enhanced if the bank in the exporter's country (the advising bank) is requested by the issuing bank to add its 'confirmation'. The exporter then has a 'confirmed irrevocable Credit' and he need look no further than his own local bank for payment. If a Credit is not 'confirmed', liability for payment rests with the issuing bank abroad, although the advising bank would usually be prepared to negotiate with recourse.

A Documentary Credit contains a detailed description of the goods: price per unit and packing; name and address of the beneficiary; port of shipment and port of destination; whether the price is FOB, CFR (cost and freight) or CIF; and whether part shipments and transhipment are allowed. In some cases, the ship will be named. Details of insurance (if CIF) and the risks to be covered will also be shown. The Credit will specify a latest date for shipment and an expiry date, which is the latest date for the presentation of documents. It will also stipulate a time-limit for presentation measured from the issue date of the Bills of Lading; in the absence of such a stipulation, banks refuse to accept documents presented later than 21 days after issuance of the Bills. The documents usually required are now described.

Invoice.   The amount must not exceed the Credit amount. If terms such as 'about' or 'circa' are used, a tolerance of 10% is allowed (in respect of quantity the tolerance is 3%). The description of the goods on the invoice and the packing must be precise and agree with the Credit. An essential part of the description is the marks and numbers on the packages. These must appear on the invoice, which should be in the name of the buyer.

Bills of Lading.   These are the document of title to the goods, without which the buyer will not be able to obtain delivery from the shipping company. The Credit will call for a full set; they are usually issued in sets of three. They must be clean, that is to say bear no superimposed clauses derogatory to the condition of the goods such as 'inadequate packing', 'used drums' or 'on deck'. Unless the Credit has specifically permitted the circumstances contained in the clause, the negotiating bank will request an indemnity. The Bills of Lading must show the goods to be 'on board'. Bills marked 'received for shipment' are not acceptable unless they bear a subsequent notation, dated and signed, stating that the goods are 'on board'. Under the regulations set out in the Uniform Customs and Practice for Documentary Credits publication No. 400 of the International Chamber of Commerce, the following Bills of Lading will be accepted:

1. Through Bills issued by shipping companies or their agents, even though they cover several modes of transport.
2. Short-form Bills of Lading which indicate some or all of the conditions of carriage by reference to a source or document other than the Bill of Lading.
3. Bills covering unitized cargoes such as those on pallets or in containers.

Unless specifically authorized in the Credit, Bills of the following type will not be accepted:

1. Bills of Lading issued by forwarding agents.
2. Bills which are issued under and are subject to a Charter Party.
3. Bills covering shipments by sailing vessels.

The Bills must be made out to the order of the shipper and endorsed in blank. If the sales contract is CIF or CFR, then the Bills must be marked 'freight paid'. The general description of the goods including marks and numbers must match the details given in the invoice. The voyage and ship, if named, must be stated in the Credit. Unless tranship- ment is expressly prohibited in the Credit, Bills indicating transhipment will be accepted provided the entire voyage is covered by the same Bill. Part-shipments are permitted unless the Credit states otherwise.

Insurance.   The policy or certificate must be as stated in the Credit and must have been issued by an insurance company or its agent. Cover notes issued by brokers are not acceptable. The details on the policy must match those on the Bills of Lading; it must also be in the same currency as the Credit and endorsed in blank. The amount covered should be at least the invoice amount — Credits usually call for invoice value plus 10%. The policy must be dated not later than the date of shipment as evidenced by the Bill of Lading. The risks covered should be those detailed in the Credit.

SGS certificate.   Issued by the Societe Generale de Surveillance SA and its affiliates, this is a preshipment inspection document. The SGS is appointed by the authorities of various countries to carry out preship- ment inspection of the quality and quantity of goods being exported and of the prices proposed to make a price comparison. In such situations, as price is related to quality and quantity, a physical examination is necessary to ensure the goods comply with the buyer's contractual requirements and conform to accepted trading standards and practice. It does not relieve buyers or sellers from the other contractual obligations. Subsequently a clean report of findings (CRF) or non-negotiable report of findings (NNRF) is issued by the SGS on satisfactory checking of documents. The SGS certificate is becoming a more commonly used document worldwide; an SGS transhipment certificate may also be required when the goods are to pass through an intermediate port en route.

According to circumstances, the Credit may call for other documents, such as consumer certificates, Certificate of Origin, quality, analysis or health certificates (which assure the buyer that the goods are as ordered), Air Waybills, railway (CIM) or road (CMR) consignment notes or post office receipts. The Credit may stipulate a last shipment date and the Bill of Lading must show shipment by that date. Extension of the shipment date automatically extends the expiry date, but not vice versa.

   The exporter, on receipt of the Letter of Credit, will check immediately the details of Credits established in their favour to see that the goods and terms agree with the sales contract and that all the necessary documents are at hand. If any amendment is required, they can approach the advising bank in good time for action to be taken before expiry.

The importer must bear in mind that once a bank's irrevocable Credit has been advised to the beneficiary, the issuing bank must honour drawings made which conform to the terms of the Credit. The application for a Documentary Credit signed by the importer legally binds him to reimburse the issuing bank for all the drawings made which conform to the terms of the Credit.

In a Documentary Credit shipment the importer must bear in mind that there are two distinct contracts — that between buyer and seller covering the goods, and that between the buyer and his banker covering the terms under which the bank has established and will honour its Documentary Credit. In dealing with Documentary Credits a bank is concerned only with the documents presented and not with the goods or services involved. Only if the beneficiary has failed to meet the terms of the Credit is any query regarding his entitlement to payment likely to arise.

Besides the basic irrevocable Credit there are revocable Credits which, as the name implies, can be cancelled or amended at any time without notice to the beneficiary. They do not constitute a legally binding undertaking by the banks concerned. Once transmitted and made available at the advising bank, however, their cancellation or modification is only effective when that bank has received notice thereof and any payment made before receipt of such notice is reimbursable by the issuing bank. The value of these Credits as security for payment is plainly doubtful. They are used mainly between parent and subsidiary companies, where a continuing series of shipments is concerned, or as an indication of good intent.

Where a buyer wishes to provide his supplier with the security of payment afforded by a Documentary Credit, but at the same time requires a period of credit, he may instruct his bank to issue a Credit calling for a Bill of Exchange drawn so many days after sight instead of the usual sight draft. This would, of course, be an irrevocable Credit. In this case the beneficiary would not receive immediate payment upon presentation of the documents as under a sight Credit, but his term Bill would be accepted by the bank. It could then be discounted in the money market at the finest rates. Thus the beneficiary would still receive payment, but the buyer would not be called upon to pay until the Bill matured.

Although it may seem that most of the advantages of Documentary Letters of Credit favour the seller, the importer has the assurance that documents will have been examined twice before being presented to him, and certainty of delivery or shipment by the date specified unless the supplier requests an amendment. Bank charges for any such amendments can be contractually designated for payment by the supplier.

Importers are often annoyed when the documents under Letters of Credit arrive at the local branch of the bank, whilst a number of other documentary collections arrive with other banks, resulting in delay whilst the documents are transferred. To obviate such an occurrence and ensure all documents are presented to the importer's own bank, all purchase orders or contracts calling for payment by documentary collection (sight D/P or D/A) should specify 'payable at (name and address of bank)'. If the supplier fails to include this data in his instructions to the collecting bank, the importer will have reasonable grounds for complaint against the supplier should delay and extra expense be incurred due to delayed presentation.

The Documentary Credit cycle
1.   Buyer and seller enter into a contract of sale calling for settlement by Documentary Credit.
2.   The buyer (applicant) requests his bank (issuing bank) to issue a Documentary Credit in favour of the seller (beneficiary). The Documentary Credit outlines the terms and conditions under which payment or negotiation or acceptance may be made.
3.   The Documentary Credit is sent to a bank in the beneficiary's country (advising bank) for onward transmission to the beneficiary.
4.   The seller should check the Documentary Credit to ensure that he can comply with all the terms and conditions.
5-6.   The seller ships the goods and presents his documents to the negotiating bank for settlement.
7.   The negotiating bank examines the documents against the Credit and if in order settles with the seller.
8-9.   The negotiating bank forwards the documents to the issuing bank claiming reimbursement as agreed between the two banks.
10-11. The issuing bank examines the documents and forwards them to its customer (the buyer) who pays for them in due course.

Checklist to ensure the Letter of Credit agrees with the terms of sale
1. Does it state that it is subject to UCP?
2. Is it irrevocable, preferably with the added confirmation of the advising bank?
3. Are the terms of settlement clearly expressed and satisfactory?
4. Where is it available? If you cannot get settlement in your own country, payment for your goods will be delayed and your security of payment reduced.
5. Does it describe correctly the goods, their weight, quantity, etc?
6. Are there any spelling errors? If there are, they should be taken up immediately with the advising bank. Any needed amendments of the Credit should then be communicated to your buyers.
7. Are the terms for despatch of the goods (e.g. FOB, CIF) as agreed in your sales contract?

8. Are all the transport details correctly stated, such as place and time of despatch, the destination, the method of carriage?
9. Are part-shipments and transhipments allowed?
10. Does it call for the correct transport documents for the method of carriage to be employed?
11. Does it state what insurance risks, if any, are to be covered and whether a policy or a certificate is required?
12. Does it require any special declarations, or endorsements or certification of documents, including references to export or import licences?
13. Can the supplier comply with the Credit terms, particularly as regards despatch and presentation time-limits and documents stipulated, bearing in mind possible difficulties and delays in obtaining outside certifications?

Importers are urged to obtain from SITPRO (Simpler Trade Procedures Board) a *Letter of Credit Checklist and Guide for Export Customers and also Importers* (£4 including postage) and the ICC publication No. 400 *Uniform Customs and Practice for Documentary Credits* available from the local Chambers of Commerce (price £12.50 including postage). Specimens of Bills of Exchange and Documentary Credits are found in *Import/Export Documentation*, pages 115, 124, 128 (see Appendix A).

7.2 CREDIT FINANCE

Import finance strategy is an area which is commanding more attention than hitherto as the number of importers and the range of financial resources available in the market place increase. Overall it effects not only the cashflow to pay for the goods, but also payment of value added tax at the port of entry (see also 'Customs planning', pages 198-212 and 247-53). Available options are as follows:

7.2.1 Buyer credit

This is available in the Trade Finance House which emerged out of the Confirming House (see pages 17-19). It is ideal for small and medium-sized importers and has the following features:

1. It provides finance for the importer to fund imports, by opening Letters of Credit where required on behalf of the importer; bank overdraft facilities are then left free to be used more effectively in other areas.
2. Cashflow may be eased by arranging for a Trade Finance House to finance goods on the importer's behalf and by taking terms of varying length, the importer can ensure that payments do not fall due all at the same time or during other preceding periods.

3. It can arrange forward exchange contracts or option contracts to minimize currency risks.
4. The Trade Finance House checks that documents from suppliers conform to the export order contract terms and helps to resolve any problems emerging from import procedure.
5. If an importer is at present taking terms from his supplier he may be able to negotiate a substantial discount by arranging for the Trade Finance House to pay a supplier on presentation of documents.

To conclude, the buyer by using a Trade Finance House can effectively increase his short-term working capital whilst reducing the amount of time devoted to checking or amending documentation.

Buyer credit is also available from banks. This involves the bank in the supplier's country providing finance for the specified period and on the currency agreed upon direct to the buyer. The supplier is paid immediately on shipment of the goods. The importer repays the financial institution providing the loan at the rate of interest set in the loan agreement.

7.2.2 Supplier credit

Supplier credit involves the overseas supplier or manufacturer granting credit terms to the buyer or importer and obtains finance from a bank or export credit agency. Payments are made to the supplier by the importer over the period of the contract and in the currency and under the terms agreed. The importer's liability is to the supplier until payment is completed. Such credit finance can be arranged with recourse (a liability on the supplier for any funds not repaid by the buyer) or without recourse (no liability on the supplier for any default in payment).

7.2.3 Export credit

Many countries have now established export credit agencies to encourage the export of goods and services. These credit facilities are offered to the exporter at fixed and preferential interest rates and enable credit finance to be made available to importers in other countries.

7.2.4 Acceptance credit

Specific banks provide acceptance credit involving the adoption of a Bill of Exchange drawn on any of its members. The 'Bank Bill' as it is called permits funds to be drawn for a set period and amount, and is particularly useful to importers of raw materials or components who have to meet their cost before the finished goods are sold. Usually a minimum is imposed when financing the scheme. The importing company draws a Bill of Exchange up to an agreed value for payment at a specified date in the future, and the bank arranges for the Bill of Exchange to 'be discounted' in the money market to one of the discount houses that specializes in this business. The sale proceeds are credited to the importer, making funds immediately available to him. When the Bill of Exchange matures, the bank pays it and debits the importing company's account for the amount.

7.2.5 Deferred payment credits

These are becoming increasingly popular where a period of credit has been agreed between buyer and seller, but the issuing bank and buyer do not wish the credit period to be represented by a Bill of Exchange. This is usually where, under local law, Bills of Exchange attract stamp duty. When documents are presented 'in order' by the seller the bank does not accept a Bill of Exchange but instead gives a letter of undertaking to the seller advising him when he will receive his money. The main drawback with this is that should the exporter wish to receive his money straight-away, he does not have a Bill of Exchange to be discounted. Such credits are very common in Spain and Italy.

7.2.6 Standby Letters of Credit

This type of credit differs from other types in that the buyer and seller hope it will never be drawn upon. They are often used as security for open account trading where the seller requires some kind of 'back-up' in the event of the buyer not paying for the goods. They normally require the issuing bank to make payment to the seller upon presentation of documents evidencing non-payment by the importer. They are also commonly used in some countries as a substitute for a bank guarantee which, due to the regulations in that country, are not generally acceptable. A prime example of this is the USA. Standby Letters of Credit have the advantage of being subject to the *Uniform Customs and Practice for Documentary Credits*, ICC publication No. 400, whereas at the moment there are no internationally agreed regulations for bank guarantees.

7.2.7 Back-to-back credits

Back-to-back credits arise in circumstances similar to those of the transferable credit and particularly where both the supplier and the buyer are overseas. The middleman receives a credit in his favour from the buyer and asks his bank to establish a credit in favour of his supplier against the security of the credit in his own favour. Hence there are two separate credits instead of one as in the case of a transferable credit, and this can create problems in the matching of documents and credit terms.

7.2.8   Revolving credits

Revolving credits are used where a series of shipments are made at intervals and the parties wish the programme to proceed without interruption. A credit is established for a certain sum and quantity of goods with a provision that, when a shipment has been made and documents presented and paid, the credit is automatically renewed in its original form so that another shipment can be made.

7.2.9   Counter trade

Counter trade (loosely known as barter) is a form of foreign trade in which the sale of goods or services to a country is limited contractually to an obligation to buy goods or services from that country. It is practised in over 100 countries and particularly common in less developed countries (LDCs) and Eastern Bloc countries. Counter trade negotiations involve international banks closely.

Pressure for this type of trade arises through lack of convertible currency, political pressures and the desire to use the marketing skills of the West to sell goods. Recently, even certain developed countries have been seeking counter trade deals.

Barter, the direct exchange of goods for goods under a single commercial contract without the involvement of money, has been conducted from time immemorial. Its practice in modern times is fairly rare. LDCs sometimes barter their primary products such as oil and timber for consumer products or capital equipment.

Counterpurchase is more common in international trade between Western developed countries on the one hand, and the LDCs and the centralized East European economies on the other. This differs from barter in that the payment for imports into an LDC is met from the proceeds of an export contract. Two separate contracts exist under normal commercial terms, one for the goods exported to the LDC, and one for the counterpurchase goods. Both contracts are normally concluded between unrelated parties with the convertible currency realized under the counter-commodity contract being used to settle the original export. As a variation of this concept, the goods exported can be settled in a minor currency, with the exporter agreeing to buy the goods from the LDC in return for a major trading currency, up to a given percentage of the main contract. The second contract may be with an entirely different company or foreign trade organization within the LDC or East European country.

Compensation or buy-back trade is tied to the sale of capital equipment and plant, and involves the buy-back of the product produced by the original equipment. This type of arrangement usually involves large projects for, say, chemical or fertilizer plants.

Switch deals result from imbalances on clearing accounts set up between central or government-owned foreign trade banks under bilateral trade agreements. They are arrangements whereby intermediaries are able to utilize clearing account credits to finance exports from third countries, thus restoring equilibrium to the clearing account.

7.2.10 Factoring

The practice of using factoring companies by exporters is very much on the increase. Their prime function is to administer the sales ledgers and collect payments once the goods have been shipped. Such factoring companies provide a complete range of services which cover those aspects of exporting, so leaving the manufacturer free to concentrate on export production and sales. For a small service charge of between 0.75% and 2% of turnover, they will provide multicurrency and multilingual sales accounting backed by credit management, which is exercised in the customer's country by the factor's own employees or agents. Also included in this service charge is 100% protection against losses due to the insolvency of the customer and, in some cases, protection against political risk and exchange rate fluctuations. Factoring cannot effectively meet the particular needs of every industry and the most suitable companies are likely to have an expanding turnover in excess of £100 000 and to be selling consumer goods, light industrial products or services on short-term credit.

The advantages of using a factoring service are: the saving of time in running a sales ledger, the savings on cost of postage, telephones and telex and overseas bank charges; involvement with only one debtor — the factoring company; the availability of credit facilities for the buyer on 100% of the value of approved sales; the removal of responsibility for collecting overdue accounts or making provision for bad debts by the seller; the ability to predict the seller's cashflow with confidence; the facility of the seller to draw cash in advance of payments being received from the buyer; and finally the ability to obtain cash discounts from suppliers using money generated from the advance payment facility. This method is popular in the European and North American markets.

7.2.11 Forfeiting

Forfeiting is a method of international trade finance involving the discounting of bank-guaranteed overseas trade bills or notes. It has no recourse to the exporter as he surrenders or relinquishes his right in return for cash payment from the forfeiter. In such circumstances the exporter agrees to surrender his rights to claims for payment on goods or services which have been delivered to the buyer. Any type of trade debt can be forfeited (i.e. surrendered for cash) but the most common is trade payee Bill of Exchange accepted by the buyer or promissory notes from the buyer. A forfeiter can provide finance for any type and duration of trade transaction but usually credit is provided for the export of capital goods which require finance for periods of between 3 and 7 years.

7.3 INTERNATIONAL EXCHANGE RATES

The subject of foreign exchange relates to the exchange of various currencies one for another. On the practical side it concerns the methods of settling foreign debts, the means of payment and the services of banks and brokers. Settlement of debts between parties in the same country is quite simply effected by the payment of money, which the creditor is prepared to accept as it is the legal tender of the country. Where the payer or recipient live in different countries and use different currencies, however, there arises the need for a system of conversion — the foreign exchange market. Unlike the markets in commodities or stocks and shares, the foreign exchange market has no centre but consists merely of telephonic communications between dealers (at the banks) and brokers.

7.3.1 Rate of exchange

The price of one currency in terms of another is called the rate of exchange; it is the number of units of one currency that will be exchanged for a given number of units of another currency. Hence rates against sterling are the number of foreign currency units to the pound. A glance at the financial press shows that two closing rates are quoted for each currency; the higher is the market's buying rate for that currency and the lower the market's selling rate. Transactions between dealers are conducted at approximately those rates. A banker who is asked to buy or sell foreign currency relies upon the market for cover, and the prices at which he can obtain this cover are market rates. Hence in quoting to his customer he bases his rates on those ruling in the market, adjusted to make provision for profit.

The market rates quoted in the press are 'spot' rates, i.e. those applied to transactions for completion immediately or at the latest within 2 working days from the date of the deal. As currency is a commodity like any other, its price will be governed by the interaction of demand and supply and hence by short- and long-term factors influencing buyers and sellers. The short-term factors fall into two categories — commercial and financial.

Commercial operations relate to trade in goods and services which make up the current account of the balance of payments and give rise to payments and receipts in various currencies, thereby determining supply and demand in the foreign exchange markets. Where a country's total purchases exceed its sales, there will be an excess supply of its currency, which will cause its price to decrease; in other words the rate of exchange will fall. Expectations of future movements in exchange rates give rise to 'leads and lags'; a debtor will pay a foreign currency debt before it is due if he expects that currency to appreciate in value (lead) or delay payment if he expects it to depreciate (lag).

Financial operations come under a variety of headings:

Stock exchange operations.   The purchase of securities on foreign stock exchanges (bourses) by private or corporate investors in order to yield a return or in the expectation of a capital appreciation. These are portfolio investments as opposed to 'industrial' investments, which represent capital placed by manufacturers in subsidiary or associated enterprises abroad.

Banking operations.   The transfer of funds by bankers for investment or deposit in foreign centres.

Speculation.   Transactions based on the expectation that the exchange rate of a particular currency will change in response to some political or natural event. Whether the operator buys or sells a currency depends on whether he anticipates a rise or fall in value.

Interest payments.   Interest on loans and dividends from investment.

Loan payments.   The issue of a loan in one country on behalf of a borrower in another gives rise to a payment across the exchanges from the country of the lender to that of the borrower, which will have an adverse impact on the exchange rate of the lending country's currency and cause that of the borrowing country to appreciate. This effect would be offset if the proceeds of the loan were used to purchase goods or services from the lending country. Upon repayment of the loan the reverse effect will occur.

Intergovernmental transfers.   Governments borrow from and lend to each other in the same way as private individuals and trading companies; the payments resulting from such loans have the same effect as that outlined above.

Exchange stabilization. Exchange rate movements are controlled by varying the relation between supply and demand. These operations are usually directed at keeping fluctuations to a minimum, although sometimes a government may deliberately seek to raise or lower the exchange rate of its currency.

7.3.2 Forward exchange

In view of the increasing amount of business conducted on credit terms, it is quite likely that an importer will be liable to pay the supplier in the latter's currency at a future date or to receive foreign currency at a future date from a buyer. With floating exchange rates the importer is vulnerable to any changes in currency values that may occur in the interval between conclusion of the contract and the date on which payment is due. It is to provide cover against such exchange risks that the 'forward exchange' market came into existence. The merchant contracts with a bank to purchase or sell one currency in exchange for another at a predetermined rate on an agreed future date. He thus knows how much he will eventually pay or receive in his own currency, and any intervening fluctuations in the exchange rate will not affect him.

Forward contracts may be 'fixed' or 'option'. A fixed forward is a contract with a specific performance date. A forward option stipulates a period of time during which performance is to take place, the actual date then being chosen by the customer. It should be clearly understood that the 'option' is not whether the customer deals or not; he is fully committed to the transactions. It relates only to the date on which he takes or delivers the currency concerned.

Forward rates
The rates for forward exchange deals are quotes as a premium or discount on the spot rate, i.e. an amount above or below spot; sometimes they are at 'par' with spot. For example, if the forward dollar—sterling rate is quoted at a discount on the spot rate (measured in the conventional way as the number of dollars to a pound) then, in terms of dollars, sterling is cheaper forward than spot. Conversely, if the forward rate is at a premium, sterling is dearer forward than spot. Forward margins (discount or premium) are determined by interest rate differentials and by market expectations of future spot exchange rates. Currencies in which interest rates are relatively low tend to be dearer forward than spot in terms of currencies in which interest rates are relatively high. The press usually quotes forward margins for 1, 3 and 6 months forward, but by arrangement with the bank it is possible to cover for longer periods, depending on the currency concerned.

A customer who has contracted to buy foreign currency but finds that he no longer requires it will still have to take delivery of the currency at the agreed forward rate; he can then sell it back to the bank at the ruling spot rate. Similarly, if the customer has not received the foreign currency he has contracted to sell, he will have to buy the amount required at the ruling spot rate for delivery to the bank. In practice, the bank may merely debit or credit the difference to the customer's account. Where circumstances cause a delay in fulfilment of a contract it may often be extended to an adjusted rate by arrangement with the bank.

Details of the current sterling and spot forward table rates are found in the financial press from which the following data on 27-03-90 was obtained.

Bank spot selling rate	1.6295	
Subtract premium	0.0089	
	1.6206	One month forward sale rate
Bank spot buying rate	1.6305	
Subtract premium	0.0087	
	1.6218	One month forward purchase rate

In this example, the US dollar is at a premium over sterling. This means that under the forward contract, the UK exporter will receive more sterling for his US dollar receipts in one month's time than he would if he exchanged at the spot rate now. Conversely, the importer would have to pay more sterling in one month's time to settle his currency payments.

From the same table source we can calculate the 1 month forward rate for the Portugese Escudos.

Bank spot selling rate	2.4495	
Add discount	0.0011	
	2.4506	One month forward sale rate
Bank spot buying rate	2.4595	
Add discount	0.0030	
	2.4625	One month forward purchase rate

In this example the Portugese Escudos is at a discount to sterling. This means the UK exporter, under the forward contract, will receive less sterling for the Portugese Escudos receipts in one month's time than if exchange had taken place at the spot rate now. The importer, however, will have to pay less sterling in 1 month's time to settle currency payments.

Forward exchange rates are not forecasts by banks of what spot rates will actually be in the future. Premium and discounts are based chiefly on the differences in interbank interest rates obtainable on the Euro-currencies involved. If an importer, say, arranged with his bank a 1 month forward contract to buy US $10 000 in exchange for sterling, then the bank could, for example, either purchase US $10 000 on the foreign exchange market at spot and place the dollars on deposit for one month, or borrow the equivalent amount in sterling for 1 month. In 1 month's time, when the forward contract matured the bank would pay the importer the US $10 000 previously held on deposit, or receive the sterling from the importer and repay the loan, as appropriate.

The interest factor which determines the 1 month premium or discount is calculated on the cost to the bank for borrowing sterling for 1 month and the interest received for placing US dollars on deposit. The 'pound spot and forward' example above shows the US dollar at a premium to sterling for 1 month. The bank in this instance would charge the importer a premium of 0.89 cent because it has paid more interest on the sterling borrowing than it has received on the US dollar deposit.

If an exporter arranged with his bank a 1 month forward contract to sell US $10 000 in exchange for sterling, then the bank could, for example, either borrow US $10 000 for 1 month, or sell US $10 000 for sterling on the foreign exchange market at spot and place the sterling equivalent on deposit for 1 month. In 1 month's time, when the forward contract matured the bank would receive from the exporter US dollars and repay the borrowing, or pay the exporter the sterling previously held on deposit. The bank would give the exporter a premium of 0.87 cent because it received more interest from its deposit in sterling than was paid on the dollar loan.

From the above it will be seen that the forward exchange market enables the ordinary merchant to protect himself against fluctuations in exchange rates. Problems can still arise, however, where expenditure and receipts are expressed in a number of different currencies. One example of this is found in connection with freight charges. For the sake of convenience a conference's rates of freight are expressed in a single currency called the 'tariff currency', usually the US dollar. Nevertheless, freight can be paid in another currency, so that agreement has to be reached on the basis for conversion of the sum involved. Where adjustments in relevant currency values have resulted in a reduction in the rates of freight or increases in shipowners' operating costs, it has been the practice of conferences to increase the freight or to introduce or increase a 'currency adjustment factor' (CAF) and/or bunker adjustment factor (BAF) (see page 69). A shipowner naturally calculates in terms of his own currency and if it depreciates against the tariff unit he seeks to impose a surcharge to protect the real value of his revenue in relation to his expenditure, which may be in a variety of other currencies.

There has been a tendency to regard the CAF as a means of keeping ratios of past rates of exchange fixed for all time. Changes in the terms of trade owing to the different rates of inflation in various countries have not been taken into account when calculating rates for sea-freight. Relationships between currencies have, however, changed considerably. When the value of sterling was falling the system favoured the UK exporter in terms of freight rates; when sterling began to appreciate, however, shipowners in other countries applied a currency adjustment. The situation became more complicated when rates of exchange were allowed to float and the dollar was effectively devalued. The system which had stood the test of all the upheavals in exchange rates began to show signs of strain. The heart of the problem is that if there were a parity of CAFs it would be to the disadvantage of UK shippers, but continental European shippers argue that if basic rate parity is maintained then CAF parity should also be the rule. If the present CAF disparity is permitted then basic rate disparity should also be introduced. The various conferences serving different areas of the world have reacted to changing circumstances in different ways and a final solution to the problem has yet to be found.

7.3.3 Currency options

In considering exchange rates it is appropriate to consider currency options. Basically a currency option is the right to buy or sell a currency against delivery of a base currency at an agreed exchange rate. The buyer of the option has the right to exercise this option at any date up to and including an agreed date, but he has no obligation to do so. The buyer of the option pays a premium for the provision of this right.

Currency options are true options and are different in kind from option date forward contracts; the latter provide an option only as to the date when exchange shall take place, but require exchange at some time within the option period. True options may be regarded as 'whether to exchange' options as opposed to 'when to exchange' options.

A 'call' option provides the right to buy the currency and sell the base currency at the agreed rate; a 'put' option provides the right to sell the currency and buy the base currency at the agreed rate. For example:

1. deutschmark call against sterling (can buy marks);
2. yen call against dollars (can buy yen);
3. sterling put against dollars (can sell sterling);

4. Swiss francs put against sterling (can sell Swiss francs).

In economic terms a currency option is an essential form of insurance against movements in exchange rates. In this regard it may be seen as an alternative to forward cover in the foreign exchange market for import and export trade. However, since the holder is not obliged to exercise the option, it is particularly ideal for covering contingent cashflows, such as those arising when tendering for a contract. The advantages of currency options are as follows:

1. Where cashflow is hedged by a forward contract, the company achieves protection against adverse currency movements; the downside risk is eliminated. Unfortunately, this method also eliminates any upside potential that otherwise would have accrued to the company if exchange rates had moved in its favour. By contrast, a principal advantage of an option is that it provides protection against downside risk in the same way as a forward contract; however, since there is no obligation to exercise the option, the upside potential is retained.
2. The option buyer knows at the outset what his 'worst case' will be: having paid the premium no further expense is payable. When the main objective is simply to limit downside risk, this is a powerful advantage. In many commercial applications, the option premium can be built into the pricing process, thus fixing minimum margins.
3. Since there is no obligation to exercise an option, options are ideal for hedging contingent cashflows which may or may not materialize, such as tenders.
4. Options may be used as a 'ratchet' to lock up profit to date on a currency position while retaining any remaining upside potential.

Options may be also used as an alternative to forward contracts to hedge trade payables and receivables in currency. However, the 'ideal' use for currency options is in a tender. Here a firm makes an offer to supply at a fixed currency price and holds this offer open for a certain period. During this period the firm is at risk from currency movements, but cannot economically take out forward cover; to do so could give rise to a loss if the order were lost. Effectively, the tenderer gives his potential customer a currency option for as long as the offer remains open; the only way he can achieve precise cover is by the use of another, offsetting option.

Most 'wholesale' currency option business takes place through specialist options exchanges, such as the Philadelphia Stock Exchange, where standard contracts are traded in similar manner to futures exchanges with specified contract amounts, delivery dates and other parameters. More recently, currency options have started to become available from certain banks in London and New York. Bank options may be more flexible than those traded on exchanges as they can be tailor-made to particular strike prices, expiration dates and amounts to suit the customer and need not be constructed by any externally-defined contract specification. In the future the currency option market is likely to expand.

7.4 LONDON INTERNATIONAL FINANCIAL FUTURES EXCHANGE (LIFFE)

The London International Financial Futures Exchange market was opened in London in 1982 to provide facilities for dealing in futures contracts covering interest rates and currencies — known generally as financial futures. A financial futures contract is an agreement to buy or sell a standard quantity of a specific financial instrument at a future date and at a price agreed between the parties through open outcry on the floor of an organized exchange. The following are the characteristics of the contract:

1. **Standard quantity**: each contract for a given type of financial instrument is for the same standard quantity, e.g. $1 million.
2. **Specific financial instrument**: the contract specification lays down not only the type of financial instrument — for example, a 3 month time deposit, a 20 year gilt-edged stock or a foreign currency — but also its quality in terms of such items as coupon rate and maturity.
3. **Future date**: the delivery of the amounts specified in the contract must take place during a specified month in the future.
4. **Open outcry**: all transactions must be executed on the floor of the exchange and prices are instantly available to all participants.

It is because fixtures contracts are standardized, with buyer and seller knowing exactly what they are trading, that they can be freely bought and sold at any time on the exchange where they are traded. One other important characteristic of a futures exchange is that whilst all financial futures transactions must have a buyer and seller, their obligation is not to each other but to the clearing house. After a transaction is recorded the clearing house substitutes itself for the other party and becomes the seller to every buyer and the buyer to every seller. In this way it achieves its primary role, which is to guarantee the performance of every transaction made on the floor.

Financial futures are used for two purposes — hedging and trading. Hedging is used to reduce the risk of loss through adverse price movements in interest rates or currency rates by taking a position in futures contracts that is equal and opposite to an existing or anticipated position in the cash market. Everyone in the business community is a potential user of financial futures to hedge their asset or liability positions. Hedging is of benefit to banks, other financial institutions, pension funds, corporate treasurers and professional City houses, brokers and dealers.

7.5 COMPUTERIZED INTERNATIONAL BANKING

7.5.1 MidTrade

A survey carried out 2 years ago among importers and exporters in the UK showed that the services being provided by the major banks were lacking in important areas. They complained, in particular, about import Letters of Credit and export collections. Concern was voiced about levels of accuracy in the banking system and consequent delays in both documents and flow of funds. Importers had difficulty in monitoring their Letters of Credit (L/C) once they had left the UK and exporters had trouble getting information regarding the status of outstanding bills. The problems were compounded by the vast administrative job involved in processing tens of thousands of L/Cs and collection was paper-intensive, resource-consuming and error-prone.

The Midland Bank recognized that the internal and external problems were interrelated and that the development of an integrated computerized processing system would benefit both the bank and its customers. The result is MidTrade, an automated processing and information system which allows for the transfer of previously paper-based records on to computer. MidTrade was launched on February 1989 after a major collaborative effort between the operations, systems and marketing departments of the bank. A major financial investment was involved but customers are not charged extra to pay for the improvements in service and benefits that the system brings.

A mainframe computer is accessed directly by terminals at Midland Bank premises in nearly 40 strategic locations. Details of L/Cs and collections are input by operators and can be updated or accessed at the touch of a button. From one single entry which is checked, data is replicated by the system to produce all necessary advice letters, payment messages and accounting details. The integrated nature of the system with the bank's communications and accounting systems negates the need for re-keying and hence reduces errors to the absolute minimum.

These features have provided solutions to the problems previously experienced: greater accuracy is achieved; the system enables Midland Bank's staff to respond quicker to customer enquiries — up-to-the-minute details can be called up on screen while the customer is on the phone; and finally, there is a faster flow of advices of L/Cs to beneficiaries overseas which enables them to begin manufacture or ship the goods earlier than might otherwise have been the case.

There are other benefits specific to export collections. MidTrade automatically generates tracers — enquiries of overseas banks — which can often lead to cash proceeds arriving up to 14 days sooner than they would otherwise have done, and consequently saving money for Midland's exporting customers. For example, with interest costs at 15%, if £25 000 arrives 1 day earlier it saves the customer more than £10. To make the export collection process even quicker, customers can send their documents and instructions directly to the overseas bank, and send a copy of the instructions to the Midland Bank for entry into MidTrade. The system also accepts SPEX-generated documentation.

Comprehensive monthly export collection status reports are made available to Midland's major customers. These reports highlight details of unaccepted and overdue items, country and customer payment performances together with summaries of country and currency exposure. Benefits specific to import letters of credit include sight and term status reports which enable customers to follow the full life-cycle of a transaction in addition to providing currency exposure and facility usage detail. Customers benefit from the improvements in the critical areas of accuracy, speed, timeliness and the ready availability of information.

The MidTrade facility is a market leader. In addition to it being fully integrated and so obviating the need to re-key transactions, access to the system by its operators extends to nearly 40 international banking centres throughout the UK and customers will be able to direct all their transactions via their local centre. The provision of local access in this way answers hitherto unfulfilled customer demand. A major advantage to buyers is that the import L/C customers will be able to access MidTrade direct from terminals in their own premises with the loading of information being made off-line. There will be no need to post or deliver instructions to the bank. Once the details are entered by the customer they will be retained and reproduced as necessary by the system. There will be no need for Midland Bank operators to print out hard copy and then re-key before transmission overseas, as is the case with many other systems. Midland's other MidTrade related plans for the future include developments in electronic data interchange and electronic mail. There is no doubt the system will grow in popularity as the importer and re-exporter realizes the benefits MidTrade offers to the market.

7.5.2 Electronic data interchange

A major development emerged in 1986 with the UN go-ahead for international standards for paperless trading.

Major trading powers, including the EEC, EFTA, the USA and the USSR have taken a unanimous decision to open the way for paperless trading — the use of standard electronic messages between computers to replace the masses of paperwork generated by national and international trade transactions. The agreement, which is supported by trade bodies like IATA and the ICC and is being keenly followed by Japan, means that for the first time a common international standard for paperless trading, or electronic data interchange (EDI), has been adopted by most of the world's prominent trading nations.

A United Nations' working party reached agreement in Geneva following 10 months' intensive development work by a joint European and North American group of experts called UN-JEDI. This group has achieved a major breakthrough in international trade terms, because paper-based trade procedures (which, according to UN estimates, account for around 7% of the value of goods shipped) are inefficient and costly, and EDI will now begin to render many of them obsolete. It will result in the progressive reduction or elimination of inefficient and expensive paperwork used by exporters and importers, and all other relevant parties such as carriers and customs authorities, and their replacement by the direct exchange between computers of structured business data.

EDI requires two basic components: a syntax and a data element directory. The former is the equivalent of grammar in a language; the latter the equivalent of the vocabulary. International EDI has been frustrated in the past, however, because these components were based on differing national standards. The syntax (or grammar) component has been developed and won unanimous agreement from all participant countries and trade organizations. The scheme will be submitted for acceptance by the International Standards Organization (ISO). The data element directory (or vocabulary), already an ISO standard, will also now be substantially revised and its flexibility enhanced.

The implications of these developments will become very extensive in the long term for international trade documentation in all its areas, including finance.

7.6 CONCLUSION

The subject of import finance, with special reference to the importer, is a vast one. Readers are urged to consult their bank to obtain professional advice and identify the options available to meet their needs. Additionally, it is prudent to keep the payment methods and procedures under constant review to take full advantage of the new opportunities available. Financial and import planning and strategy determination are important considerations (see pages 247-50). The importer keen to know more of the subject is recommended to read *Finance of International Trade* by A. Watson (see Appendix A).

8 *Cargo insurance*

Marine insurance is defined in the *Marine Insurance Act, 1906*, as 'a contract whereby the insurer undertakes to indemnify the assured in a manner and to the extent thereby agreed, against marine losses, that is to say, the losses incidental to marine adventure'. Hence this includes cargo insurance involving the maritime conveyance of merchandise from one country to another. It would be wrong not to include a chapter on cargo insurance in a book of this nature, but the reader must realize that it is only possible to deal briefly with the salient parts of this extensive subject. For further study the student is recommended to read one of the excellent cargo insurance textbooks available.

This chapter deals with the practical considerations which affect financial protection of goods in transit to buyer's premises. The advantages which accrue from a proper appreciation of the role cargo insurance plays in the transference to others of those risks to which goods consigned by sea and air are exposed must be thoroughly understood by the importer (buyer). Cargo insurance must be seen as an indispensable adjunct to overseas trade.

8.1 IMPORTERS' STRATEGY

During the past 10 years there has been a tendency worldwide for an increasing number of importers to undertake their own insurance and thereby save hard currency, facilitate claims procedure and have complete control over the cost of such provision. The responsibility for arranging insurance at various stages of the transit is a matter of negotiation between the buyer and seller. The principal points for consideration are the following:

The insured value. The amount covered must be at least the invoiced value of the goods; 110% of the invoiced value is commonplace, but it may be more. In situations where the goods are bought under CIF terms, the buyer may instruct the seller in the required amount or arrange a 'top-up' himself. Particular attention needs to be given to inland freight charges from the seaport or airport and VAT. The possibility exists of opting for an 'increased value' insurance for the extra charges incurred and thereby obtaining a separate cover at a lower rate of premium relative to the voyage or flight.

Risk covered. This must include transport of goods from the seller's warehouse to the docks or airport, storage while awaiting loading and customs clearance, time spent on board ship, road, rail or air transport, off-loading and storage on arrival and final transport to the buyer. Usually the seller's insurance cover ceases at the destination airport or seaport. The extra cover to embrace the delivery transit to the importer's premises, warehouse, including storage or ultimate customer DES or aircraft is for the buyer's account. Insurance cover must be made for the storage of the goods in the buyer's warehouse and subsequent distribution.

Terms of purchase. The basis on which the goods are bought as defined in Incoterms 1990 reflects the responsibilities of the buyer and seller in the execution of the contract (see Chapter 10). In particular the insurance cover provisions are specified and whether they are for the buyer's or seller's account. Transit insurance must be established as the responsibility of the shipper/seller/consignor or the buyer/receiver/consignee; the importer in doubt should contact an insurance broker.

Some countries, particularly Eastern Bloc states, only sell under CIF terms and hence the buyer has no option to undertake any insurance provision. It is important under such arrangements to establish the extent of the insurance cover, including provision for surveys and claims and arrange for any top-up at the buyer's expense.

The terms under which the buyer can arrange his own insurance include Ex Works, FCA, CFR, FOB, (see Appendix E). With the development of combined transport operation FCA, CPT, CIP are becoming more common and the buyer must decide which favours him most.

Terms of payment. Most payment of the goods is due on shipment or presentation of the documents (see page 98). However, situations do emerge whereby a period of credit ranging from 30 to 60 days exists and the seller has a residual interest in the goods until payment is made. Advice should be sought on insurance cover which would be for the buyer's account.

Commodity policies. Some goods may require extra insurance cover, e.g. antiques, livestock, foodstuffs, nuclear fuels, etc. Adequate cover must be sought and any advice sought from an insurance broker or trade association.

Overland carriage.   A high volume of business is now conveyed by road and rail with the maritime portion of the transit being a small element in the schedule. It is essential that adequate cover be obtained for the land element of the carriage with regard to the carrier's consignment note and whether the buyer's transport is undertaking part of the haulage. Again, the insurance broker or a trade association can give advice.

Buyer's own policy.   Regular importers are urged to contact an insurance broker and obtain an open cover policy which will offer favourable premiums for volume business (see pages 129-30).

8.2   CARGO INSURANCE MARKET

There are no fixed rates in marine insurance and the actual premium for a particular ship or cargo is assessed on the incidence of losses in that trade and the risks that the ship and other conveyances conveying the cargo are likely to undergo. This process of assessing the premium is known as underwriting and the marine insurance contract is embodied in a document called a policy. Marine insurance is undertaken by insurance companies or by Lloyd's underwriters — primarily the latter, through a broker.

Lloyd's of London is a society of underwriters specializing in the insurance of marine and similar risks. It had its origin in the seventeenth century when shipowners, merchants and underwriters met at Edward Lloyd's coffee house in London. Lloyd's was incorporated by Act of Parliament in 1871 and is governed by an elected committee. The Corporation of Lloyd's, which incidentally has no connection with Lloyd's Register of Shipping, does not accept insurance or issue policies. Briefly, the Corporation provides the facility for its members to transact the business of insurance. These members, who are known as underwriting members (or 'names') currently number more than 26 000 and have an absolutely separate and unlimited liability in respect of all risks written in their name. For the purposes of trading these underwriting members are grouped into what are known as 'syndicates'. These syndicates are of varying size and the monetary capacity and strength of each is based upon the individual wealth pledged by its underwriting members. Currently there are over 400 syndicates trading in the Lloyd's market. The insurance business, or risks, undertaken by each syndicate are accepted by an underwriter who, in acting for his syndicate, commits his underwriting members to the risks written by him.

The Corporation of Lloyd's provides the various departments necessary for the conduct of such a large organization on their own premises. Separate departments are maintained for the signing of policies, the settlement of claims, the collection of general average refunds, salvage and recoveries from third parties, and for the payment of claims abroad. The

Corporation is also responsible for the provision of a Lloyd's agent in most ports of importance. Other important activities include the publication of *Lloyd's List*, a daily shipping paper, and many other technical publications.

The broker plays a leading role in the process of underwriting, the public have no direct access to the underwriter. Having learnt the needs of his client, the broker prepares the 'slip' which is the basis of the proposed policy, presents it to likely underwriters and secures the best terms for insurance, collecting the initials of various underwriters until the risk is completely insured. When the risk is completely insured, the broker informs his client and subsequently a policy is issued on behalf of the underwriters involved. It should be noted that the broker is the agent of the assured and as such is subject to the common law of agency that if, due to his negligence, his principal (the assured) is prejudiced, the principal may sue him for damages. It costs the assured absolutely nothing to utilize the services of a broker who is paid his fee — brokerage — by the underwriter(s) with whom he places his principal's business.

Lloyd's agents, which are established at almost every port in the world, have the following salient duties:

1. Protecting the interests of underwriters (Lloyd's or otherwise) according to instructions which may be sent to them, for example, by endeavouring to avoid fraudulent claims.
2. Rendering advice and assistance to masters of shipwrecked vessels.
3. Informing Lloyd's about any casualties which may occur in their district and about arrivals and departures.
4. Appointing surveyors to inspect damaged vessels and granting certification of seaworthiness when called upon to do so by masters of vessels which have suffered damage.
5. Notifying London headquarters of all information of relevant interest which may come to their notice.
6. Surveying or appointing surveyors when called upon by consignees of cargo or by underwriters to survey damage, and issuing reports stating the cause, nature and extent of all damage. Lloyd's agents will survey and issue reports in connection with damaged goods at the request of any interested party on the payment of a fee, quite apart from any question of insurance. All reports issued by Lloyd's agents are made 'without prejudice' and subject to the terms, conditions and amount of any policy of insurance.

Whilst it is true to say that the bulk of marine insurance is effected at Lloyd's, a significant proportion of cover is provided by insurance companies specializing in marine insurance. Overall, there are about 100 such companies with the bulk of them situated in London and Liverpool. The premium rates can vary significantly, reflecting their experience and assessment of the risks involved. The Corporation of Lloyd's has an immense reputation throughout the world and nearly half its business is transacted from abroad.

8.3 FUNDAMENTAL PRINCIPLES OF CARGO INSURANCE

The three fundamental principles of insurance are insurable interest, good faith and indemnity. This applies to all aspects of marine insurance but, in the case of cargo, there is a distinct variation in the application of the principle to insurable interest.

8.3.1 Insurable interest

Basically, a person has an insurable interest in a marine adventure when he stands in any legal or equitable relation to the adventure or to any insurable property at risk therein in consequence of which he may:

1. benefit by the safety or due arrival of the insurable property; or
2. be prejudiced by its loss or by damage thereto or by the detention thereof; or
3. incur liability in respect thereof.

The subject matter insured in connection with insurable interest is usually either ship, goods or freight, although it may sometimes be an interest arising from one of these, for example, profit, wages or disbursements.

A good example of insurable interest is absolute ownership of the subject matter insured, but there are a number of other circumstances in which a person may possess an insurable interest. For instance, persons responsible for goods whilst in their charge have an insurable interest in respect of their legal liability for such goods, even if the owner himself has effected a full insurance. Of course, the owner could not recover from his insurers and also from the third party. If he recovers from the insurers his rights against third parties must be subrogated to them (see below). Again, if goods are consigned to an agent for sale on commission, the agent has an insurable interest because, if the goods are lost, he will be precluded from earning his commission on their sale.

Various other forms of insurable interest exist.

A defeasible or contingent interest
A defeasible interest is one which ceases during the currency of the risk for reasons other than maritime perils, e.g. the exercise of an option or election, such as when the commodity ownership changes hands during the course of the transit. A contingent interest is one which may be acquired during the currency of a risk through the operation of some

contingency; an example is a buyer acquiring an interest in the merchandise during the course of the transit.

Bottomry and respondential bonds
Bottomry is the advancement of money in time of necessity to the master on the security of a vessel and freight being earned, or on a vessel, freight and cargo. Money advanced in bottomry bonds is only repayable in the event of the safe arrival of the vessel. Hence the rate of interest is comparatively high. Moreover, the bond is void at law if it agrees to repay the money in the event of the vessel not completing the adventure. Respondential is the similar advance of money in the security of cargo alone but such a loan is repayable even if the vessel be lost, provided the cargo is saved. Such loans are now rarely necessary.

Charges of insurance
The assured has an insurable interest in the charges of any insurance he may effect. In cargo insurance, the premiums paid form part of the value of the goods themselves. Insurance on premiums as such is normally only taken out in connection with hull risks. Where the subject matter is insured 'lost or not lost', the assured may recover although he may not have acquired his interest until after the loss unless, at the time of effecting the contract of insurance, the assured was aware of the loss and the insurer was not.

8.3.2   Good faith

In the formation of a contract of cargo insurance the utmost good faith (*uberrimae fidei*) must be observed by both the assured and insured. If either party fails to observe good faith, the other may avoid the contract. Breach of good faith may be either positive or negative in character. It may consist of either material misrepresentation, or of non-disclosure of a material fact. Such a breach does not make the contract void, but it may be avoided by the injured party. Hence the assured must disclose to the insurer, before the contract is concluded, all material circumstances which are known to the assured. A material circumstance is one which will influence the judgment of a prudent underwriter to decide whether or not to accept the risk and under what terms.

8.3.3   Indemnity

A cargo insurance policy is basically a contract of indemnity, an agreement to compensate the assured in the event of loss. The fundamental indemnity principle governing contract of marine insurance is found in the judgment Castellain v. Preston 1883, which indicated 'the replacing of the assured, after a loss, in as nearly as may be the same relative pecuniary position as if a loss had not occurred'. However, the contract of cargo insurance is not a contract of perfect indemnity, as an arbitrary valuation of the subject matter insured is almost invariably inserted in the policy as a basis of indemnity. This arbitrary valuation, in the absence of fraud, is the amount recovered by the assured if there is a total loss, though it may be more or less than perfect indemnity. In other words, the basis of indemnity under a marine policy remains constant throughout the risk.

The only practical way of conducting marine insurance is on the basis of agreed values. In the case of fire insurance it is usually an easy matter to arrive at the value of goods at the time and place of the fire, but it would be a much more difficult matter to arrive at the value of goods at the time and place where they are lost or damaged at sea. Again, bankers when financing shipments of goods require the shippers to provide cargo insurance policies fully covering them for the amount of their advance.

Whilst such agreed values must of necessity be arrived at in a somewhat arbitrary fashion, they nevertheless represent a figure which in most circumstances provides a reasonable indemnity for the assured. The normal basis of valuation is CIF, cost plus an agreed percentage, usually between say 10 and 25%, to cover a measure of anticipated profit for the buyer as well as landing charges, carriage costs, etc. Thus, if a loss occurs at the very end of the transit when all costs and charges have already been paid, the insured value does not normally provide a near-profit indemnity; if, on the other hand, it occurs at an earlier stage when some of these costs and charges have not been paid (for instance through the sinking of the carrying vessel) it would provide more than a perfect indemnity. Market fluctuations also affect this consideration. It is possible for the market value of goods, especially basic commodities, to rise or fall considerably during the course of a long transit. In the event of a rise, it could be quite possible for the insured value to represent less than the actual value of the goods at the time of a loss. The assured is then out of pocket to the extent of the higher profit than he would otherwise have made. If the cargo is under-valued, the assured is his own insurer in respect of the balance. As regards over-valuation, the use of valued policies does not enable the assured to grossly over-value the subject matter of the insurance. The value must be fixed in such a manner as to indicate that the assured only desired an indemnity.

Additional to the three main principals of cargo insurance, it is appropriate to mention briefly the doctrine of proximate cause and the principle of subrogation.

The doctrine of proximate cause is concerned solely with establishing the actual cause of loss or damage of the cargo as, in many circumstances, there may be more than one cause. In order to determine the proximate cause of a loss consideration must be given only to the most dominant and effective cause of loss, which is not necessarily the nearest cause in time. The remote causes of a loss must be ignored.

When the underwriter has paid a loss under his policy, he is entitled to place himself in the position of the assured and to take over all rights of the assured in respect of the loss he had paid. The principle is called sub-rogation. For example, if goods are jettisoned for the common safety, on paying for a total loss of the jettisoned goods, the underwriter stands in the place of the assured and is entitled to general average compensation for the jettison. The principle of subrogation is inherent in every contract of marine insurance and is linked to the principle of indemnity. Its application renders it impossible for the assured to defeat the principle of indemnity by receiving from two or more parties, sums exceeding a true indemnity.

8.4   CARGO INSURANCE POLICY

The importer will be influenced by two main factors in deciding the nature of the cargo insurance required — the actual insurable interest, and the terms of sale and type of contract. Before examining the content of the policy, it is appropriate first of all to consider the three main categories of general cargo insurance available:

1. All risks. In theory, this provides cover against all risks or loss or damage but, in reality, much depends on the type of merchandise involved. It does not extend, as specified in the Institute Cargo Clauses, to cover loss, damage, or expense proximately caused by delay or inherent vice or nature of the subject matter insured.
2. With average (WA). This type of policy provides cover against all loss or damage due to marine perils throughout the duration of the policy. It is subject, however, to any specific franchise which may be introduced into the policy, such as those below a certain specified percentage value and non-recoverable. However, when the specified amount is reached the claim is paid in full.
3. Free of particular average (FPA). This is a limited form of cargo insurance cover in that no partial loss or damage is recoverable from the insurers unless the actual vessel or craft is stranded, sunk or burnt. Under the latter circumstances, the FPA cargo policy-holder can recover any losses of the insured merchandise which was on the vessel at the time as would obtain under the more extensive WA policy. Basic-ally, the FPA policy provides coverage for total losses and general average emerging from actual 'marine perils'. For example, the total loss of an insured consignment during discharge, loading or transhipment.

8.4.1 Marine Policy Form

The SG (Standard General) Policy Form was adopted by Lloyd's in 1779 and remained with us almost without change until 1982, its use being recommended by the *Marine Insurance Act, 1906.* Following the Lloyd's lead the company market also adopted the SG Form subject to some small amendments. This old document, with its somewhat archaic phraseology specifying the attachment and termination of risk for both hull and cargo insurance, the perils insured against and the conditions of cover, was replaced on 1 January 1982 by a simple document called the Marine Policy Form. In this, the underwriters agree, in consideration of the payment of a premium specified in the schedule, to insure against loss, damage, liability or expense in the manner hereinafter specified, i.e. in accordance with the terms and conditions of the new clauses attached. All details regarding the cargo interest to be insured is contained in a schedule included in the policy. The Marine Policy and Institute clauses are subject to English law and practice.

Clauses
There are three sets of Institute Cargo Clauses: A, B and C. The clauses are presented in a manner which embraces the scope of cover and the terms of the insurance under the sub-headings: Risks covered, Exclusions, Duration, Claims, Benefit of insurance, Minimizing losses, Avoidance of delay, and Law and practice. All the differences between the three sets of clauses are contained in the first two sections (Risks covered and Exclusions), i.e. those dealing with the scope of the cover provided. All the other sections are identical in all three sets.

Risks covered.   The A clauses cover all risks of loss of or damage to the subject matter insured, subject to the stated exclusions.

The B clauses cover:

1. Loss or damage to the subject matter insured reasonably attributable to:
   (a) fire or explosion;
   (b) vessel or craft being stranded, grounded, sunk or capsized;
   (c) overturning or derailment of land conveyance;
   (d) collision or contact of vessel, craft or conveyance with any external object other than water;
   (e) discharge of cargo at port of distress;
   (f) earthquake, volcanic eruption or lightning.
2. Loss or damage to the subject matter caused by:
   (a) general average sacrifice;
   (b) jettison or washing overboard;
   (c) entry of sea, lake or river water into vessel, craft, hold,

conveyance, container, liftvan or place of storage;

(d) total loss of any package lost overboard or dropped whilst loading onto, or unloading from, vessel or craft.

The C clauses are more restricted than the B clauses — they do not cover: earthquake, volcanic eruption or lightning; washing overboard; entry of sea, lake or river water into vessel, craft, hold, conveyance, container, liftvan or place of storage; total loss of any package lost overboard or dropped whilst loading on to, or unloading from vessel or craft. Otherwise the coverage provided is the same as that provided by the B clauses. In both the B and C clauses the requirement of 'proximately caused by' has been reduced to 'reasonably attributable' for most of the risks.

All three sets cover general average and salvage charges. The 'Both-to-blame collision clause' is included in all three sets.

Exclusions.   The following are not covered by any of the three sets of clauses:

1. Loss, damage or expense attributable to wilful misconduct of the assured.
2. Ordinary leakage, ordinary loss in weight or volume, or ordinary wear and tear of the subject matter insured.
3. Loss, damage or expense caused by insufficiency or unsuitability of packing or preparation of the subject matter insured (for the purpose of this clause 'packing' shall be deemed to include stowage in a container or liftvan but only when such stowage is carried out prior to attachment of this insurance or by the assured or their servants).
4. Loss, damage, or expense caused by inherent vice or nature of the subject matter insured.
5. Loss, damage, or expense proximately caused by delay, even though the delay be caused by a risk insured against (except expenses payable under general average).
6. Loss, damage or expense arising from insolvency or financial default of the owners, managers, charterers or operators of the vessel.
7. Loss, damage or expense arising from the use of any weapon or war employing atomic or nuclear fission and/or fission or other like reaction or radioactive force or matter.
8. Loss, damage or expense arising from:
    (a) unseaworthiness of vessel or craft and/or
    (b) unfitness of vessel, craft, conveyance, container or liftvan for the safe carriage of the subject matter insured, where the assured or their servants are privy to such unseaworthiness or unfitness, at the time the subject matter insured is loaded therein. The underwriters waive any breach of the implied warranties of seaworthiness of the ship to carry the subject matter insured to destination, unless the

assured or their servants are privy to such unseaworthiness or unfitness.

9. War, civil war, revolution, rebellion, insurrection, or civil strife arising therefrom, or any hostile act by or against a belligerent power; capture, arrest, restraint, detainment (piracy excepted), and the consequences thereof or any attempt threat; derelict mines, torpedoes, bombs, or other derelict weapons of war.

10. Loss, damage or expense caused by/resulting from:
    (a) Strikers, locked-out workmen, or persons taking part in labour disturbances, riots or civil commotions.
    (b) Strikes, lock-outs, labour disturbances, riots or civil commotions.
    (c) Terrorists or any persons acting from a political motive.

Duration. The attachment and termination of the risk, i.e. cover commences when goods leave the warehouse or store at the place named in the policy for the transit and continues until delivered to consignee's or other final warehouse or store at the destination named, or upon expiry of 60 days after completion of discharge overside from overseas vessel at final port, whichever first occurs.

Claims. This section includes the 'lost or not lost' provisions stating that the assured must have an insurable interest at the time of loss and he is not to be prejudiced in the event of the loss occurring before the contract of insurance was concluded, unless he was aware of such loss. Moreover, when the transit is terminated at a different place to that originally intended, the underwriter will reimburse the assured for extra charges incurred in unloading, storing and forwarding cargo to its original destination.

The increased value clause provides that when increased value insurance has been effected the amount of the increase shall be deemed to increase the total amount insured on the cargo, and the policies involved shall bear their proportionate part of any loss in relation to their sum insured to the total amount insured.

8.5 FACTORS DETERMINING PREMIUM RATES

1. The carrying vessel. The age, classification, flag, ownership and management of the ship are important considerations.
2. Nature of the packing used. This has to be related to the mode of transport and its adequacy as a form of protection to the cargo. Air-freight and maritime container shipments tend to require less packing.
3. Type of merchandise involved. Some commodities are more vulnerable to damage than others. Additionally, one must relate this to the cover provided and experience of conveying such cargo.

4. Nature of transit and related warehouse accommodation. Generally, the shorter the transit time, the less vulnerable the cargo to damage/pilferage. Again the mode(s) of transport involved influence premium determination. Maritime containerization has tended in many trades/cargoes to reduce risk of pilferage, but the cargo still remains susceptible to damage.

5. Previous experience. If the cargo involved has been subject to significant damage or pilferage the premiums are likely to be high. In the main, the shipper and broker tend to work well together in devising methods to minimize damage and pilferage and overcome inadequate packing.

6. The extent of cover needed. This is a critical area and obviously the more extensive cover required, the higher the premium rate. For example, glassware may be insured at a high rate against all risks including breakage, or at a much lower rate excluding breakage, cracking or chipping. The degree of fragility is not the same for all commodities and obviously there cannot be a universal rate for breakage. Again the broker will advise the shipper, but much depends on terms of delivery.

7. The volume of cargo involved. A substantial quantity shipment of import cargo may obtain a more favourable premium, but much depends on the circumstances, particularly transport mode and type of packing, if any.

8.6   CARGO INSURANCE CLAIMS

Most insurance company policies require that immediate notice be given to the nearest branch or agency in the event of damage giving rise to a claim under a policy on goods. Lloyd's policies stipulate that a Lloyd's agent shall be called in should damage occur.

When notified of damage, the company's agent or Lloyd's agent appoints a suitable surveyor to inspect the goods and to report on the nature and extent of the damage. A common practice is for a report or certificate of loss incorporating the surveyor's findings to be issued to the consignees, the latter paying the fee. This is the usual procedure relative to the Lloyd's agent. This certificate of loss is included with the claim papers and, if the loss is recoverable under the insurance cover, the fee is refunded to the claimants.

In some circumstances, the claim papers are returned to the place where the insurance was effected and subsequently presented to the underwriters. However, especially where goods are sold on CIF terms and the policy is assigned to the consignees, arrangements are made for any claims to be paid at destination. In such cases, the consignees approach the agents named in the policy for payment of their claims.

Lloyd's agents undertake this service. The policy must be produced by the claimant when a marine claim is put forward because of the freedom with which the marine policy may be assigned. In circumstances where the policy or certificate of insurance has been lost or destroyed, underwriters are generally willing to settle the claim, provided that the claimant completes a letter of indemnity.

The presentation of claims is by negotiation on documents supporting the assured's case. It is very difficult to state with any degree of legal precision exactly on whom the onus of proof falls in every case, but generally speaking, the assured must be able to prove a loss by a peril against which he was insured. Once the assured has presented a prima-facie case of loss by a peril insured against, the onus is on the insurers to disprove liability.

The claims procedure will vary by circumstances and undoubtedly the buyer will secure a quicker settlement if insurance cover is effected in his own country rather than by the seller in his/her country. Details of the procedure are as follows:

1. The buyer must inform the broker or insurer of the loss in writing giving the fullest details and circumstances giving rise to the claim. Ideally for a ship or aircraft this should embrace the nature of damage or loss and possible cause, place, date, time, name of ship or aircraft and schedule, carrier's name, and any other data. Such data can be telephoned with a confirmatory telex, or letter to follow.
2. The terms under which the goods were purchased, i.e. CIF, CFR CPT, FCA, etc. This will enable the interested parties to determine their responsibilities under the claim and hasten the processing of it.
3. The company or person responsible for the loss should be identified: e.g. carrier, forwarding agent, warehouse company, seaport/airport authority or stevedores.
4. If the damage or loss was established on delivery, the delivery note should be preserved. It may be that part of the consignment is missing.
5. Retain any external packing or other material for inspection by the surveyor, together with photographic evidence and any written report.

The following documents are required when making an insurance claim and should be produced by the buyer:

1. The commercial invoice issued to the buyer together with shipping specification and/or weight notes.
2. The original Bill of Lading, Charter Party, Air Waybill, or CMR or CIM consignment note.
3. The original policy or certificate of insurance.
4. The survey report or other documentary evidence detailing the loss or damage incurred.

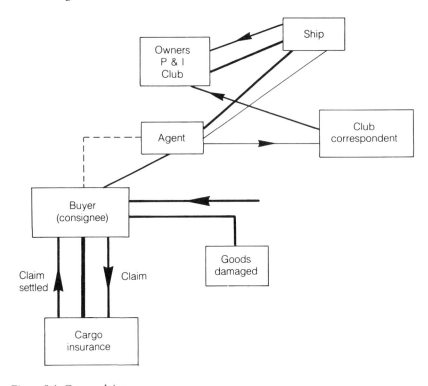

Figure 8.1 Cargo claims

5. Extended protest or extract from ships logs for salvage loss, particular average in goods, or total loss of goods for maritime consignments. This will be provided by the shipowner to determine/establish any evidence of damage/pilferage.
6. Letters of subrogation for total loss or particular average on goods.
7. Any exchange of correspondence with the carriers and other parties regarding their liability for the loss or damage.
8. Any landing account or weight notes at final destination.

Having established the documents required to deal with the claim, it is important that a code of procedure be devised to process it.

Figure 8.1 features the main elements of the cargo claim. Figure 8.2 shows the development of the cargo claim and its constituents from the factory to the buyer (consignee).

Brief details are given below of the claims procedure which involves a bulk shipment.

1. Receiver notifies his agent of damage or loss and allows the ship's agent 3 days to examine the cargo.

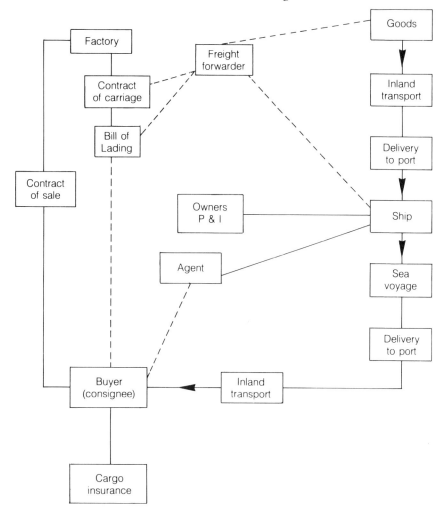

Figure 8.2 Development of a cargo claim

2. When the extent of damage is ascertained by receiver or shipowner's agent, the shipowner and P & I Club must be told.
3. A large claim may require a P & I Club surveyor or a consultant to examine the cargo. An early examination is essential and the agent must establish from ship's master and confirm with the shipowner or P & I Club, the actual name of P & I Club involved.
4. When the cargo claim facts are established, correspondence starts as detailed in Figures 8.1 and 8.2 involving interested parties: shipowner, receiver's agents, P & I Club, cargo receiver, shipowner's agent, cargo insurance company/Lloyd's, lawyers, etc.

5. The receiver's agent's role is decisive in all stages to ensure prompt settlement is obtained and quick action essential in the early stages.

It will be appreciated that circumstances will vary. The claim could emerge at the factory warehouse of the buyer rather than at the destination port as found in the example.

It is important to bear in mind that clean receipts for imported cargo acceptance are not given when the goods are in a doubtful condition, but the receipt is suitably endorsed and witnessed if possible, for example, if one package is missing. Furthermore, if the loss or damage incurred was not readily apparent at the time of taking delivery, written notice must be given to the carriers or other bailees within 3 days of delivery acceptance. It is desirable that the claim be progressed as quickly as practicable.

It is advantageous for the importer to have a good comprehension of the term general average (GA) which features in any standard maritime policy. It is defined as a 'loss arising in consequences of extraordinary and intentional sacrifices made or expenses incurred, for the common safety of the ship and cargo'. Examples of general average include jettison of cargo, damage to cargo, etc.

In the event of a shipowner declaring a general average loss, each party involved in the voyage must contribute in proportion to their interest in the maritime venture. This, of course, involves shippers who may not have suffered any damage or loss to their cargo. The cargo is only released in such a situation when the shipper or importer has given either a cash deposit or provided a general average guarantee given by the insurers. This involves signing a general average bond which confirms that the importer will pay his general average contribution as assessed in the general average adjustment drawn up by the average adjuster.

8.7 CARGO CLAIMS PREVENTION

Claims prevention is the process of devising a system to reduce or eliminate the level of claims emerging from the carriage of goods on an international transit. It is important that the buyer gives special attention to claims prevention and thereby facilitates the goods arriving in an undamaged condition and that none are missing.

Circumstances giving rise to a cargo claim may be as follows:

1. Missing goods.
2. Damaged goods.
3. Stained, mutilated or soiled goods.
4. Non-saleable goods arising through frustration of the transit such as transit delays causing perishable goods to deteriorate beyond a marketable saleable product.

5. Failure of the goods to arrive on specified date resulting in a compensation claim.
6. Inadequate packing.
7. Poor stowage.
8. Poor handling or stacking of cargo resulting in damage, crushing, etc.

To minimize the level of cargo claims it is most desirable that adequate measures be taken. The following list should not be regarded as exhaustive but merely a selection of the more important areas where measures can be taken to reduce claims:

1. Conduct transit tests to determine where delays, damage or pilferage are encountered and institute any remedial measures.
2. Improve documentation to specify circumstances of claim and reasons for claim. Comprehensive claims reports permit realistic analysis of causes and thereby produce a possible pattern of circumstances.
3. Quality control of product, transport service and packaging (see also item 4).
4. Analysis of adequacy of packaging in terms of handling and stowage and of compatibility with atmospheric conditions exposure to weather.
5. Improve security and evaluate alternative routeing, packaging, cargo packing, marking identity, etc., to avoid pilferage.
6. Improved packaging, handling and stowage techniques and/or transport mode, i.e. break-bulk to containers, to avoid breakage.
7. Evaluate the cost of alternatives to current practices and their likelihood of success.
8. Improve staff training, especially on the handling and stowage of cargo and in measures to lessen cargo claims such as completing and promptly submitting forms.
9. Devise a code of procedure to report cargo loss or damage, thereby ensuring prompt action can be taken to lessen the prospect of further claims.
10. Provision of adequate preventative claims staff resources to lessen such risk as electronic detection.
11. Introduce modern technology.
12. Produce a brochure on claims prevention, and packaging, stowage and handling techniques.
13. Initiate early discussions with the carrier(s) and other interested parties to devise remedial measures to resolve difficulties and claims encountered.

The need to deal with claims promptly and adequately cannot be overstressed. Cargo insurance premiums then remain competitive and the buyer is well-satisfied with the goods received in a quality condition.

9 *Import documentation*

An important part of import practice is a good comprehension of the various documents involved to process the import consignment — their role, limitations and likely problems. An importer's bank, freight forwarder or trade association can help with any queries.

It is the responsibility of the exporter to ensure the documents for the transport of the goods are complete, accurate and properly and promptly processed in accordance with the contract of sale. Failure to do so can frequently result in costly consequences.

The importer, however, has the responsibility for accurately completing the necessary forms for the goods to be licensed for import and cleared through customs. Improper documentation can cause goods to be impounded, warehoused or left on the quayside with consequent damage, loss and expense.

Normally the supplier arranges to deliver the goods when and where the importer requires, but much will depend on the buying terms — FOB, DDP, CIF or FCA (see Chapter 10). The documents will vary but those needed for any import transaction should be specified in the contract. Many suppliers despatch their goods through a freight forwarder (see pages 194-6) and often under consolidation arrangements which may be by air, road trailer or LCL.

The following measures ensure comprehension and efficient processing of importation documents and therefore smooth transit of consignments:

1. Ensure good liaison is maintained between the seller, buyer and their forwarding agents, and have details of their addresses, telex, fax and telephone numbers for prompt communication to resolve problems and seek clarification.
2. Check with the customs the documents required to process the imported consignment and ensure they are made available from the seller.
3. Obtain a checklist on errors likely to arise in import documentation from international banks, SITPRO, trade associations, Chambers of Commerce, etc.
4. Ensure adequate funds are available to meet VAT and customs duties

and any freight or agent charges. Check the documents to ensure charges raised are valid and are for the buyer's account and not that of the seller. If in doubt confer with the buyer initially and subsequently with the other parties.

5. Ensure the goods received conform to their description on the export invoice or carrier's consignment note — Bill of Lading or Air Waybill.
6. Ensure the correct documents are used and maximum benefit is being obtained from them. For example, there are advantages to the buyer in using the Sea Waybill rather than the Bill of Lading (see *Elements of Shipping*, pages 262-274). The buyer should be fully appraised of the benefits to the importer of using specific documents and getting the commodity description correct to obtain minimum customs payments under the tariff (see pages 79-80).
7. Develop electronic data interchange where possible and advantageous.
8. Ensure that the role and significance of original and copy documents are fully understood and the relevant convention such as Warsaw Convention, CIM, CMR, Hague-Visby-Rules etc. for the carrier's document, especially at what stage under Incoterms 1990 the title of the goods passes from the seller to the buyer.
9. The carriers documents such as the Bill of Lading, Air Waybill, Sea Waybill, etc. are likely to be completed by the importer only when the buyer takes charge of the transportation such as under the Ex Works or FCA situations.

The foregoing should be read in consultation with Chapter 11 on processing the imported consignment. In processing an import consignment involving extensive documentation, one must bear in mind there can be up to four contracts to execute: the export sales contract, the contract of carriage, the financial contract and the contract of cargo insurance. Failure to have the relevant documentation correctly completed results in late delivery as customs will refuse to clear the goods. Documentation relating to customs, insurance and finance is covered in detail in Chapters 6, 7 and 8. A study of the various consignment documents now follows.

9.1 AIR WAYBILL

The Air Waybill is the consignment note used for the carriage of goods by air. It is often called an air-freight consignment note; it is not a document of title and is not transferable or negotiable. It is basically a receipt for the goods for despatch and is prima-facie evidence of the conditions of carriage. There are usually 12 copies of each Air Waybill for distribution to the shipper, sales agent, issuing carrier (airline operator), consignee, delivery agent, airport of destination, third carrier (if applicable), second carrier (if applicable), first carrier, extra copy for carrier (when required), invoice and airport of departure. Copies 1-3 are the 'originals'.

Copies are used as circumstances demand. For example the second carrier's copy would be used only if the consignment was conveyed on another airline to complete the transit — for example, if British Airways conveyed it for the first leg of the journey and Air Canada the remainder. The conditions of carriage are found on the reverse of the Air Waybill document and are subject to the *Carriage by Air Act, 1961*. This is based on the Warsaw rules and a number of other conventions. There are supplementary provisions in the *Carriage by Air Act, 1962*. Actual liability to the IATA airline carrier is based at 250 gold francs per kg. In the UK its value is fixed by a statutory instrument from time to time in the form of the Carriage by Air (Sterling Equivalent) orders. These currently give a value of £13.63 per kg.

The standard IATA Air Waybill, used worldwide, is the most important feature of the simplified system of documentation for international air-freight. A single Air Waybill covers carriage over any distance, by as many airlines as may be required to complete the transportation. When goods carried by one airline for part of the journey are transferred to another airline, the original Air Waybill is sent forward with the consignment from point of original departure to the final destination.

The exporter is responsible for the correctness of the particulars and statements relating to the goods in the Air Waybill. There is an indemnity to the carrier in the case of inaccuracies. Provision of the requisite documents required by customs is also the exporter's duty. There is an indemnity to the carrier if the exporter fails to do so.

A new 'universal' Air Waybill (Fig. 9.1) was introduced from 1 January 1984 and its use is mandatory. It is compatible with the United Nations layout key and can be used for both domestic and international transits. The new universal Air Waybill contains the following information:

1. The place and date of its execution.
2. Names of the departure and destination airports.
3. The names and addresses of the consignor, consignee and the first carrier (airline).
4. A description of the goods.
5. The number of packages with marks, weights, quantity and dimensions.
6. The total freight amount prepaid and/or to pay is precisely defined, and the rate.
7. The declared value for customs purposes, likewise for carriage and the currency.

220 ∣ 3 1 7 (342   220-3187 6342

Shipper's Name and Address	Shipper's account Number

Not negotiable
Air Waybill*
(Air Consignment note)
Issued by
Deutsche Lufthansa AG,
D-5000 Köln 21, Von-Gablenz-Straße 2—6   Member of International
                                                        Air Transport Association

⊖ **Lufthansa**

Copies 1, 2 and 3 of this Air Waybill are originals and have the same validity

Consignee's Name and Address	Consignee's account Number

It is agreed that the goods described herein are accepted in apparent good order and condition (except as noted) for carriage **subject to the Conditions of Contract on the reverse hereof. The shipper's attention is drawn to the notice concerning carrier's limitation of liability.** Shipper may increase such limitation of liability by declaring a higher value for carriage and paying a supplemental charge if required.
Carrier maintains cargo liability insurance to protect itself against claims for which it is legally liable.

Issuing Carrier's Agent Name and City	Accounting Information

Agent's IATA Code	Account No.	

Airport of Departure (Addr. of first Carrier) and requested Routing

to	By first Carrier Routing and Destination	to	by	to	by	Currency	CHGS Code	WT/VAL PPD COLL	Other PPD COLL	Declared Value for Carriage	Declared Value for Customs

Airport of Destination	Flight/Date For Carrier Use only	Flight/Date	Amount of Insurance	**Insurance** — If Carrier offers insurance and such insurance is requested in accordance with conditions on reverse hereof, indicate amount to be insured in figures in box marked amount of insurance

Handling Information

No of Pieces RCP	Gross Weight	kg lb	Rate Class Commodity Item No.	Chargeable Weight	Rate Charge	Total	Nature and Quantity of Goods (incl. Dimensions or Volume)

Prepaid	Weight Charge	Collect	Other Charges

	Valuation Charge		Insurance premium

| | Tax | | |

	Total other Charges Due Agent		Shipper certifies that the particulars on the face hereof are correct and that insofar as any part of the consignment contains dangerous goods, such part is property described by name and is in proper condition for carriage by air according to the applicable Dangerous Goods Regulations.

| | Total other Charges Due Carrier | |

Signature of Shipper or his Agent

Total prepaid	Total collect

Currency Conversion Rates	cc charges in Dest. Currency

Executed on	(Date)	at	(Place)	Signature of Issuing Carrier or its Agent

For Carriers Use only at Destination	Charges at Destination	Total collect Charges

220-3187 6342

* Luftfrachtbrief (nicht begebbar) — eine verbindliche Übersetzung dieses Frachtbriefformulars (einschließlich der Vertragsbedingungen) in die deutsche Sprache liegt bei allen Lufthansa Frachtbüros aus.

Original 3 (for shipper)

Form 8277 C-85 (CGN XC 2) · Printed in the Fed. Rep. of Germany

Figure 9.1 Air Waybill, reproduced by kind permission of Lufthansa.

8. The date of the flight.
9. Details of any special route to be taken.
10. The signature of the shipper or his agent.
11. The signature of the issuing carrier (airline operator) or his agent.
12. Details of the booked flight and actual flight(s) incorporating the first, second and third carriers.

Efficient service depends on the accuracy and completeness of the Air Waybill. Hence shippers themselves must give clear and complete forwarding instructions to the airline or agent. To facilitate this procedure they may use the Shipper's Letter of Instruction, a standardized form which may be obtained from any airline, approved IATA cargo agent or forwarder.

At departure airports the Air Waybill is a contract of carriage, a receipt for goods, it provides a unique reference for handling inventory control and documentation reference, it includes a description of goods and full rating information, it includes special handling requirements, and provides basic details for aircraft manifest (list of cargo details). Post-flight information includes a document source for revenue collection, interlining accounting and proration, and cargo statistics. At destination airports the Air Waybill provides a basic document for notification to consignee, customs clearance and delivery to consignee. Additionally it is a source document for accounting clearance and delivery charges. Where more than one package is involved, the carrier can require the consignor to make out separate Air Waybills. The air consignment note must be printed in one of the official languages of the country of departure. Erasures are not admissible, but alterations can be made provided they are authenticated by the consignor's signature or initials. If quantities, weights, or values are altered, they must appear in words as well as figures.

An increasing volume of air-freight is now conveyed under consolidation with the freight forwarder sponsoring the overall consignment. It may involve a hundred individual consignments concerning various consignors/consignees. Under such consignments, the freight forwarder attaches to the Master Air Waybill the cargo manifest detailing the fullest information on each of the consignments despatched. In such circumstances the freight forwarder issues a 'House Air Waybill' to the shipper to confirm details of despatch by air which facilitates payment for the goods.

Under a Documentary Letter of Credit, certain specific information or instructions to be shown on the Air Waybill may be requested by the importer. This usually includes: names and addresses of the exporter, importer and the first carrier; the names of the airports of departure and destination together with details of any special route; the date of the flight, the declared value of the merchandise for customs purposes; the number of packages with marks, weights, quantity and dimensions; the freight charge per unit of weight or volume; the technical description of the goods (not the commercial description); whether the freight charge has been prepaid or will be paid at the destination; the signature of the exporter (or his agent), the place and date of issue; and finally the signature of the issuing carrier (or his agent).

In the next few years further modernization of air-freight documentation will take place. This includes the move to an automated information system. As computers are acquired by shippers, agents, handling companies, customs offices and others, a new approach to documentation and procedures is required. Additionally required are the development of a neutral Air Waybill numbering system (valid on all IATA airlines); use of bar codes for automatic verifications; automated information systems so that airlines and stations can adequately communicate with each other; standard data elements; standard message formats; and new codes and procedures.

It is important the importer comprehends that the Air Waybill is not a document of title but merely a receipt issued by an airline for goods despatched by air. Hence unlike a Bill of Lading, the Air Waybill is not required at destination airport to claim the goods when they have cleared through customs.

9.2 ATA CARNETS

The buyer or importer may become involved in the temporary importation of a product, for example when the exporter wishes to despatch samples and exhibits to the buyer for evaluation. This is usually undertaken by an ATA carnet. The exporter undertakes all the arrangements for the process which is classified as a temporary export and re-import. There is no need to pay import duties and taxes or to lodge bonds or guarantee with the customs authorities of the countries into which the importation occurs. The classes of goods broadly covered by the carnet include commercial samples, goods for exhibition purposes and professional equipment. ATA carnets are used worldwide and usually issued by Chambers of Commerce.

9.3 BILLS OF EXCHANGE (see also Chapter 7)

Under the terms of the *Bills of Exchange Act, 1882*, a Bill of Exchange has been defined as 'an unconditional order in writing addressed by one person to another, signed by the person giving it, requiring the person to whom it is addressed to pay, on demand, or at a fixed or determinable future time, a sum certain in money or to the order of a specified person or bearer'. Drafts can be drawn either at sight (payment to be made on demand or on presentation) or at a particular 'tenor' ('usance') (payment to be made at a fixed or determinable future date, usually within 180 days of sight of the Bill of Exchange by the drawer, or within 180 days of the date of the draft). Special Bank of England approval is needed for credit periods exceeding 180 days under an export sales contract. The general procedure for Letters of Credit is for drafts to be drawn on a bank, but some Credits require them to be drawn on the importer. Drafts can be drawn in pairs called 'first' and 'second' Bills of Exchange.

The Bill of Exchange is a popular way of arranging payment. The most usual procedure is for the exporter (seller) to hand the Bill of Exchange together with the documents to the exporter's (seller's) bank who will send them to a bank overseas for 'collection'. The overseas bank will notify the buyer of the arrival of the documents and will release them to him subject to one of two conditions. Firstly, if the Bill is drawn at 'sight' the buyer pays the amount of the Bill in full, or secondly if the Bill is drawn payable after a certain number of days, the buyer accepts the Bill, i.e. he signs across the Bill his agreement to pay the amount in full at due date.

The main benefit of this method of payment is that the exporter (seller) can maintain control of the goods until the importer (buyer) has agreed to pay for them. However, there is still no absolute guarantee the importer (buyer) will pay, but legal procedures exist in most countries to recover money owing against Bills of Exchange.

The Bill of Exchange contains the following data:

1. The date.
2. A specific sum, which should agree with the amount on the export invoice.
3. The 'tenor', that is, whether at sight or at a stated period after sight or at a fixed date.
4. The name of the drawee.
5. The name and signature of the drawer.
6. The name of the payee or order or bearer.
7. The endorsement of the payee where applicable.

Overall, the Bill of Exchange should be so worded to conform to what is laid down in the credit.

The following discrepancies tend to arise in processing Bills of Exchange and should be avoided: (a) document drawn incorrectly or for a sum different to the credit amount; (b) designation of the signature on the document not specified if required, e.g. director or partner.

9.4 BILLS OF LADING

A Bill of Lading is a receipt for goods shipped on board a vessel, signed by the person (or his agent) who contracts to carry them, and stating the conditions in which the goods were delivered to (and received by) the ship. It is not the actual contract, which is inferred from the action of the shipper or shipowner in delivering or receiving the cargo, but forms excellent evidence of the terms of the contract. It is a document of title to the goods which is the subject of the contract between the buyer (importer) and seller (exporter).

9.4.1 Acts and Rules governing Bills of Lading

The Bills of Lading Act, 1855 established the following details relevant to this document:

1. It preserved the right of the original shipper to '*stoppage in transitu*' (in transit). Moreover, not only did it give the right of conditional endorsement and of reserving the '*jus disponendi*' (law of disposal) but also the unpaid seller could resume possession of the goods by exercising the right of 'stoppage *in transitu*'.
2. It established the principle of transferability, permitting the transfer of a Bill of Lading from the holder to a person to whom the property in the goods passes, together with any rights and liabilities incorporated in the document.
3. It provided that once the Bill of Lading has been issued, it is prima-facie evidence that the goods have been shipped.

Subsequent legislation emerged through the Hague Rules in September 1921. These Rules were agreed at an international convention at Brussels on 25 August 1924 and gave effect in the United Kingdom to the *Carriage of Goods by Sea Act, 1924 (COGSA)*. They are officially known as 'The International Convention for the Unification of Certain Rules relating to Bills of Lading' and govern liability for loss or damage to goods carried under a Bill of Lading. The main effect of COGSA was that it radically changed the legal status of the shipowner by imposing on him a precise liability and giving precisely defined rights and remedies in place of previous freedom. The Rules apply to all outward (export) shipments from any nation which ratified them. They apply almost universally wherever they have not been superseded by the Hague–Visby Rules (see below). Their main features are as follows:

1. It lays down minimum terms under which a carrier may offer for the carriage of all goods, other than live animals, non-commercial goods (such as personal and household effects), experimental shipments and goods carried on deck where the Bill of Lading is claused to indicate such carriage.

2. The carrier (shipowner) has to exercise due diligence to provide a seaworthy vessel. The basic principle is that the carrier is only liable for loss or damage caused by his own negligence or that of his servants, agents or subcontractors. However, the carrier is still protected in three cases where the loss or damage has been caused by negligence: negligence in navigation; negligence in the management of the vessel (as opposed to the care of the cargo); and fire, unless by the actual fault of privity of the carrier.

3. Liability is limited to the following per package: Australia A $200, Canada C $500, West Germany DM 1250, Greece DR 8000, Japan Y100 000, USA US$500, USSR R250, UK £100.

In 1967 a further international conference adopted some revisions to the Hague Rules, principally affecting their limitation. The amended rules are officially known as the Brussels Protocol signed on 23 February 1968 and known as the Hague-Visby Rules and contained in the United Kingdom by the *Carriage of Goods by Sea Act, 1971.* The Special Drawing Rights Protocol, adopted in February 1984, placed all the contracting states' carriers under a liability per package/weight of SDR 2 per kg or SDR 666.67 per package or unit, whichever is the greater. Countries involved (Autumn 1987) are Belgium, Denmark, Finland, Italy, Netherlands, Norway, Poland, Spain, Sweden and the UK.

The 1968 Convention came into effect on 23 June 1977 and the contracting states applying the Hague-Visby Rules (Autumn 1987) include Belgium, Denmark, Ecuador, Egypt, Finland, France, East Germany, Italy, Lebanon, Holland, Norway, Poland, Singapore, Spain, Sri Lanka, Sweden, Switzerland, Syria, Tonga, the UK and West Germany. The Visby amendment applies to all Bills of Lading where the port of shipment is a ratifying nation, or the place of issue of the Bill of Lading is in a ratifying nation, or where the Bill of Lading applies Hague-Visby Rules contractually.

In March 1978 at a further international conference in Hamburg, a new set of rules termed the Hamburg Rules was proposed. If adopted, the Hamburg rules will radically alter the liability which shipowners have to bear for loss or damage to goods. The main differences between the Hamburg Rules and Hague-Visby Rules are given below:

1. The carrier will be liable for loss, damage, or delay to the goods occurring in his charge unless he proves that 'he, his servants, or agents took all measures that could reasonably be required to avoid the occurrence and its consequences'.

2. The carrier is liable for delay in delivery if, 'the goods have not been delivered at the port of discharge provided for under the Contract of Carriage within the time agreed expressly upon or, in the absence of such agreement, within the time which it could be reasonable to

require of a diligent Carrier having regard to the circumstances of the case'.

3. The dual system for calculating the limit of liability either by reference to package or weight as set out in the Hague-Visby Rules has been readopted but the amounts have been increased by about 25% to SDR 835 per package and SDR 2.5 per kg.
4. The Hamburg Rules cover all contracts for the carriage by sea other than Charter Parties.
5. They cover live animals and deck cargo.
6. They apply to both imports and exports.

The Rules will come into effect 1 year after ratification or accession by 20 nations and by Autumn 1987 11 nations had acceded — Barbados, Chile, Egypt, Hungary, Lebanon, Morocco, Romania, Senegal, Tanzania, Tunisia and Uganda.

9.4.2 Details contained in a Bill of Lading

1. The name of the shipper (usually the exporter).
2. The name of the carrying vessel.
3. Full description of the cargo (provided it is not bulk cargo) including any shipping marks, individual package numbers in the consignment, contents, cubic measurement, gross weight, etc.
4. The marks and numbers identifying the goods.
5. Port of shipment.
6. Port of discharge.
7. Full details of freight, including when and where it is to be paid — whether freight paid or payable at destination.
8. Name of consignee or, if the shipper is anxious to withhold the consignee's name, shipper's order.
9. The terms of the contract of carriage.
10. The date the goods were received for shipment and/or loaded on the vessel.
11. The name and address of the notified party (the person to be notified on arrival of the shipment, usually the buyer).
12. Number of Bills of Lading signed on behalf of the master or his agent, acknowledging receipt of the goods.
13. The signature of the ship's master or his agent and the date.

9.4.3 Types and forms of Bills of Lading

Shipped (on board) Bill of Lading.   Under the *Carriage of Goods by Sea Act, 1924*, the shipper can demand that the shipowner supplies Bills of Lading proving that the goods have been actually shipped. For this reason, most Bill of Lading forms are already printed as shipped bills and commence with the wording: 'shipped in apparent good order and condition'. It confirms the goods are actually on board the vessel. This is the most satisfactory type of receipt and it is stressed the importer will normally require the exporter to produce Bills of Lading as evidence that goods have been shipped on board.

Received for shipment Bill of Lading.   This arises where the word 'shipped' does not appear on the Bill of Lading. It merely confirms that the goods have been handed over to, and are in the custody of the shipowner. The cargo may be in a dock, warehouse or transit shed or even inland. The Bill has, therefore, not the same meaning as a 'shipped' Bill and the buyer under a CIF contract will not accept such a Bill for ultimate financial settlement through the bank unless provision has been made in the contract. Forwarding agents will invariably avoid handling 'received for shipment Bills' for their clients unless special circumstances obtain.

Through Bills of Lading.   In many cases it is necessary to employ two or more carriers to get the goods to their final destination. The on-carriage may be either by a second vessel or by a different form of transport.

Stale Bills of Lading.   It is important that the Bill of Lading is available at the port of destination before the goods arrive or, failing this, at the same time. Bills presented to the consignee or buyer or his bank after the goods are due at the port are said to be stale. A cargo cannot normally be collected by the buyer (importer) without the Bill of Lading and the late arrival of this all-important document may have undesirable consequences such as warehouse rent, etc.

Groupage Bill of Lading.   Forwarding agents are permitted to 'group' together particular compatible consignments from individual consignors to various consignees, usually situated at the same destination, and despatch them as one consignment. The shipowner will issue a groupage Bill of Lading, whilst the forwarding agent, who cannot hand to his principals the shipowners' Bill of Lading, will issue to the individual shippers a certificate of shipment sometimes called 'house Bill of Lading'. At the destination, another agent working in close liaison with the agent forwarding the cargo will break-bulk the consignment and distribute the goods to the various consignees. This practice is on the increase, usually involving the use of containers (LCL shipments) and particularly evident in the continental trade and deep-sea container services.

Transhipment Bill of Lading.   This type is issued usually by shipping companies when there is no direct service between two ports, but when the shipowner is prepared to tranship the cargo at an intermediate port at his expense.

Clean Bill of Lading.   Each Bill of Lading states: 'in apparent good order and condition', which of course refers to the cargo. If this statement is not modified by the shipowner, the Bill of Lading is regarded as 'clean' or 'unclaused'. By issuing clean Bills of Lading, the shipowner admits his full liability of the cargo described in the Bill under the law and his contract. This type is much favoured by banks for financial settlement purposes.

Claused Bills of Lading.   If the shipowner does not agree with any of the statements made in the Bill of Lading he will add a clause to this effect, thereby causing the Bill of Lading to be termed as 'unclean', 'foul', 'dirty', or 'claused'. There are many recurring types of such clauses including: inadequate packaging; unprotected machinery; second-hand cases; wet or stained cartons; damaged crates; cartons missing, etc. The clause 'shipped on deck at owner's risk' may thus be considered to be a clause under this heading. This type of Bill of Lading is usually unacceptable to a bank.

Negotiable Bills of Lading.   If the words 'or his or their assigns' are contained in the Bill of Lading, it is negotiable. There are, however, variations in this terminology, for example, the word 'bearer' may be inserted, or another party stated in the preamble to the phrase. Bills of Lading may be negotiable by endorsement or transfer. Basically the Bill of Lading is a negotiable document which allows the goods to be transferred by endorsement and delivery. This situation allows one or other parties to the transaction control over title to the goods and on this basis Letters of Credit tend to stipulate certain types of Bill of Lading in order for this control to be exercised. Examples are given below:

1. Bill of Lading completed as follows:
   Shipper Box in B/L — Actual shipper (exporter)
   Consignee Box in B/L — Actual consignee (buyer)
   Notify Box in B/L — Consignee or importer's agent at port of arrival

This situation permits the consignee to present himself or agent to take delivery of the goods. In the event of the agent so doing the Bill of Lading would be endorsed on the back of the document.

2. To order of bank involving completion of Bill of Lading as follows:
   Shipper Box in B/L — Actual shipper (exporter)

Consignee Box in B/L — To the order of Bank

Notify Box in B/L — Consignee, buyer (importer)

In such circumstances the bank carries out the endorsement and thereby exercises control over the goods. Hence if the bank wishes to ensure the buyer has actually paid for the goods before he takes delivery the bank may endorse the Bill of Lading when payment is made.

3. 'To order' Bills of Lading requires document to be completed as follows:

Shipper Box in B/L — Shipper (exporter)

Consignee Box in B/L — To order

Notify in Box in B/L — Consignee, buyer (importer)

In this situation the shipper must stamp and sign the Bill of Lading in order for the title of goods to be transferred to the consignee. Hence the Bill of Lading is not valid to the buyer unless the endorsement is made. It is a useful safeguard against Bills of Lading accidentally transmitted to buyers directly. In such a situation the buyer could not take delivery of the goods and the Bill of Lading would have to be returned to the shipper for endorsement and presentation to the bank. Bills of Lading completed in this manner are described as 'to order bank endorsed'.

Non-negotiable Bills of Lading.   When the words 'or his or their assigns' are deleted from the Bills of Lading, the Bill is regarded as non-negotiable. The effect of this deletion is that the consignee (or other named party) cannot transfer the property or goods by transfer of the Bills. This particular type is seldom found and will normally apply when goods are shipped on a non-commercial basis, as with household effects.

Container Bills of Lading.   Containers are now playing an increasing role in international shipping and container Bills of Lading are becoming more common in use. They cover the goods from port-to-port or from inland point of departure to inland point of destination (e.g. inland clearance depot to container base).

Straight Bill of Lading.   An American term used to describe the Sea Waybill.

Combined transport Bill of Lading.   A Bill of Lading issued by a combined transport operator that covers the multi-modal transport on a door to door basis in one contract of carriage. The combined transport operator undertakes to perform in his own name the performance of the

Code Name: "COMBICONBILL"

Shipper

Combined Transport BILL OF LADING
N e g o t i a b l e   B/L No.

Reference No.

Consigned to order of

Notify address

Place of receipt			
Ocean vessel	Port of loading		
Port of discharge	Place of delivery	Freight payable at	Number of original Bs/L
Marks and Nos.	Quantity and description of goods	Gross weight, kg	Measurement, m³

Particulars above declared by Shipper

Freight and charges

RECEIVED the goods in apparent good order and condition and, as far as ascertained by reasonable means of checking, as specified above unless otherwise stated.

The Carrier, in accordance with the provisions contained in this document,

a) undertakes to perform or to procure the performance of the entire transport from the place at which the goods are taken in charge to the place designated for delivery in this document, and

b) assumes liability as prescribed in this document for such transport.

One of the Bs/L must be surrendered duly endorsed in exchange for the goods or delivery order.

IN WITNESS whereof TWO (2) original Bs/L have been signed, if not otherwise stated above, one of which being accomplished the other(s) to be void.

Place and date of issue

Note:
The Merchant's attention is called to the fact that according to Clauses 11 to 13 of this B/L, the liability of the Carrier is, in most cases, limited in respect of loss of or damage to the goods and delay.

Signed for the Carrier

Printed and sold by
Fr. G. Knudtzon Ltd., 55, Toldbodgade, Copenhagen,
by authority of The Baltic and International Maritime Conference,
Copenhagen. Copyright.

56-0

As agent(s) only   p.t.o.

Figure 9.2 Combined Transport Bill of Lading, reproduced by kind permission of Baltic and International Maritime Conference.

COMBINED TRANSPORT BILL OF LADING

Adopted by The Baltic and International Maritime Conference in January, 1971
Code Name: "COMBICONBILL"

I. GENERAL PROVISIONS

1. **Applicability.** Notwithstanding the heading "Combined Transport Bill of Lading", the provisions set out and referred to in this document shall also apply, if the transport as described on the face of the B/L is performed by one mode of transport only.

2. **Definitions.** "Carrier" means the party on whose behalf this B/L has been signed. "Merchant" includes the Shipper, the Receiver, the Consignor, the Consignee, the Holder of this B/L and the Owner of the Goods.

3. **Carrier's Tariff.** The terms of the Carrier's applicable Tariff at the date of shipment are incorporated herein. Copies of the relevant provisions of the applicable Tariff are available from the Carrier upon request. In the case of inconsistency between this B/L and the applicable Tariff, this B/L shall prevail.

4. **Time Bar.** All liability whatsoever of the Carrier shall cease unless suit is brought within 11 months after delivery of the goods or the date when the goods should have been delivered.

5. **Law and Jurisdiction.** Disputes arising under this B/L shall be determined at the option of the Claimant by the courts and subject to Clause 12 of this B/L in accordance with the law at

(a) the place where the Carrier has his habitual residence or his principal place of business or the branch or agency through which the contract of combined transport was made, or

(b) the place where the goods were taken in charge by the Carrier or the place designated for delivery. No proceedings may be brought before other courts unless the parties expressly agree on both the choice of another court or arbitration tribunal and the law to be then applicable.

II. PERFORMANCE OF THE CONTRACT

6. **Sub-contracting.**

(1) The Carrier shall be entitled to sub-contract on any terms the whole or any part of the carriage, loading, unloading, storing, warehousing, handling and any and all duties whatsoever undertaken by the Carrier in relation to the goods.

(2) For the purposes of this contract and subject to the provisions in this B/L, the Carrier shall be responsible for the acts and omissions of any person of whose services he makes use for the performance of the contract of carriage evidenced by this document.

7. **Methods and Routes of Transportation.**

(1) The Carrier is entitled to perform the transport in any reasonable manner and by any reasonable means, methods and routes.

(2) In accordance herewith, for instance, in the event of carriage by sea, vessels may sail with or without pilots, undergo repairs, adjust equipment, drydock and tow vessels in all situations.

8. **Optional Stowage.**

(1) Goods may be stowed by the Carrier by means of containers, trailers, transportable tanks, flats, pallets, or similar articles of transport used to consolidate goods.

(2) Containers, trailers and transportable tanks, whether stowed by the Carrier or received by him in a stowed condition from the Merchant, may be carried on or under deck without notice to the Merchant.

9. **Hindrances etc. Affecting Performance.**

(1) The Carrier shall use reasonable endeavours to complete the transport and to deliver the goods at the place designated for delivery.

(2) If at any time the performance of the contract as evidenced by this B/L is or will be affected by any hindrance, risk, delay, difficulty or disadvantage of whatsoever kind, and if by virtue of sub-clause (1) the Carrier has no duty to complete the performance of the contract, the Carrier (whether or not the transport is commenced) may elect to

(a) treat the performance of this contract as terminated and place the goods at the Merchant's disposal at any place which the Carrier shall deem safe and convenient; or

(b) deliver the goods at the place designated for delivery.

In any event the Carrier shall be entitled to full freight for goods received for transportation and additional compensation for extra costs resulting from the circumstances referred to above.

III. CARRIER'S LIABILITY

10. **Basic Liability.**

(1) The Carrier shall be liable for loss of or damage to the goods occurring between the time when he receives the goods into his charge and the time of delivery.

(2) The Carrier shall, however, be relieved of liability for any loss or damage if such loss or damage arose or resulted from:

(a) The wrongful act or neglect of the Merchant.

(b) Compliance with the instructions of the person entitled to give them.

(c) The lack of, or defective conditions of packing in the case of goods which, by their nature, are liable to wastage or to be damaged when not packed or when not properly packed.

(d) Handling, loading, stowage or unloading of the goods by or on behalf of the Merchant.

(e) Inherent vice of the goods.

(f) Insufficiency or inadequacy of marks or numbers on the goods, covering, or unit loads.

(g) Strikes or lock-outs or stoppage or restraints of labour from whatever cause whether partial or general.

(h) Any cause or event which the Carrier could not avoid and the consequence whereof he could not prevent by the exercise of reasonable diligence.

(3) Where under sub-clause (2) the Carrier is not under any liability in respect of some of the factors causing the loss or damage, he shall only be liable to the extent that those factors for which he is liable under this clause have contributed to the loss or damage.

(4) The burden of proving that the loss or damage was due to one or more of the causes, or events, specified in (a), (b) and (h) of sub-clause (2) shall rest upon the Carrier.

When the Carrier establishes that in the circumstances of the case, the loss or damage could be attributed to one or more of the causes, or events, specified in (c) to (g) of sub-clause (2), it shall be presumed that it was so caused. The Merchant shall, however, be entitled to prove that the loss or damage was not, in fact, caused either wholly or partly by one or more of the causes or events.

11. **The Amount of Compensation.**

(1) When the Carrier is liable for compensation in respect of loss of or damage to the goods, such compensation shall be calculated by reference to the value of such goods at the place and time they are delivered to the Merchant in accordance with the contract or should have been so delivered.

(2) The value of the goods shall be fixed according to the commodity exchange price or, if there be no such price, according to the current market price or, if there be no commodity exchange price or current market price, by reference to the normal value of goods of the same kind and quality.

(3) Compensation shall not, however, exceed 30 Francs per kilo of gross weight of the goods lost or damaged. A Franc means a unit consisting of 65.5 milligrammes of gold of millesimal fineness 900'.

(4) Higher compensation may be claimed only when, with the consent of the Carrier, the value for the goods declared by the consignor which exceeds the limits laid down in this clause has been stated in this B/L. In that case the amount of the declared value shall be substituted for that limit.

12. **Special Provisions.**

(1) Notwithstanding anything provided for in clauses 10 and 11 of this B/L, if it can be proved where the loss or damage occurred the Carrier and/or the Merchant shall, as to the liability of the Carrier, be entitled to require such liability to be determined by the provisions contained in any international convention or national law, which provisions

(a) cannot be departed from by private contract, to the detriment of the Claimant, and

(b) would have applied if the Merchant had made a separate and direct contract with the Carrier in respect of the particular stage of transport where the loss or damage occurred and received as evidence thereof any particular document which must be issued if such international convention or national law shall apply.

(2) Insofar as the Hague Rules contained in the International Convention for the Unification of Certain Rules relating to Bills of Lading, dated 25th August, 1924, do not apply to carriage by sea by virtue of the foregoing provisions of this clause, the liability of the Carrier in respect of any carriage by sea shall be determined by that Convention. The Hague Rules shall also determine the liability of the Carrier in respect of carriage by inland waterways as if such carriage were carriage by sea. Furthermore, they shall apply to all goods, whether carried on deck or under deck.

13. **Delay, Consequential Loss, etc.** If the Carrier is held liable in respect of delay, consequential loss or damage other than loss of or damage to the goods, the liability of the Carrier shall be limited to the freight for the transport covered by this B/L, or to the value of the goods as determined in Clause 11, whichever is least.

14. **Notice of Loss.** Unless notice of loss of or damage to the goods and the general nature of it be given in writing to the Carrier at the place of delivery before or at the time of the removal of the goods into the custody of the person entitled to delivery thereof under this B/L, or if the loss or damage be not apparent, within six consecutive days thereafter, such removal shall be *prima facie* evidence of the delivery by the Carrier of the goods as described in this B/L.

15. **Defences and Limits for the Carrier.**

(1) The defences and limits of liability provided for in this B/L shall apply in any action against the Carrier for loss or damage to the goods whether the action be founded in contract or in tort.

(2) The Carrier shall not be entitled to the benefit of the limitation of liability provided for in Clause 11 sub-clause (3), if it is proved that the loss or damage resulted from an act or omission of the Carrier done with intent to cause damage or recklessly and with knowledge that damage would probably result.

16. **Defences and Limits for Servants, etc.**

(1) If an action for loss or damage to the goods is brought against a servant, agent or independent contractor, such person shall be entitled to avail himself of the defences and limits of liability which the Carrier is entitled to invoke under this contract.

(2) However, if it is proved that the loss or damage resulted from an act or omission of this person, done with intent to cause damage or recklessly and with knowledge that damage would probably result, such person shall not be entitled to the benefit of limitation of liability provided for in Clause 11 sub-clause (3).

(3) Subject to the provisions of Clause 11 sub-clause (3), of Clause 15 sub-clause (2) and of sub-clause (2) of this clause, the aggregate of the amounts recoverable from the Carrier and his servants, agents or independent contractors shall in no case exceed the limits provided for in this document.

IV. DESCRIPTION OF GOODS

17. **Carrier's Responsibility.**

This B/L shall be *prima facie* evidence of the receipt by the Carrier of the goods as herein described in respect of the particulars which he had reasonable means of checking. In respect of such particulars, proof to the contrary shall not be admissible, when this document has been transferred to a third party acting in good faith.

18. **Shipper's Responsibility.** The Shipper shall be deemed to have guaranteed to the Carrier the accuracy, at the time the goods were taken in charge by the Carrier, of the description of the goods, marks, number, quantity and weight, as furnished by him, and the Shipper shall indemnify the Carrier against all loss, damage and expenses arising or resulting from inaccuracies in or inadequacy of such particulars. The right of the Carrier to such indemnity shall in no way limit his responsibility and liability under this B/L to any person other than the Shipper.

V. FREIGHT AND LIEN

19. **Freight.**

(1) Freight shall be deemed earned on receipt of the goods by the Carrier and shall be paid in any event.

(2) The Merchant's attention is drawn to the stipulations concerning currency in which the freight and charges are to be paid, rate of exchange, devaluation and other contingencies relative to freight and charges in the relevant tariff conditions. If no such stipulation as to devaluation exists or is applicable the following clause to apply:

If the currency in which freight and charges are quoted is devalued between the date of the freight agreement and the date when the freight and charges are paid, then all freight and charges shall be automatically and immediately increased in proportion to the extent of the devaluation of the said currency.

(3) For the purpose of verifying the freight basis, the Carrier reserves the right to have the contents of containers, trailers or similar articles of transport inspected in order to ascertain the weight, measurement, value, or nature of the goods.

20. **Lien.** The Carrier shall have a lien on the goods for any amount due under this contract and for the costs of recovering the same, and may enforce such lien in any reasonable manner.

VI. MISCELLANEOUS PROVISIONS

21. **General Average.**

(1) General Average to be adjusted at any port or place at the Carrier's option, and to be settled according to the York-Antwerp Rules 1974, this covering all goods, whether carried on or under deck. The Amended Jason Clause as approved by BIMCO to be considered as incorporated herein.

(2) Such security including a cash deposit as the Carrier may deem sufficient to cover the estimated contribution of the goods and any salvage and special charges thereon, shall, if required, be submitted to the Carrier prior to delivery of the goods.

22. **Dangerous Goods.**

(1) When the Merchant hands goods of a dangerous nature to the Carrier, he shall inform him in writing of the exact nature of the danger and indicate, if necessary, the precautions to be taken.

(2) Goods of a dangerous nature which the Carrier did not know were dangerous, may, at any time or place, be unloaded, destroyed, or rendered harmless, without compensation; further the Merchant shall be liable for all expenses, loss or damage arising out of their handing over for carriage or of their carriage.

(3) If any goods shipped with the knowledge of the Carrier as to their dangerous nature shall become a danger to the ship or cargo, they may in like manner be landed at any place or destroyed or rendered innocuous by the Carrier without liability on the part of the Carrier except to General Average, if any.

23. **Both-to-Blame Collision Clause.**

The Both-to-Blame Collision Clause as adopted by BIMCO to be considered incorporated herein.

24. **Shipper-packed Containers, etc.**

(1) If a container has not been filled, packed or stowed by the Carrier, the Carrier shall not be liable for any loss of or damage to its contents and the Merchant shall cover any loss or expense incurred by the Carrier, if such loss, damage or expense has been caused by

(a) negligent filling, packing or stowing of the container;

(b) the contents being unsuitable for carriage in container; or

(c) the unsuitability or defective condition of the container unless the container has been supplied by the Carrier and the unsuitability or defective condition would not have been apparent upon reasonable inspection at or prior to the time when the container was filled, packed or stowed.

(2) The provisions of paragraph (1) of this clause also apply with respect to trailers, transportable tanks, flats and pallets which have not been filled, packed or stowed by the Carrier.

Figure 9.2 (contd) Combined Transport Bill of Lading, reproduced by kind permission of Baltic and International Maritime Conference.

combined transport. Hence it is issued by a carrier who contracts as a principal with the merchant to effect a combined transport. It is ideal for container movements. An example of a combined transport Bill of Lading (negotiable) is found in Figure 9.2.

Combiconbill. With the development of combined transport operations, an increasing volume of both liner cargo trade and bulk cargo shipments will be carried involving the Bill of Lading being issued in association with a selected Charter Party. An example is found in the Combined Transport Bill of Lading 1971 — code name 'Combiconbill' issued with selected Charter Parties. (See also pp. 359—368 of *Elements of Shipping*.)

9.4.4   Processing the consignment under a Bill of Lading

Once the shipper or his agent becomes aware of the sailing schedules of a particular trade, through the medium of sailing cards or some form of advertisement, he communicates with the shipowner with a view to booking cargo space on the vessel or container. Provided satisfactory arrangements have been concluded, the shipper forwards the cargo. At this stage, it is important to note that the shipper always makes the offer by forwarding the consignment, while the shipowner either accepts or refuses it. Furthermore, it is the shipper's duty, or that of his agent, to supply details of the consignment; normally, this is done by completing the shipping company's form of Bill of Lading and the shipping company then signs the number of copies requested.

When the goods have been received on board the ship the Bill of Lading is dated and signed by, or on behalf of, the carrier, usually by the master of the ship or his agent, and stamped 'freight paid' or 'freight payable at destination' as appropriate. If the cargo is in good condition and everything is in order, no endorsement will be made on the document and it can be termed a 'clean' Bill of Lading. Conversely, if the goods are damaged or a portion of the consignment is missing, the document will be suitably endorsed by the master or his agent and the Bill of Lading will be considered 'claused' or 'unclean'. The complete set of Bills of Lading is then returned to the exporter (seller) for prompt despatch to the importer (buyer). The buyer must have a negotiable Bill of Lading with which to clear the goods at the port of destination.

Bills of Lading are made out in sets, the number of which varies according to the trade. Generally, it is two or three, one of which will probably be forwarded immediately, and another by a later mail in case the first is lost or delayed. In some trades, coloured Bills of Lading are used, to distinguish the original (signed) Bills from the copies which are purely for record purposes. The reverse of the Bill of Lading bears the terms and conditions of the contract of carriage. The clauses on most Bills of Lading are similar in effect if not in wording.

Where the shipper has sold the goods on Letter of Credit terms established through a bank, or when he wishes to obtain payment of his invoice before the consignee obtains the goods, he will pass the full set of original Bills to his bank, who will in due course arrange presentation to the consignee against payment. The financial role of the Bill of Lading is explained in Chapter 7.

The shipowner or his agent at the port of destination will require one original Bill of Lading to be presented to him before the goods are handed over to the buyer. Furthermore, he will normally require payment of any freight due, should this not have been paid at the port of shipment. When one of a set of Bills of Lading has been presented to the shipping company, the other Bills in the set lose their value.

In the event of the Bill of Lading being lost or delayed in transit, the shipping company will allow delivery of the goods to the person claiming to be the consignee, if he gives a letter of indemnity. This is normally countersigned by a bank and relieves the shipping company of any liability should another person eventually come along with the actual Bill of Lading.

Many Bills of Lading are consigned 'to order' and in such situations are endorsed, normally on the reverse, by the shipper. If the consignee is named, the goods will only be released to him, unless he transfers his right by endorsement subject to the Bill of Lading providing for this.

It is important to the importer to ensure that when goods are shipped CIF or CFR terms, that freight is paid and the Bill of Lading is marked accordingly.

The following items are common discrepancies found in Bills of Lading when being processed and should be avoided. Such discrepancies can be lessened by good liaison between the seller and buyer, and other relevant parties.

1. Document not presented in full sets when requested.
2. Alterations not authenticated by an official of the shipping company or their agents.
3. Bill of Lading not clean when presented, such as, when it is endorsed regarding damaged condition of the specified cargo or inadequate packing thereby making it unacceptable to a bank for financial settlement purposes.
4. Document not endorsed 'on board' when so required.
5. The 'on board' endorsement is not signed or initialled by the carrier or agent and likewise not dated.
6. Bill of Lading is not 'blank' endorsed if drawn to order.
7. Document fails to indicate whether 'freight paid' as stipulated in the credit arrangements, i.e. CFR or CIF contracts.

8. Bill of Lading not marked 'freight pre-paid' when freight charges are included in the invoice.
9. Bill of Lading made out 'to order' when the Letter of Credit stipulates 'direct to consignee' or vice versa.
10. Document dated later than the latest shipping date specified in the credit.
11. Not presented within 21 days after date of shipment or such lesser time as prescribed in the Letter of Credit.
12. Bill of Lading details merchandise other than that prescribed.
13. Rate at which freight is calculated, and the total amount, is not shown when credit requires such data to be given.
14. Cargo has been shipped 'on deck' and not placed in the ship's hold. Basically, 'on deck' claused Bills of Lading are not acceptable when clean on-board Bills of Lading are required.
15. Shipment made from a port or to a destination contrary to that stipulated.
16. Other types of Bills of Lading presented, although not specifically authorised. For example, Bills of Lading issued under a Charter Party, or forwarding agents' Bills of Lading are not accepted unless specially authorized in the Letter of Credit.

9.4.5   The common short-forms of Bills of Lading and Sea Waybills and the Liner Waybill

The common short-form Bill of Lading is identical in legal and practical terms to the traditional Bills, but is more simple and can be used with any shipping line. The document covers shipper or forwarder and provides Bills from port to port and through-transport including container Bills of Lading. It does not cover combined transport Bills of Lading which are almost always completed by the combined transport operator.

The common short-form Bill of Lading is fully negotiable and the normal Bill of Lading lodgement and presentation procedures remain unchanged. However, instead of the mass of small print on the reverse, there is an approved 'short-form' clause on the face which incorporates carriers' standard conditions with full legal effect. It is not used extensively for inward shipments to the UK.

The common short-form Sea Waybill has the following salient features which are similar in many ways to the common short-form Bill of Lading:

1. It is a common document upon which the shipper adds the name of the contracting carrier to be used.
2. It is a non-negotiable document consigned to a named consignee and

not requiring presentation to obtain possession of the goods at destination.

3. It is a 'received for shipment' document, with an option for use as a shipped document.

4. It is described as a 'short-form' document because of the use of an abridged standard clause on the face of the document which incorporates the conditions of carriage of the contracting carrier. The change eliminates the need to reprint documents to accommodate changes and conditions.

5. It facilitates earlier release of the goods (if received for shipment) and thereby reduces delays associated with negotiability. Moreover, it helps the speedier flow of goods to the consignee. One must bear in mind the named consignee is not required to produce the Sea Waybill to obtain possession of the goods at destination.

The commercial and financial feasibility of using the Sea Waybill clearly rests with the shipper or consignee and is dependent upon the type of transaction involved. The Sea Waybill is the natural choice for trading between multinational companies and associated companies, and also for open account sales (see Chapter 7). However, it can be used additionally in many cases involving banking transactions, and even under Letters of Credit providing the Credit is suitably worded.

The point at which Sea Waybills are released will depend upon whether the document is 'received for shipment' or 'shipped on board'. In signing Sea Waybills, the carrier or his agent is required to insert the carrier's cable address within the signature or date stamp. If a 'received for shipment' document was issued and cargo was subsequently short-shipped or a carrier's clause required (for example, to indicate that damage was sustained whilst the goods were on the quay) then a qualification report should be issued to the shipper, consignee and those concerned within the carrier's organization; information concerning such reports should also be made available to insurers on request. Use of the 'shipped' option would, however, obviate the need for a qualification report, and, in such circumstances the normal Bill of Lading procedures would apply.

If a 'shipped on board' document was issued, then the 'shipped' option should be such that, if the document was to be presented under a Documentary Credit, it satisfies *Uniform Customs and Practice for Documentary Credits* (1984 revision). This refers to a procedure whereby Sea Waybills can be endorsed to specify that the goods mentioned have been loaded on board or shipped on a named vessel, the 'loading on board' date being specified.

The Sea Waybill is used increasingly as buyers and sellers realize its benefits. Currently the Comite Maritime International is devising a set of rules acceptable to carriers, bankers, insurers and merchants which will further enhance the international popularity of the Waybill. It is envisaged the rules will become operational by the early 1990s.

The Liner Waybill is a non-negotiable document. It usually embodies the Hague-Visby Rules and can be sent forward with the goods allowing the importer immediate delivery.

Bills of Lading are dealt with in detail in Chapter 12 of *Elements of Shipping* (see Appendix A).

9.5 BLACKLIST CERTIFICATE

A number of countries require evidence that goods do not originate from a particular country with whom they are at war or with whom they have strained political relations. Statements regarding the registration of the carrying vessel and/or ports of call prior to delivery may also be a requirement.

9.6 CARGO INSURANCE POLICY AND CERTIFICATE

It is most important to have insurance cover against loss or damage that may occur during shipment. The export sales contract with the buyer must clearly state who is responsible for arranging the insurance at all stages from the time the merchandise leaves the exporter's premises until the buyer takes possession. This embraces transportation of the goods to the seaport, airport, or inland clearance depot; the period during which the merchandise is stored awaiting shipment or loading; the periods whilst the goods are on board the ship, aircraft or other conveyance such as the through international road transport; the off-loading and storage on arrival; and finally transportation to the buyer. This involves primarily Incoterms 1990 which are fully dealt with in Chapter 10.

The cargo insurance policy may only be issued by the insurer and is usually in a standard form covering the customary risk for any voyage or flight. The form of policy in general use today is fully explained in Chapter 8. Individual policies for single shipments are rarely used by regular importers because a new policy would have to be obtained for each shipment. However, insurance certificates based on the overall policy may be issued and are far more common than the policy.

The principal points for consideration by the buyer relative to the insurance of the goods are detailed below:

1. Insured value: the amount covered must be at least the invoiced value of the goods; 110% of the invoiced value is normal, but this may sometimes be more.
2. Risk to be covered: this must include transport of the goods from

warehouse to docks or airport, storage while awaiting loading, the time spent on board the sea, road, rail or air transport, off-loading and storage on arrival, and final transport to the buyer.

3. The need for an extension to the policy in case of delay at any stage of transit must also be kept in mind.

The insurance certificate must contain the same details as the policy with the slight difference that it will carry a shortened version of the provisions of the policy under which it is issued and should be signed by the policy holder. Generally, it must contain:

1. the name and signature of the insurer;
2. the name of the assured;
3. the endorsement of the assured when applicable so that the rights to claim may be transferred;
4. a description of the risk covered;
5. a description of the consignment;
6. the sum or sums to be insured;
7. the place where claims are payable together with the name of the agent to whom claims may be directed.

For processing an international consignment the policy must also:

1. cover the risk detailed in the credit arrangements;
2. be in a completed form;
3. be in a transferable form;
4. be dated on or before the date of the document evidencing despatch, for example, of Bill of Lading;
5. be expressed in the same currency as that of the Credit.

The insurance policy/certificate must avoid the following discrepancies when presented under a Letter of Credit:

1. insufficient cover or risks mentioned in the credit not included;
2. insurance not issued in the currency of the credit;
3. not endorsed and/or signed;
4. dated later than date of shipment or despatch;
5. goods incorrectly described;
6. alterations not authenticated;
7. not in a transferable form when required;
8. carrying vessel's name not recorded;
9. no cover for transhipment when Bills of Lading indicate it will take place.

When a policy is called for under a Letter of Credit, a certificate is not acceptable. However, a policy is acceptable when a certificate is requested. Broker's cover notes are not acceptable unless specifically permitted in the Credit.

An increasing number of buyers (importers) are undertaking the cargo insurance arrangements and funding it as found at the CFR contract. It offers many advantages to the buyer, including saving hard currency, complete control of all insurance provision and claims, and usually it is cheaper. Many importers have 'open' or floating cover for the whole of their international trade. The importer should ensure that the main policy allows claims to be paid anywhere in any agreed currency. Moreover, claims which can only be settled and paid in the country of shipment are likely to be protracted and unsatisfactory. Hence the merit of the buyer undertaking the insurance provision arrangements.

9.7   CERTIFICATE OF HEALTH

A Certificate of Health is usually required when agricultural or animal products are imported. The certificate is issued and signed by the health authority in the supplier's country. Agricultural and animal products require a certificate stating that they comply with UK health regulations, details of which are available from Ministry of Agriculture Fisheries and Foods, Government Buildings, Hook Rise, South Kingston by-pass, Surbiton, Surrey KT6 7NF.

9.8   CERTIFICATE OF ORIGIN

The Certificate of Origin specifies the quantity and value of the goods together with their place of manufacture. It must be completed by the supplier and authenticated by a Chamber of Commerce or similar authorizing organization in the supplier's country. Goods which also qualify for preferential rates of customs duty under the Generalized System of Preferences (GSP) require a special certificate of origin in GSP Form A to establish entitlement to these rates. Any errors in the form should be authenticated by the signatory and endorsed by a competent authority. The person who signs on behalf of the exporter or his agent must be authorized to do so with his signature being registered with the issuing authority (usually a Chamber of Commerce). The certificate of origin includes the: name and address of exporter; name and address of importer; description of goods; country of origin of the goods; signature and seal or stamp of the certifying body.

It is important the certificate of origin is signed and worded exactly as specified in the Credit. Details of goods requiring a Certificate of Origin are available from HM Customs and Excise.

9.9 CERTIFICATES OF QUALITY AND QUANTITY CONTROL

An overseas importer may need such documents, but they are more likely to be a requirement of an overseas government wishing to protect its foreign exchange position. Such documents are particularly common in the African states.

9.10 CHARTER PARTY

A Charter Party (Fig. 9.3) is a contract whereby a shipowner agrees to place his ship, or part of it, at the disposal of a merchant or other person (known as the charterer), for the carriage of goods from one port to another port on being paid freight, or to let his ship for a specified period, his remuneration being known as hire money. The terms, conditions and exceptions under which the goods are carried are set out in the Charter Party.

A very large proportion of the world's trade is carried in 'tramp' vessels. It is quite common to find that one cargo will fill a whole ship and, in these circumstances, one cargo owner or one charterer will enter into a special contract with the shipowner for the hire of his ship. Such a contract is known as a Charter Party. There are basically two types of Charter Parties: demise and non-demise.

A demise or 'bareboat' Charter Party arises when the charterer is responsible for providing the cargo and crew, whilst the shipowner merely provides the vessel. In consequence, the charterer takes full responsibility for the operation of the vessel, and pays all expenses incurred. A demise Charter Party may extend from a few weeks to several years.

A non-demise Charter arises when the shipowner provides the vessel and crew, whilst the charterer merely supplies the cargo. It may be a voyage charter for a particular voyage, in which the shipowner agrees to carry cargo between specified ports for a pre-arranged freight. The majority of tramp cargo shipments are made on a voyage charter basis. Alternatively, it may be a time charter for a stated period or voyage for a remuneration known as hire money. The shipowner continues to manage the vessel, both under non-demise voyage or time Charter Parties under the charterer's instructions. With a time charter, it is usual for the charterer to pay port duties, fuel costs and overtime payments incurred in an endeavour to obtain faster turn-rounds. It is quite common for liner companies to supplement their services by taking tramp ships on time charter, but this practice may lessen as containerization develops.

There are several types of non-demise voyage charter and these are

1. Shipbroker	RECOMMENDED THE BALTIC AND INTERNATIONAL MARITIME CONFERENCE UNIFORM GENERAL CHARTER (AS REVISED 1922 and 1976) INCLUDING "F.I.O." ALTERNATIVE, ETC. (To be used for trades for which no approved form is in force) CODE NAME: "GENCON" Part I
	2. Place and date
3. Owners/Place of business (Cl. 1)	4. Charterers/Place of business (Cl. 1)
5. Vessel's name (Cl. 1)	6. GRT/NRT (Cl. 1)
7. Deadweight cargo carrying capacity in tons (abt.) (Cl. 1)	8. Present position (Cl. 1)
9. Expected ready to load (abt.) (Cl. 1)	
10. Loading port or place (Cl. 1)	11. Discharging port or place (Cl. 1)

12. Cargo (also state quantity and margin in Owners' option, if agreed; if full and complete cargo not agreed state "part cargo") (Cl. 1)

13. Freight rate (also state if payable on delivered or intaken quantity) (Cl. 1)	14. Freight payment (state currency and method of payment; also beneficiary and bank account) (Cl. 4)
15. Loading and discharging costs (state alternative (a) or (b) of Cl. 5; also indicate if vessel is gearless)	16. Laytime (if separate laytime for load. and disch. is agreed, fill in a) and b). If total laytime for load. and disch., fill in c) only) (Cl. 6) a) Laytime for loading
17. Shippers (state name and address) (Cl. 6)	b) Laytime for discharging c) Total laytime for loading and discharging
18. Demurrage rate (loading and discharging) (Cl. 7)	19. Cancelling date (Cl. 10)

20. Brokerage commission and to whom payable (Cl. 14)

21. Additional clauses covering special provisions, if agreed.

It is mutually agreed that this Contract shall be performed subject to the conditions contained in this Charter which shall include Part I as well as Part II.
In the event of a conflict of conditions, the provisions of Part I shall prevail over those of Part II to the extent of such conflict.

Signature (Owners)	Signature (Charterers)

19-0   Printed and sold by Fr. G. Knudtzon Ltd., 55, Toldbodgade, Copenhagen, by authority of The Baltic and International Maritime Conference (BIMCO), Copenhagen.

Figure 9.3 Glencow Charter Party, reproduced by kind permission of the Baltic and International Maritime Conference.

1. It is agreed between the party mentioned in Box 3 as Owners of the 1
steamer or motor-vessel named in Box 5, of the gross/nett Register 2
tons indicated in Box 6 and carrying about the number of tons of 3
deadweight cargo stated in Box 7, now in position as stated in Box 8 4
and expected ready to load under this Charter about the date in- 5
dicated in Box 10, and the party mentioned in Box 4 as Charterers in Box 4 6
that: 7
The said vessel shall proceed to the loading port or place stated 8
in Box 10 or so near thereto as she may safely get and lie always 9
afloat, and there load a full and complete cargo (if shipment of deck 10
cargo agreed same to be at Charterers' risk) as stated in Box 12 11
(Charterers to provide all mats and/or wood for dunnage and any 12
separations required, the Owners allowing the use of any dunnage 13
wood on board if required) which the Charterers bind themselves to 14
ship, and being so loaded the vessel shall proceed to the discharg- 15
ing port or place stated in Box 11 as ordered on signing Bills of 16
Lading or so near thereto as she may safely get and lie always 17
afloat and there deliver the cargo on being paid freight on delivered 18
or intaken quantity as indicated in Box 13 at the rate stated in 19
Box 13. 20

2. **Owners' Responsibility Clause**
Owners are to be responsible for loss of or damage to the goods 21
or for delay in delivery of the goods only in case the loss, damage 22
or delay has been caused by the improper or negligent stowage of 23
the goods (unless stowage performed by shippers/Charterers or their 24
stevedores or servants) or by personal want of due diligence on the 25
part of the Owners or their Manager to make the vessel in all respects 26
seaworthy and to secure that she is properly manned, equipped and 27
supplied or by the personal act or default of the Owners or their 28
Manager. 29
And the Owners are responsible for no loss or damage or delay 30
arising from any other cause whatsoever, even from the neglect or 31
default of the Captain or crew or some other person employed by the 32
Owners on board or ashore for whose acts they would, but for this 33
clause, be responsible, or from unseaworthiness of the vessel on 34
loading or commencement of the voyage or at any time whatsoever. 35
Damage caused by contact with or leakage, smell or evaporation 36
from other goods or by the inflammable or explosive nature or in- 37
sufficient package of other goods not to be considered as caused 38
by improper or negligent stowage, even if in fact so caused. 39
40

3. **Deviation Clause**
The vessel has liberty to call at any port or ports in any order, for 41
any purpose, to sail without pilots, to tow and or assist vessels in 42
all situations, and also to deviate for the purpose of saving life and/ 43
or property. 44
45

4. **Payment of Freight**
The freight to be paid in the manner prescribed in Box 14 in cash 46
without discount on delivery of the cargo at mean rate of exchange 47
ruling on day or days of payment, the receivers of the cargo being 48
bound to pay freight on account during delivery, if required by Cap- 49
tain or Owners. 50
Cash for vessel's ordinary disbursements at port of loading to be 51
advanced by Charterers if required at highest current rate of ex- 52
change, subject to two per cent. to cover insurance and other ex- 53
penses. 54
55

5. **Loading Discharging Costs**
(a) Gross Terms
The cargo to be brought alongside in such a manner as to enable 56
vessel to take the goods with her own tackle. Charterers to procure 57
and pay the necessary men on shore or on board the lighters to do 58
the work there, vessel only heaving the cargo on board. 59
If the loading takes place by elevator, cargo to be put free in vessel's 60
holds, Owners only paying trimming expenses. 61
Any pieces and or packages of cargo over two tons weight, shall be 62
loaded, stowed and discharged by Charterers at their risk and expense. 63
The cargo to be received by Merchants at their risk and expense 64
alongside the vessel not beyond the reach of her tackle. 65
66
67
(b) F.i.o. and free stowed trimmed
The cargo to be brought into the holds, loaded, stowed and or trim- 68
med and taken from the holds and discharged by the Charterers or 69
their Agents, free of any risk, liability and expense whatsoever to the 70
Owners. 71
The Owners shall provide winches, motive power and winchmen from 72
the Crew if requested and permitted; if not, the Charterers shall 73
provide and pay for winchmen from shore and or cranes, if any. (This 74
provision shall not apply if vessel is gearless and stated as such in 75
Box 15). 76
77
* *indicate alternative (a) cr (b), as agreed, in Box 15.* 78

6. **Laytime** 79
(a) Separate laytime for discharging and loading
The cargo shall be loaded within the number of running hours as 80
indicated in Box 16, weather permitting, Sundays and holidays ex- 81
cepted, unless used, in which event time actually used shall count. 82
The cargo shall be discharged within the number of running hours 83
as indicated in Box 16, weather permitting, Sundays and holidays ex- 84
cepted, unless used, in which event time actually used shall count. 85
86
(b) Total laytime for loading and discharging
The cargo shall be loaded and discharged within the number of total 87
running hours as indicated in Box 16, weather permitting, Sundays and 88
holidays excepted, unless used, in which event time actually used 89
shall count. 90
91
(c) Commencement of laytime (loading and discharging)
Laytime for loading and discharging shall commence at 1 p.m. if 92
notice of readiness is given before noon, and at 6 a.m. next working 93
day if notice given during office hours after noon. Notice at loading 94
port to be given to the Shippers named in Box 17. 95
Time actually used before commencement of laytime shall count. 96
Time lost in waiting for berth to count as loading or discharging 97
time, as the case may be. 98
99
* *indicate alternative (a) or (b) as agreed, in Box 16.* 100

7. **Demurrage** 101
Ten running days on demurrage at the rate stated in Box 18 per 102
day or pro rata for any part of a day, payable day by day, to be 103
allowed Merchants altogether at ports of loading and discharging. 104

8. **Lien Clause** 105
Owners shall have a lien on the cargo for freight, dead-freight, 106
demurrage and damages for detention. Charterers shall remain re- 107
sponsible for dead-freight and demurrage (including damages for 108
detention), incurred at port of loading, Charterers shall also remain 109
responsible for freight and demurrage (including damages for deten- 110
tion) incurred at port of discharge, but only to such extent as the 111
Owners have been unable to obtain payment thereof by exercising 112
the lien on the cargo. 113

9. **Bills of Lading** 114
The Captain to sign Bills of Lading at such rate of freight as 115
presented without prejudice to this Charterparty, but should the 116
freight by Bills of Lading amount to less than the total chartered 117
freight the difference to be paid to the Captain in cash on signing 118
Bills of Lading. 119

10. **Cancelling Clause** 120
Should the vessel not be ready to load (whether in berth or not) on 121
or before the date indicated in Box 19, Charterers have the option 122
of cancelling this contract, such option to be declared, if demanded, 123
at least 48 hours before vessel's expected arrival at port of loading. 124
Should the vessel be delayed on account of average or otherwise. 125
Charterers to be informed as soon as possible, and if the vessel is 126
delayed for more than 10 days she is stated to be 127
expected ready to load, Charterers have the option of cancelling this 128
contract, unless a cancelling date has been agreed upon. 129

11. **General Average** 130
General average to be settled according to York-Antwerp Rules, 131
1974. Proprietors of cargo to pay the cargo's share in the general 132
expenses even if same have been necessitated through neglect or 133
default of the Owners' servants (see clause 2). 134

12. **Indemnity** 135
Indemnity for non-performance of this Charterparty, proved damages, 136
not exceeding estimated amount of freight. 137

13. **Agency** 138
In every case the Owners shall appoint his own Broker or Agent both 139
at the port of loading and the port of discharge. 140

14. **Brokerage** 141
A brokerage commission at the rate stated in Box 20 on the freight 142
earned is due to the party mentioned in Box 20. 143
In case of non-execution at least ⅓ of the brokerage on the estimated 144
amount of freight and dead-freight to be paid by the Owners to the 145
Brokers as indemnity for the latter's expenses and work. In case of 146
more voyages the amount of indemnity to be mutually agreed. 147

15. **GENERAL STRIKE CLAUSE** 148
Neither Charterers nor Owners shall be responsible for the con- 149
sequences of any strikes or lock-outs preventing or delaying the 150
fulfilment of any obligations under this contract. 151
If there is a strike or lock-out affecting the loading of the cargo, 152
or any part of it, when vessel is ready to proceed from her last port 153
or at any time during the voyage to the port or ports of loading or 154
after her arrival there, Captain or Owners may ask Charterers to 155
declare, that they agree to reckon the laydays as if there were no 156
strike or lock-out. Unless Charterers have given such declaration in 157
writing (by telegram, if necessary) within 24 hours, Charterers shall 158
have the option of cancelling this contract. If part cargo has already 159
been loaded, Owners must proceed with same, (freight payable on 160
loaded quantity only) having liberty to complete with other cargo 161
on the way for their own account. 162
If there is a strike or lock-out affecting the discharge of the cargo 163
on or after vessel's arrival at or off port of discharge and same has 164
not been settled within 48 hours, Receivers shall have the option of 165
keeping vessel waiting until such strike or lock-out is at an end 166
against paying half demurrage after expiration of the time provided 167
for discharging, or of ordering the vessel to a safe port where she 168
can safely discharge without risk of being detained by strike or lock- 169
out. Such orders to be given within 48 hours after Captain or Owners 170
have given notice to Charterers of the strike or lock-out affecting 171
the discharge. On delivery of the cargo at such port, all conditions 172
of this Charterparty and of the Bill of Lading shall apply and vessel 173
shall receive the same freight as if she had discharged at the 174
original port of destination, except that if the distance of the sub- 175
stituted port exceeds 100 nautical miles, the freight on the cargo 176
delivered at the substituted port to be increased in proportion. 177

16. **War Risks ("Voywar 1950")** 178
(1) In these clauses "War Risks" shall include any blockade or any 179
action which is announced as a blockade by any Government or by any 180
belligerent or by any organized body, sabotage, piracy, and any actual 181
or threatened war, hostilities, warlike operations, civil war, civil com- 182
motion, or revolution. 183
(2) If at any time before the Vessel commences loading, it appears that 184
performance of the contract will subject the Vessel or her Master or 185
crew or her cargo to war risks at any stage of the adventure, the Owners 186
shall be entitled by letter or telegram despatched to the Charterers, to 187
cancel this Charter. 188
(3) The Master shall not be required to load cargo or to continue 189
loading or to proceed on or to sign Bill(s) of Lading for any adventure 190
on which or any port at which it appears that the Vessel, her Master 191
and crew or her cargo will be subjected to war risks. In the event of 192
the exercise by the Master of his right under this Clause after part or 193
full cargo has been loaded, the Master shall be at liberty either to 194
discharge such cargo at the loading port or to proceed therewith. 195
In the latter case the Vessel shall have liberty to carry other cargo 196
for Owners' benefit and accordingly to proceed to and load or 197
discharge such other cargo at any other port or ports whatsoever, then 198
backwards or forwards, although in a contrary direction to or out of or 199
beyond the ordinary route. In the event of the Master electing to 200
proceed with part cargo under this Clause freight shall in any case 201
be payable on the quantity delivered. 202
(4) If at the time the Master elects to proceed with part or full cargo 203
under Clause 3, or after the Vessel has left the loading port, or the 204

Figure 9.3 (contd)

last of the loading ports, if more than one, it appears that further 205
performance of the contract will subject the Vessel, her Master and 206
crew or her cargo, to war risks, the cargo shall be discharged, or if 207
the discharge has been commenced shall be completed, at any safe 208
port in vicinity of the port of discharge as may be ordered by the 209
Charterers. If no such orders shall be received from the Charterers 210
within 48 hours after the Owners have despatched a request by 211
telegram to the Charterers for the nomination of a substitute discharg- 212
ing port, the Owners shall be at liberty to discharge the cargo at 213
any safe port which they may, in their discretion, decide on and such 214
discharge shall be deemed to be due fulfilment of the contract of 215
affreightment. In the event of cargo being discharged at any such 216
other port, the Owners shall be entitled to freight as if the discharge 217
had been effected at the port or ports named in the Bill(s) of Lading 218
or to which the Vessel may have been ordered pursuant thereto. 219

(5) (a) The Vessel shall have liberty to comply with any directions 220
or recommendations as to loading, departure, arrival, routes, ports 221
of call, stoppages, destination, zones, waters, discharge, delivery or 222
in any other wise whatsoever (including any direction or recom- 223
mendation not to go to the port of destination or to delay proceeding 224
thereto or to proceed to some other port) given by any Government or 225
by any belligerent or by any organized body engaged in civil war, 226
hostilities or warlike operations or by any person or body acting or 227
purporting to act as or with the authority of any Government or 228
belligerent or of any such organized body or by any committee or 229
person having under the terms of the war risks insurance on the 230
Vessel, the right to give any such directions or recommendations. If, 231
by reason of or in compliance with any such direction or recom- 232
mendation, anything is done or is not done, such shall not be deemed 233
a deviation. 234

(b) If, by reason of or in compliance with any such directions or re- 235
commendations, the Vessel does not proceed to the port or ports 236
named in the Bill(s) of Lading or to which she may have been 237
ordered pursuant thereto, the Vessel may proceed to any port as 238
directed or recommended or to any safe port which the Owners in 239
their discretion may decide on and there discharge the cargo. Such 240
discharge shall be deemed to be due fulfilment of the contract of 241
affreightment and the Owners shall be entitled to freight as if 242
discharge had been effected at the port or ports named in the Bill(s) 243
of Lading or to which the Vessel may have been ordered pursuant 244
thereto 245

(6) All extra expenses (including insurance costs) involved in discharg- 246
ing cargo at the loading port or in reaching or discharging the cargo 247
at any port as provided in Clauses 4 and 5 (b) hereof shall be paid 248
by the Charterers and or cargo owners, and the Owners shall have 249
a lien on the cargo for all moneys due under these Clauses. 250

17. GENERAL ICE CLAUSE 251
Port of loading 252

(a) In the event of the loading port being inaccessible by reason of 253
ice when vessel is ready to proceed from her last port or at any 254
time during the voyage or on vessel's arrival or in case frost sets in 255
after vessel's arrival, the Captain for fear of being frozen in is at 256
liberty to leave without cargo, and this Charter shall be null and 257
void. 258

(b) If during loading the Captain, for fear of vessel being frozen in, 259
deems it advisable to leave, he has liberty to do so with what cargo 260
he has on board and to proceed to any other port or ports with 261
option of completing cargo for Owners' benefit for any port or ports 262
including port of discharge. Any part cargo thus loaded under this 263
Charter to be forwarded to destination at vessel's expense but 264
against payment of freight, provided that no extra expenses be 265
thereby caused to the Receivers, freight being paid on quantity 266
delivered (in proportion if lumpsum), all other conditions as per 267
Charter. 268

(c) In case of more than one loading port, and if one or more of 269
the ports are closed by ice, the Captain or Owners to be at liberty 270
either to load the part cargo at the open port and fill up elsewhere 271
for their own account as under section (b) or to declare the Charter 272
null and void unless Charterers agree to load full cargo at the open 273
port. 274

(d) This Ice Clause not to apply in the Spring. 275

Port of discharge 276

(a) Should ice (except in the Spring) prevent vessel from reaching 277
port of discharge Receivers shall have the option of keeping vessel 278
waiting until the re-opening of navigation and paying demurrage, or 279
of ordering the vessel to a safe and immediately accessible port 280
where she can safely discharge without risk of detention by ice. 281
Such orders to be given within 48 hours after Captain or Owners 282
have given notice to Charterers of the impossibility of reaching port 283
of destination. 284

(b) If during discharging the Captain for fear of vessel being frozen 285
in deems it advisable to leave, he has liberty to do so with what 286
cargo he has on board and to proceed to the nearest accessible 287
port where she can safely discharge. 288

(c) On delivery of the cargo at such port, all conditions of the Bill 289
of Lading shall apply and vessel shall receive the same freight as 290
if she had discharged at the original port of destination, except that if 291
the distance of the substituted port exceeds 100 nautical miles, the 292
freight on the cargo delivered at the substituted port to be increased 293
in proportion. 294

Figure 9.3 (contd)

given below. It will be seen that they all deal with the carriage of goods from a certain port or ports to another port or ports and the difference between them arise mainly out of payment for the cost of loading and discharging and to port expenses. They are quite common today and in each case the shipowner pays the port charges.

Gross form of Charter.   This is probably the most common form of Charter used by tramp ships today. In this form, the shipowner (in return for a higher freight) meets the cost of employing the stevedores at either the loading port or the port of discharge, or both.

Net terms.   Under these terms the cargo is loaded and discharged at no cost to the shipowner. The cost of stevedores at the loading port is borne by the shipper and, at the port of discharge, by the receiver. The term net terms is not in common use but is generally referred to as 'free in and out' (FIO) with exactly the same meaning.

FIO Charter.   Under this Charter the cargo is loaded and discharged at no cost to the shipowner. The cost of stevedores at the loading port is borne by the shipper and at the port of discharge by the receiver.

Liner terms.   Under this Charter usually found in the short sea trade, the shipowner is responsible for loading, stowing and discharging the cargo. Usually the shipowner selects and appoints the stevedores, but this can be an area of discussion during the fixture negotiations.

Lump sum Charter.   In this case, the charterer pays a lump sum of money for the use of the ship and the shipowner guarantees that a certain amount of space (that is, bale cubic metres) will be available for cargo, along with the maximum weight of cargo that the vessel will be able to carry. A lump sum Charter may be on either a gross or an FIO basis. Such a charter is very useful when the charterer wishes to load a mixed cargo — the shipowner guarantees that a certain amount of space and weight will be available and it is up to the charterer to use that space to his best advantage.

There are, of course, numerous variations that may be made to the above broad divisions and this is a matter for negotiation when the vessel is being 'worked' for future business. For example, the gross and FIO Charters may be modified to an FOB (free on board) Charter meaning that the charterer pays for the cost of loading and the shipowner pays for the cost of discharge, or alternatively the Charter may be arranged on the basis of free discharge, that is, the charterer pays for the cost of discharging. The same general terms of contract are found in all the above types of Charter.

A substantial proportion of the Charters in this country are negotiated through a shipbroker on the Baltic Exchange in London. The role of this exchange is explained in Chapter 12. The negotiations are carried out by word of mouth in the exchange, not by letter, and when the contract has been concluded the vessel is said to be 'fixed'. The Charter Party is then prepared and signed by the two parties or their agents. In addition to the trade to and from this country, a large number of cross voyages, that is, from one foreign country to another, are fixed on the London market, quite often to a vessel owned in yet another foreign country. There is no compulsion to conduct negotiations through a shipbroker on the Baltic Exchange. Many negotiations are conducted direct between charterer and shipowner. It is a matter for the shipowner's judgement whether he engages a shipbroker to conduct his negotiations direct with the charterer. Obviously, when the shipbroker is negotiating a series of voyage charters for his principal, the shipowner will endeavour to reduce to an absolute minimum the number of ballast voyages. These arise between termination of one voyage charter for example at Rotterdam, and commencement of the next voyage charter, for example, at Southampton, involving a ballast voyage from Rotterdam to Southampton.

It will be appreciated that the terms and conditions of a Charter Party will vary according to the wishes of the parties to the contract. Nevertheless, the former Chamber of Shipping of the United Kingdom (now designated General Council of British Shipping) together with the Baltic and International Maritime Conference have approved a number of Charter Parties (about 50) for certain commodities in specified trades, including primarily the tramp trades (e.g. coal, wheat, timber, and ore). The parties to the contract are free to make any amendments to such Charter Parties to meet their needs and there is no obligation to use any particular Charter Party for a particular trade.

The subject of chartering is dealt with extensively in Chapter 15 of *Elements of Shipping* (see Appendix A).

9.11 COMBINED TRANSPORT DOCUMENTS

The development of combined transport operations with its many advantages (Chapter 9 of *Economics of Shipping Practice and Management*, see Appendix A) will continue throughout the decade. This involves the container shipment, the through road haulage service, the through rail service, and so on. The documents concerned embrace the Combiconbill — combined transport Bill of Lading (see pp. 149-50) — which is the carriage of goods by at least two modes of transport; the CMR (Convention relative au contract de transport internationale des Marchandises par vois de Route), a consignment note involving the conveyance of goods on a through international road haulage service (see p. 147) or the CIM (Convention Internationale concernant le transport de Marchandises par chemin de fer), a consignment note involving the conveyance of goods on a through international rail service (see p. 146). Moreover the FIATA (International Federation of Forwarding Agents Association) have introduced the FIATA combined transport Bill of Lading which is widely used by their members (Chapter 15 of *Elements of Shipping*, see Appendix A).

In the 1970s an attempt was made to draft a convention to cover loss or damage to goods carried under a combined transport document. It was known variously at different stages as the Tokyo–Rome rules, the Tokyo rules, and the TCM convention. Regretfully it failed to gain adequate support and subsequently the International Chamber of Commerce revised particular elements of it, with the result that the final draft was published as the 'ICC rules for a Combined Transport Document'. The United Nations Conference on Trade and Development (UNCTAD) was unhappy with this situation, however, and decided to intervene with an international convention to govern combined transport. It was finally adopted at an international conference in Geneva in May 1980 as the 'United Nations Convention on International Multi-modal Transport of Goods' or as more commonly known 'UNCTAD MMO'. Like the Hamburg Rules, if adopted it is likely to increase the carrier insurance costs, which will probably result in increased freight rates without any corresponding reduction in cargo insurance premiums. Some 30 countries need to ratify it before acceptance and by the Autumn 1987 it had the support of only four countries.

A development in recent years emerging from combined transport operation is the non vessel operating carrier (NVOC) or non vessel operating common carrier (NVOCC). This may involve container (FCL or LCL) movement or trailer transits. The carrier issues Bills of Lading for the carriage of goods on ships which he neither owns or operates. Usually, a freight forwarder issues a 'house' Bill of Lading for a container or trailer movement or, if a UK–Continental trailer trade, a CMR consignment note. A carrier defined by maritime law is one offering an international cargo transport service.

9.12   CONVENTION ON THE CONTRACT FOR THE INTERNATIONAL CARRIAGE OF GOODS BY ROAD (CMR)

The international convention concerning the carriage of goods by road (CMR) came into force in the UK in October 1967. It permits the carriage of goods by road under one consignment note under a common code of conditions applicable to the following countries: Austria, Belgium, Bulgaria, Czechoslovakia, Denmark, East Germany, Finland,

France, Greece, Hungary, Italy, Luxembourg, Netherlands, Norway, Poland, Portugal, Romania, Spain, Sweden, Switzerland, UK, West Germany, and Yugoslavia. Additionally, by Orders in Council, the convention has been extended to cover the Isle of Man, the Isle of Guernsey and Gibraltar. It applies to all international carriage of goods by road for reward to or from a contracting party. It does not apply to traffic between the UK and the Republic of Ireland.

The convention applies to every contract for the carriage of goods by road in vehicles for reward when the place of taking over the goods and the place designated for delivery are situated in two different countries, of which at least one is a contracting party. Thus, any international road journey for hire or reward (own account is not subject to the convention) which either starts or finishes in the UK will be subject to CMR unless one of the following limited exemptions apply: postal despatch; funeral consignments; personal effects — household removals; movement of own goods, i.e. non-commercial cargo; movements between the UK and Eire and vice versa.

The contract of carriage, found in the CMR consignment note, is established when it is completed by the sender and carrier with the appropriate signatures and/or stamp being recorded thereon. The senders and carrier are entitled respectively to the first and third copies of the consignment note, and the second copy must accompany the goods. If the goods have to be loaded in different vehicles, or are of different kinds, or are divided into different lots, either party has the right to require a separate consignment note to be made out in respect of each vehicle or each kind or lots of goods. The CMR consignment note is not a negotiable or transferable document or document of title.

The consignment note must contain the following particulars: the date when and the place where it is made out; the names and addresses of the sender, the carrier and the consignee; the place and date of taking over the goods, and the place designated for delivery; the ordinary description of the nature of the goods and the method of packing and, in the case of dangerous goods, their generally recognized description; the number of packages and their special marks and numbers; the gross weight of the goods or their quantity otherwise expressed; charges relating to the carriage including supplementary charges, customs duties, etc; the requisite instructions for customs and other formalities; and a statement that the carriage is subject, notwithstanding any clause to the contrary, to the provisions of the convention.

Further, the consignment note must contain the following particulars where applicable: a statement that transhipment is not allowed; the charges which the sender undertakes to pay; the amount of 'cash on delivery' charges; a declaration of the value of the goods; a declaration of the amount representing any special interest in delivery; the sender's instructions to the carrier regarding insurance of the goods; the agreed time-limit for the carriage; a list of the documents handed to the carrier; where the carrier has no reasonable means of checking the number of packages and their marks and numbers, or the apparent condition of the goods and their packaging, any reservations about accuracy must be entered in the consignment note, specifying the grounds on which they are based; where the sender requires the carrier to check the gross weight of the goods or their quantity otherwise expressed or the contents of the packages, the carrier must enter the results of such checks; any agreement that open-unsheeted vehicles may be used for the carriage of the goods.

The parties may enter any other useful particulars in the consignment note.

The sender is liable for all expenses, loss and damage sustained by the carrier by reason of the inaccuracy or inadequacy of certain specified particulars which the consignment note must contain, or by reason of the inaccuracy or inadequacy of any other particulars or instructions given by him. The carrier is liable for all expenses, loss and damage sustained by the person entitled to dispose of the goods as a result of the omission of the statement that the contract is subject to the convention. For the purposes of the convention, the carrier is responsible for the acts and omissions of his agents and servants and any other persons whose services he uses for the performance of the carriage as long as those agents, servants or other persons are acting within the scope of their employment.

There is a duty on the carrier:

1. to check the accuracy of the statements in the consignment note as to the number of packages and their marks and numbers, and the apparent condition of the goods and their packaging;
2. if the sender so requires it, to check the gross weight of the goods or their quantity otherwise expressed or the contents of the packages;
3. to check the statement that the contract is subject to the convention is properly included in the consignment note.

The sender is responsible for the accuracy and adequacy of documents and information which he must either attach to the consignment note or place at the carrier's disposal for the purposes of customs or other formalities which have to be completed before delivery of the goods. There is a duty on the sender:

1. to ensure that the goods are properly packed;
2. in the case of dangerous goods, to inform the carrier of the exact nature of the danger and indicate, if necessary, the precautions to be taken;
3. to ensure the accuracy and adequacy of certain specified particulars

which the consignment note must contain and of any other particulars or instructions given by the sender to the carrier.

The statutory provisions are embodied in the *Carriage of Goods by Road Act, 1965*. A CMR consignment note is shown in Fig. 9.4. The CMR consignment note must be carried on all hire-and-reward journeys involving an international transit. The CMR states that three copies must be completed: one for the exporter, one which accompanies the goods and the third for retention by the carrier.

9.13 EXCHANGE PERMIT

The Exchange Permit is particularly found in the Middle Eastern trades and is usually associated with the issue of an import licence. They are generally issued by government departments, Chambers of Commerce, or Chambers of Industry to authorize import of a specific commodity. They are a means of regulating the flow of specific commodity imports and the funds associated with them.

9.14 EXPORT INVOICING

There is a continual stream of new overseas import regulations along with new developments and a constant issue of new forms. Accordingly, the requisite invoice for a particular market should be checked by the importer; serious delays will be encountered in processing the order through customs in the buyer's country if the incorrect form is used. Details of the various types of invoices are now examined.

Commercial invoice. The suppliers invoice is the basic document required by the buyer: sufficient copies (at least three), legalized by a Chamber of Commerce or a Foreign Consulate where necessary, should be prepared to meet the requirements of HM Customs and in a format specified by the importing country for use by their customs authorities. This document is the claim for payment for the goods under the contract. The commercial invoice gives details of the goods and is issued by the seller (exporter). It forms the basis of the transaction between the seller and buyer. Usually it bears the exporter's own headed invoice form stationery. The invoice gives a description of the goods, stating prices and terms exactly as specified in the credit packing details, as well as shipping marks. Where there are several packages in one consignment, the invoice is usually accompanied by a packing list. Overall, it contains the following information:

1. Name and address of buyer (importer) and seller (exporter).
2. Buyer's reference, i.e. order number, indent number, etc.

899506

COPY 1 SENDER
COPY 2 CONSIGNEE
COPY 3 CARRIER

Approved by FTA RHA SITPRO UK 1981

*NB FOR
DANGEROUS
GOODS

INDICATE
1. CORRECT
TECHNICAL
NAME (PROPER
SHIPPING
NAME)
2. HAZARD
CLASS
3. UN NUMBER
4. FLASHPOINT
(IF ANY)
IN °C.

730

LETTRE DE VOITURE INTERNATIONALE (CMR) **INTERNATIONAL CONSIGNMENT NOTE**

Sender (Name, Address, Country) Expéditeur (Nom, Addresse, Pays) 1	Customs Reference/Status Reference/designation pour mise en douane 2
	Senders Agents Reference Référence de l'expéditeur/de l'agent 3
Consignee (Name, Address, Country) Destinataire (Nom, Addresse, Pays) 4	Carrier (Name, Address, Country) Transporteur (Nom, Addresse, Pays) 5
Place & date of taking over the goods (place, country, date) Lieu et date de la prise en charge des marchandises (Lieu, pays, date) 6	Successive Carriers Transporteurs successifs 7
Place designated for delivery of goods (place, country) Lieu prévu pour la livraison des marchandises (lieu, pays) 8	This carriage is subject, notwithstanding any clause to the contrary, to the Convention on the Contract for the International Carriage of Goods by Road (CMR) Ce transport est soumis nonobstant toute clause contraire à la Convention Relative au Contrat de Transport International de Marchandises par Route (CMR)

Marks & Nos, No & Kind of Packages, Description of Goods* Marques et Nos, No et nature des colis, Désignation des marchandises* 9	Gross weight (kg) Poids Brut (kg) 10	Volume (m³) Cubage (m³) 11

Carriage Charges Prix de transport 12	Sender's Instructions for Customs, etc Instructions de l'Expéditeur (optional) 13

Reservations Reserves 14	Documents attached Documents Annexes (optional) 15	
	Special agreements Conventions particulières (optional) 16	
Goods Received/Marchandises Recues 17	Signature of Carrier/Signature du transporteur 18	Company completing this note Société émettrice 19
		Place and Date/Signature Lieu et date/Signature 20

Figure 9.4 CMR Consignment Note.

3. Number and types of packages.
4. Weights and measurements of the consignment.
5. Place and date of issue.
6. Details of actual cost of freight and insurance if so requested.
7. Total amount payable, embracing price of goods, freight, insurance and so on.
8. The export and/or import licence number.
9. The contents of individual packages.
10. The method of despatch.
11. Shipment terms.
12. Letter of Credit number and details, if so requested.
13. Country of origin of goods.
14. Signature of exporter.

It is a document rendered by one person to another in regard of goods which have been sold. Its primary function is as a check for the buyer (importer) against charges and delivery. With regard to insurance claims, and for packing purposes, it is useful evidence to verify the value and nature of the goods and in certain circumstances it is evidence of the contract between the two parties. For example, packing not up to specification may give underwriters redress against the sellers. The invoice is not necessarily a contract of sale; it may be so if it contains all the material terms in writing. On the other hand, it may not be a complete memorandum of the contract of sale and, therefore, evidence may be given to vary the contract which is inferred therefrom. In many cases the commercial invoice forms the export sale contract.

A useful detail in an invoice is the Customs Co-operation Council Nomenclature — a classification number for all goods subject to customs tariffs in international trade — which enables customs to identify quickly the goods for statistical and clearance purposes.

Consular invoice.   The importing authorities of some countries require consular invoices, especially those which enforce *ad valorem* import duties. This applies particularly in South America. The invoices are specially printed documents obtainable from consulates which must be completed exactly in accordance with requirements and certified by the consul of the country to which the goods are consigned. This is done at the nearest convenient consular office to the seaport, airport or ICD of departure by the seller. The invoices are issued at the consular office and a fee is payable on certification which is often based on a percentage value of the commercial invoice value of the goods. The consul of the importing country retains one copy, returns one copy to the shipper, and forwards further copies to the customs authorities in his own country. The consular invoice may be used in some circumstances as a

Certificate of Origin. In some situations the regulations of the countries of import can be met simply by having the invoice legalized, i.e. stamped by the relevant consulate.

Customs invoices. Customs invoices may be required by the authorities of the importing country. An adequate number should be provided for the use of the customs authorities overseas.

Pro forma invoice. When an overseas trade contract is negotiated, it is customary for a 'contract of sale' to be arranged by the submission of a pro forma invoice, which is basically a catalogue or list which specifies goods for sale. The buyer communicates his interest to the seller in the form of an offer to buy goods as advertized and acceptance of this offer is communicated in a commercial invoice submitted by the seller. Overall, it is confirmation of the export order. It outlines the main responsibilities of both parties to the contract and enables each to check these are in accordance with the terms negotiated. It includes the following:

1. A full description of the goods — the price, the quality and the quantity plus any special packing or shipping requirements.
2. Licences. Buyers will find that a licence to import into the country of destination is more often required than export licences; the latter are only required for a very restricted list of goods. Hence it is desirable that an exporter receives a copy of any essential import licence in order to be aware of its conditions, and in particular to ensure goods are shipped and arrive at their destination within the validity of the licence.
3. Terms of payment.
4. Insurance. The terms of sale (Incoterms 1990) will specify the responsibilities of both buyer and seller. If insurance is the responsibility of the exporter, he should arrange for all goods to be 'held covered' for the voyage or flight and during a period of warehousing at the destination.

The pro forma invoice may be required in advance for Letter of Credit purposes. The following discrepancies relating to processing pro forma invoices under Letters of Credit do arise and should be avoided:

1. Value exceeds Credit amount.
2. Amount differs from that of Bill of Exchange.
3. Prices of goods not as indicated in Credit.
4. Omission of the price basis and shipment terms, e.g. FOB, CIF or CFR.

5. Inclusion of charges not specified in the Credit.
6. Invoice not certified, notarized or signed as required by Credit.
7. Buyer's name differs from that mentioned in the Credit.
8. Invoice not issued by the exporter.
9. Invoice does not contain declaration required under the Credit.
10. Description of goods differs from that in the Credit.

The following items require particular attention by the exporter to ensure the goods reach the importer within the delivery schedule.

1. Invoice description of the goods should agree exactly with the Documentary Letter of Credit.
2. The invoice must be addressed to the importer.
3. The invoice should include the exact licence and/or certificate numbers required by the Credit.
4. The invoice must show the terms of shipment mentioned in the Credit.

9.15 INTERNATIONAL CONVENTION CONCERNING THE CARRIAGE OF GOODS BY RAIL (CIM)

The international convention concerning the carriage of goods by rail (CIM) has existed in some form since 1893. It permits the carriage of goods by rail under one document, a consignment note (not negotiable), under a common code of conditions applicable to 29 countries mainly situated in Europe and the Mediterranean areas of Africa. It embraces the maritime portion of the transit subject to it being conveyed on shipping lines as listed under the convention. Advantages of the CIM throughout rail consignment involving a container or train ferry wagon include through rates under a common code of conditions, simplified documentation and accountancy, flexibility of freight payment, no intermediate handling (usually) nor customs examination in transit countries and through transits. The latest COTIF/CIM convention came into force in May 1985 and was ratified by 34 countries, mainly European.

The CIM consignment note (Fig. 9.5) is completed by the shipper, agent or originating rail carrier and has six copies — the original of the consignment note, the invoice, the arrival note, the duplicate of the consignment note, the duplicate of the invoice, and a supplementary copy. The following information must be recorded on the CIM:

1. The date and originating rail station of the consignment.
2. The name and address of the sender and the consignee.
3. The originating rail station accepting consignment and the station or place designated for delivery.
4. The ordinary description of the nature of the goods and method of

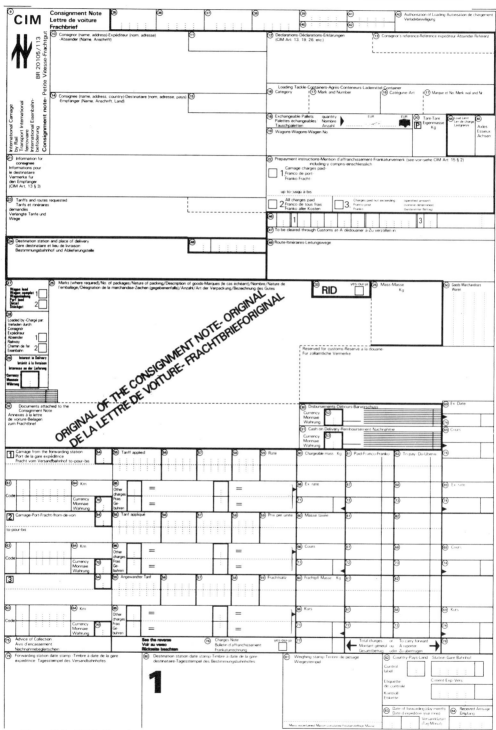

Figure 9.5 CIM Consignment Note, reproduced by kind permission of the British Railways Board.

packing and, in the case of dangerous goods, their generally recognized description.

5. The gross weight of the goods or their quantity.
6. The charges relating to the carriage.
7. The requisite instructions for customs and other formalities.

The foregoing may also be required under a Letter of Credit.

It is likely that the use of international rail freight will increase under 1992 Single Market Entity and Channel Tunnel provision.

9.16 LETTERS OF INDEMNITY

If for some reason the Bill of Lading is missing or has not been received by the importer when the buyer wishes to collect the goods, the shipping company will only release the goods if the buyer provides them with a Letter of Indemnity. This absolves the shipping company of all responsibility for and consequences arising from their releasing the goods without the Bill of Lading. Additionally, the Letter of Indemnity will give an undertaking that the importer will produce the Bill of Lading as soon as possible. Most shipping companies require the bank to sign the form of indemnity. The bank will either issue the Letter of Indemnity themselves or add their endorsement to an existing Letter.

9.17 PACKING LIST

The packing list gives the contents of each individual package. In particular it will include the number and kind of packages, their contents, overall net and gross weight usually in kilograms, the dimensions and the volume. The document is often referred to as a packing note and may feature the package marking. HM Customs require a packing list at the time of importation unless such data is on the commercial invoice.

9.18 PARCEL POST RECEIPT

This is issued by the post office for goods sent by parcel post. It is both a receipt and evidence of despatch. It is not a document of title and goods should be consigned to the party specified in the Documentary Credit. An airmail label should be fixed to a postal receipt in respect of air parcel post despatch; alternatively the post office should stamp the receipt 'air parcel'. Overall, it is a cheap method of delivery for small consignments and the post office can provide insurance if required.

PACKING SPECIFICATION

OGEL OZALID GROUP (EXPORT) LIMITED

Shipping Marks	Invoice to

Customer's Order Reference	Exporters Order Reference and Date	Invoice Reference	Page No.

Package Type	Number	Containing	Gross Kilos	Nett Kilos	Measurements

Figure 9.6 Packing Specification, reproduced by kind permission of Ozalid Group Export Ltd.

9.19 PRESHIPMENT INSPECTION CERTIFICATE

An increasing number of shippers and various organizations, authorities and governments throughout the world are now insisting that the goods are inspected for quality, quantity being exported and the comparison of price(s) proposed and market price(s) at the time of shipment. Organizations which undertake such work - which can extend to transhipment en route — include the Societe Generale de Surveillance (SGS) and Ship Classification Societies such as Bureau Veritas.

The SGS representative will examine the goods at the place of manufacture or assembly prior to despatch. This is to ensure they comply with the description found in the export sales contract, Bill of Lading or export invoice. Subsequently the goods will be examined as they are loaded into the container or loaded onto the ship. In situations where a seller is at variance with SGS opinion, he may present his position to the SGS principals, either directly or through his importer.

If everything is in order a clean report of findings (CRF) will be issued by SGS to their principals. This is required together with other commercial documents such as Bill of Lading, Letter of Credit, invoice in order to obtain payment via the commercial bank and/or customs clearance import. If a non-negotiable report of findings (NNRF) is issued by SGS, the seller (exporter) may opt to discuss the matter with the principal involved who remains the final arbiter. Such a situation arises where goods are shipped before SGS inspection has taken place. In due course SGS will issue the pre-shipment inspection certificate to confirm the goods have been supplied in accordance with the contract.

The SGS do not have the right to approve or prevent shipment of the goods. The opinion expressed by SGS is given after all the factors are provided by the seller, information given in good faith but without any liability to the seller for any loss, damage, or expense arising from the issuance of Report of Findings. Currently some 35 countries require that both Letter of Credits and contracts relevant to the import of goods contain a condition that a Clean Report of Findings covering quality, quantity and price must be presented along with other documents required to negotiate payment. The system has been introduced for the following reasons:

1. To minimize the loss of foreign exchange through over-invoicing, concealed commission payments, and illegal money transfers.
2. To minimize losses of revenue and duty payments through under invoicing.
3. To reduce evasion of import controls and help combat smuggling.
4. To help control landed prices and therefore control local inflation.

5. To avoid dumping of cargo through the incidence of shipping sub-standard goods.
6. To avoid the incidence of loss through shipment of underweight cargo or short shipments.

The pre-shipment certificate is not a mandatory requirement in the UK but some buyers (importers) require it.

9.20   PHYTOSANITARY (PLANT HEALTH) CERTIFICATE

The importation of all planting material, forest trees and other trees and shrubs, and certain raw fruit and vegetables must be accompanied by a Phytosanitary Certificate in most countries. In some countries the importation of certain species of plants from certain areas of the world is prohibited. Application for such certificates should be made to the agricultural department of the exporting country who will issue them in compliance with the *Import and Export (Plant Health) (Great Britain) order, 1980* and the *Import and Export of Trees, Wood and Bark (Health) Great Britain order, 1980*. However, the importation of certain species of plants from certain parts of the world is prohibited.

9.21   SHIPS DELIVERY ORDER

A Ships Delivery Order is a written, legally-recognized authority to deliver goods to a named party in exchange for the original Bill of Lading usually at the port of destination. It is issued at the port of destination and is subject to all the terms and conditions of the carrier's Bill of Lading. It must not contain any reservations or clauses other than those appearing in the Bill of Lading except where increased obligations or extra cost may be incurred in giving delivery beyond the Bill of Lading.

The Delivery Order should be addressed to the ship's master, and proves useful, for example, when the buyer does not wish to know the identity of the supplier abroad for trade reasons. It is important the document is endorsed by the party to whom it is made out. However, if it is issued in one port, for delivery in another, and the freight is payable at destination, the order would then be 'consigned' to the carrier's agent to ensure that it is presented and released before collection of the goods is authorized.

9.22   TIR CARNETS

The UK is a party to the Customs Convention in the International Transport of Goods under cover of TIR Carnets (TIR conventions 1959 and 1975) which is designed to facilitate the international transport of goods on road vehicles by simplifying customs requirements. It covers road vehicles, semi-trailers and containers (road- or rail-borne, including those of demountable body type).

The guaranteeing association which issues the TIR carnet guarantees the duty payable in the goods carried under the cover of the carnet. The TIR is a customs facility which enables goods in customs-sealed vehicles and customs-sealed containers to transit intermediate countries with the minimum of formalities. It is recognized by over 50 countries worldwide including the USA, USSR and Australia.

9.23 VETERINARY CERTIFICATE/HEALTH CERTIFICATE

This may be required when livestock or domestic animals are imported. It should be signed by the appropriate health authority in the exporter's country and is required by UK Customs at the time of importation.

9.24 WEIGHT LIST

In some countries, a Weight List document is required. This merely gives details of the weight of the consignment.

Readers are reminded that customs documentation is dealt with on pages 77-90 and dangerous cargo on pages 53-4. The importer keen to develop a deeper knowledge of the subject is urged to study my book *Import/Export Documentation* (see Appendix A).

10 *Incoterms 1990*

Our study of import practice would not be complete without an in-depth evaluation of Incoterms 1990. The need for every importer to have thorough knowledge of Incoterms 1990 cannot be over-stressed, and likewise the sales and marketing personnel who negotiate the export sales contract terms on behalf of the buyer. The booklet *Incoterms 1990* No. 350 is available from local Chambers of Commerce who devised the terms and update them regularly.

The role of the ICC is to promote the world economy with particular emphasis on the expansion of international trade, and investment. National economic growth is encouraged to generate expansion of world trade. The objective of the ICC is the integration of the business community's approach to world economic progress and problems. The ICC is represented in 96 countries and works through all its National Committees and Councils.

An international trade deal can involve up to four contracts and the importer (buyer) must have a broad understanding of each of them. The four contracts are: the contract of carriage, the export sales contract (usually involving Incoterms 1990), the insurance contract, and the contract of finance. (See ICC booklet No. 400 on *Uniform Customs and Practice for Documentary Credits*, price £12.50). There are three main areas of uncertainty in international trade contracts and their interpretation — the uncertainty as to which country's law will be applicable to their contracts; the difficulty emerging from inadequate and unreliable information; and the serious problem of the diversity of interpretation of the various trade terms. The latter point can involve costly litigation and loss of much goodwill when a dispute over the interpretation of such terms arises.

The role of Incoterms 1990 is to give the business person a set of international rules for the interpretation of the more commonly used terms such as FOB, CIF and Ex Works in foreign trade contracts. Such a range of terms enables the business person to decide which is the most suitable for their needs, knowing that the interpretation of such terms will not vary by individual country.

It must be recognized, however, that it is not *always* possible to give a precise interpretation. In such situations one must rely on the custom of the trade or port. Business persons are advised to use terms which are subject to varying interpretations as little as possible and to rely on the well-established, internationally-accepted terms. To avoid any misunderstandings or disputes the parties to the contract are well advised to keep trading customs of individual countries in mind when negotiating their export sales contract. However, parties to the contract may use Incoterms as the general basis of their contract, but may specify variations of them or additions to them relevant to the particular trade or circumstances. An example is the CIF (cost insurance freight) plus war risk insurance. The seller would base his quotation accordingly. Special provisions in the individual contract between the parties will override anything in the Incoterm provisions.

A point to bear specially in mind is the need for caution in the variation, for example, of CFR (cost and freight), CIF (cost insurance freight) or (DDP) Delivered Duty Paid; the addition of a word or letter could change the contract and its interpretation. It is essential that any such variation be explicitly stated in the contract to ensure each party to the contract is aware of its obligations and acts accordingly.

The buyer (importer) and seller (exporter) parties to the contract must especially bear in mind that Incoterms only define their relationship in contract terms, and has no bearing directly or indirectly on the carriers obligations to them as found in the contract of carriage. However, the law of carriage will determine how the seller should fulfil his obligation to deliver the goods to the carrier on board the vessel as found in FOB, CFR, and CIF. A further point to bear in mind by the seller and buyer is that there is no obligation for the seller to procure an insurance policy for the buyer's benefit. However, in practice many contracts request the buyer or seller to so arrange insurance from the point of departure in the country of despatch, to the point of final destination chosen by the buyer.

Incoterms 1990 can be divided into recommended usages by modes of transport as under — all modes (i.e. combined transport), EXW, FCA, CPT, CIP, DAF, DDP; conventional port/sea transport only FAS, FOB, CFR, CIF, DES, DEQ. Incoterms 1990 reflect the changes and development of international distribution during the past decade, especially the development of combined transportation and associated documentation together with electronic data interchange. In analysing each term the seller and buyer should identify the following aspects:

Seller
1. Supplying good(s) in conformity with the contract.
2. Licences and authorizations.

3. Place of delivery (not delivery of the goods).
4. Carriage of goods contract and insurance.
5. Documentation and notice to the buyer.
6. Transfer of risks.
7. Transfer and division of costs.
8. Checking, packages, marking.
9. Other obligations.

Buyer
1. Licences and authorizations.
2. Notices, receipt of documents.
3. Taking delivery.
4. Transfer of risks.
5. Transfer and division of costs.
6. Other obligations.

The use of Bills of Lading is now becoming less common in the liner trade and is being replaced by non-negotiable documents such as Sea Waybills, Liner Waybills, freight receipts and combined or multi-modal transport documents. Ultimately the transmission of such information will be by automatic dataprocessing techniques. SITPRO are very much involved in such developments.

10.1 FACTORS DETERMINING CHOICE OF INCOTERMS

Personnel involved in negotiating the sales contract have a wide choice in selecting the cargo delivery term most acceptable to the sale. The prime consideration is to ensure that each party to the contract is clearly aware of their obligation to ensure the consignment is despatched without impeding the transit arrangements. The following factors are relevant in the evaluation of the choice of the cargo delivery term:

1. Basically the buyer is the stronger party in such negotiations especially as he has to fund the carriage charges directly through his payment to the carrier under FOB or indirectly through CIF to the seller. This is a fundamental point the buyer must always bear in mind.
2. The buyer has the opportunity of controlling the transit arrangements when he concludes the arrangements, and funds them direct with the carrier. He may, through other contracts, be able to get a discount through the volume of business generated to the trade or route.
3. An increasing number of third world countries, COMECON and Eastern Bloc countries now follow a policy of directing all cargoes onto their national shipping line or airline. This saves hard currency

and develops their shipping and airline companies. It also reflects in many situations cargo preference laws enforced by the buyer's government as part of their trading policy.

4. The seller, under CIF terms, can maximize the national income from such a sale and thereby despatch the consignment on the seller's national shipping line or airline, and likewise obtain insurance cover through brokers.

Overall, the most decisive factors to employ in determining the most acceptable Incoterm are experience of the trading market and the development of a good business relationship between seller and buyer on a long-term basis.

10.2   DESCRIPTION OF INCOTERMS 1990

10.2.1   EXW Ex Works (named place)

This term means maximum involvement by the buyer in arrangements for the conveyance of the consignment to the specified destination. The exporter merely makes the goods available by an agreed date at his factory or warehouse. The seller minimizes his obligations whilst the buyer obtains the goods at the lowest possible price, by arranging to use his national shipping line or airline and by securing insurance cover in his own country. This eliminates the need to fund such provisions using hard currency and thereby improves the importer's trade balance. This practice is much on the increase nowadays, particularly by third world, COMECON and Eastern Bloc nations. The seller's obligations cease when the buyer accepts the goods at the factory or warehouse. It is usual for the buyer to appoint an agent in the seller's country to look after all the collection, transportation, insurance and documentation arrangements, possibly in consultation with the national shipping line or airline.

The term provides two options: Ex Works 'cleared for export', and Ex Works 'uncleared for export'. The following is based on uncleared for export.

The principal obligations of the seller include: to supply the goods in accord with the contract of sale; to make available the goods to the buyer at the customary delivery point, or as specified in the contact of sale to enable the goods to be conveyed on the transport unit arranged by the buyer; to provide at his expense the necessary packing (if any) to enable the buyer to convey the goods on the specified transport; to give the buyer prompt notice when the goods will be available for collection; to bear all risk and expense of the goods until they have been placed at the disposal of the buyer as specified in the contract of sale; to render the buyer on request every assistance to provide, in the country of delivery or cargo origin, all the relevant documentation required in the process of exportation.

Obviously the responsibilities of the buyer are more extensive. These include: to take delivery of the cargo and to pay for the goods in accord with the contract of sale terms: to fund any preshipment inspection expense; to bear all the cost and risk of the goods from the time they have been placed at his disposal by the seller in accord with sales contract terms; to fund any customs duties and taxes arising through exportation; to bear additional costs incurred and related risks inherent through the failure of the buyer to give instructions about the place of delivery within the prescribed period; to fund all costs in obtaining the documents required for the purpose of importation and exportation and for passing through the countries of transit. This term should not be used where according to regulations of the country of export the buyer cannot obtain directly or indirectly the export licence. In such a situation the FCA term should be used.

10.2.2 FOB Free on Board (named port of shipment)

Under such terms the goods are placed in the ship by the seller at the specified port of shipment detailed in the sales contract. The risk of loss of, or damage to, the goods is transferred from the seller to the buyer when the goods pass over the ship's rail. Under such terms the seller bears all the cost and the risk of conveyance up to the ship's rail and the buyer accepts the residue of the transit cost, including sea-freight and insurance. This term is used frequently in international trade and is to the advantage of the buyer because the cargo can be conveyed on his national shipping line, thereby ensuring it is funded by the national currency. Insurance provision can likewise be arranged in his own country with similar benefit. It is usual for the buyer to appoint an agent in the seller's country to look after the preshipment, documentation, insurance, etc. arrangements in consultation with the shipping company.

The principal seller's obligations found in a FOB sales contract include: to supply the goods in accord with the contract of sale; to deliver the cargo on the named vessel at the specified port of shipment within the agreed period or on the agreed date and in so doing promptly inform the buyer; to provide at his expense any export licence or other governmental authorization necessary for the export of goods; to bear all costs and risks of the goods until such time as the cargo has effectively passed over the ship's rail at the named port; to provide at his expense the customary packing of the goods unless it is the custom of the trade to ship the cargo unpacked; to pay the cost of any cargo scrutiny prior to the delivery of the cargo; to supply at seller's expense the requisite documentation as proof of delivery of the goods alongside the named vessel; to provide the buyer on request and at buyer's expense with the Certificate of Origin; to supply the buyer on request and at buyer's expense every assistance to obtain Bills of Lading/Sea Waybill and other documentation issued in the country of shipment or origin necessary for the importation process both in transit countries and the destination country.

The buyer's responsibilities are extensive. These include: to arrange at his own expense and risk preshipment cargo inspection arrangements; to bear all cost and risk of the cargo from the time it has passed the ship's rail at port of shipment and to pay the price as specified in the sales contract; to bear all the cost and risk emerging from the failure of the shipowner to fulfil the contracted preshipment arrangements (such as the cargo being shut out) — this is subject to the seller making the cargo available at the loading berth in accord with the sales contract; in the event of the buyer failing to give preshipment details to the seller within the prescribed period all additional cost and risk to be borne by the buyer; to pay all cost to the seller to obtain Bills of Lading, Certificate of Origin, consular documents and any other documentation required to process the cargo through importation both in transit countries and in the country of destination. This term may only be used for Water Transport. When the ship's rail serves no practical purpose, such as roll on/roll off or container traffic the FCA term should be used.

10.2.3 CFR Cost and Freight (named port of destination)

Under this term the seller must pay the costs necessary to bring the goods to the named port of shipment, the risk of loss of, or damage to, the goods, as well as of any additional expenses, is transferred from the seller to the buyer when the goods pass the ship's rail. This is identical to CIF except that the buyer is responsible for funding and arranging the cargo insurance.

The seller's obligations in CFR include: to supply the goods in accord with the contract of sale terms; to arrange and pay for the conveyance of the goods to the specified port of destination by the customary route and fund any unloading charges at the destination port; to provide and pay for any export licence or other governmental authorization necessary to export the cargo; to arrange and pay for, on specified date or period, the cargo loading at the agreed port (if no such loading date or period is quoted, such a task to be undertaken within a reasonable period); to bear all the cargo risk until such time as it passes over the ship's rail at the port of shipment; to supply promptly and pay for the clean shipped negotiable Bill of Lading for the agreed destination port, together with any invoice of the goods shipped; to provide and pay for the customary packing of the goods unless it is the custom of the trade to ship the cargo unpacked; to fund any cargo scrutiny prior to loading the cargo; to pay any cost of dues and taxes incurred relative to the process of exportation in respect of the cargo prior to shipment; to provide the buyer on request and at the buyer's expense, a Certificate of Origin and consular invoice; to render the buyer on request and at the buyer's expense and risk every assistance to obtain any documents required in the country of shipment or transit countries necessary for the conveyance of the cargo to its destination.

A point for the seller to note especially with the CFR term is the need to supply a full set of clean on board or shipped Bills of Lading. If the Bill of Lading contains a reference to the Charter Party, the seller must also provide a copy of the latter. The buyer must ensure these provisions are complied with by the seller.

The factors relevant to the buyer include: acceptance of the documents as tendered by the seller (subject to their conformity with the terms of the contract) and payment of the goods etc., as specified in the contract of sale; to receive the goods at the port of destination and, with the exception of the sea-freight, all the costs and charges incurred during the voyage(s); to fund all unloading expenses at destination port including lighterage, wharfage, etc. unless such costs have been included in the freight or collected by the shipowner at the time freight was paid; to fund any pre-shipment cargo inspection arrangements; to undertake all the risk when the cargo has passed the ship's rail at the departure port; in the event of the buyer failing to give instructions (by the specified date or within agreed period) relative to destination port, all additional cost and risk will be borne by the buyer subject to the goods being duly appropriated to the contract; to pay all the costs to obtain the Certificate of Origin and consular documents; to meet all charges to provide any other documentation specified relative to processing the consignment in the country of shipment or transit countries; to pay all customs duties and other taxes raised at the time of importation; to obtain and pay for any import licence or related documentation required at the time of importation.

In the CFR contract sale the buyer can arrange the cargo insurance in his own country thereby saving foreign currency. Many importers are tending to favour this arrangement. This term should only be used for sea and inland water transport. When the ship's rail serves no practical purpose as in the case of roll on/roll off or container traffic, the CPT term should be used.

10.2.4   CIF Cost, Insurance, Freight (named port of destination)

This is a popular cargo delivery arrangement. The seller, in addition to CFR obligations, is obliged to procure marine insurance against the risk of loss of, or damage to, the goods in transit. In other words, the seller contracts with the insurer and pays the insurance premium.

The salient features of the contract as far as the seller is concerned include: to supply the goods in accord with contract of the sale terms; to arrange and pay for the carriage of the goods to the specified destination port by the customary route and to fund any unloading charges at the destination port; to provide and pay for any export licence or other governmental authorization necessary to export the cargo; to arrange and pay for, on specified date or within an agreed period, the cargo loading at the agreed port (if no such loading date or period is quoted such a task to be undertaken within a reasonable period); to inform the buyer promptly when loading is completed; to arrange and pay for insurance of the cargo in a transferable form against the risk of loss or damage during the transit — such cover shall be Institute Cargo Clauses (Institute of London Underwriters) and embrace the CIF price plus 10% and the insurance will be in the currency of the contract; to bear all the risk of goods until they have effectively passed the ship's rail at the port of shipment; to supply to the buyer promptly, at the seller's expense, a clean negotiable 'shipped on board' Bill of Lading for the agreed port of destination and insurance policy or certificate of insurance; to provide and pay for the customary packing of the goods unless it is the custom of the trade to ship the goods unpacked; to pay the cost of any cargo scrutiny prior to loading the cargo; to bear any cost of dues and taxes incurred relative to the process of exportation in respect of the cargo prior to shipment; to provide the buyer on request and at the buyer's expense a Certificate of Origin and consular invoice; to render the buyer on request and at the buyer's expense every assistance to obtain any documents required in the country of shipment or transit countries necessary for the conveyance of the cargo throughout the transit. A point to bear in mind concerning the insurance cover is that the seller has to procure marine insurance against the buyer's risk of loss or damage to the goods during the carriage against minimum coverage and destruction.

The responsibilities of the buyer include: acceptance of the documents as tendered by the seller (subject to their conformity with the terms of the contract) and payment of the goods, as specified in the contract of sale; to fund any pre-shipment cargo inspection arrangements; to receive the goods at the agreed destination port and to bear, with the exception of the freight and marine insurance, all costs and charges incurred during the voyage(s); to fund all unloading expenses at the port of destination, including lighterage and wharfage, unless such costs have been included in the freight or collected by the shipowner at the time freight was paid; to undertake all the risk when the cargo has passed the ship's rail at the departure port; in the event of the buyer failing to give instructions, by the specified date or within an agreed period, relative to the port of destination, all additional cost and risk will be borne by the buyer subject to the goods being duly appropriated to the contract; to pay all the costs in obtaining a Certificate of Origin and consular documents; to meet all charges to provide any other documentation specified relative to processing the consignment in the country of shipment or transit countries; to pay all customs duties and other taxes raised at the time of importation; and obtain at his expense any import licence or related documentation required at time of importation.

The CIF terms enable the seller to obtain the maximum income from the sales contract with the insurance and freight charges contributing to the invisible exports if the goods are carried on the national shipping line and the insurance is effected in the country of origin. This term should only be used for sea and inland water transport. When the ship's rail serves no practical purpose as in the case of roll on/roll off or container traffic, the CIP term should be used.

10.2.5 DES Delivered Ex Ship (named port of destination)

This sales contract term is not used extensively. It obliges the seller to make the goods available to the buyer on board the vessel at the destination port as specified in the sales contract. The seller has to bear the full cost and risk involved to bring the goods to the destination port.

The seller's main obligations include: to supply the goods in accord with contract of sale terms; to make the goods available to the buyer on board the vessel at the agreed destination port to enable the cargo to be conveniently discharged; to bear all the risk and expense of the cargo conveyance to the destination port until promptly collected by the buyer; to provide and pay for the customary packing of the goods unless it is the custom of the trade to ship the goods unpacked; to pay the cost of any cargo scrutiny prior to collection of the cargo by the buyer; to inform promptly the buyer of the expected date of arrival of the vessel and to provide the buyer with a Bill of Lading and any other documents necessary to enable the buyer to take delivery of the consignment; to provide the buyer on request and at the buyer's expense the Certificate of Origin and consular invoice; to render the buyer on request and at the buyer's expense every assistance to provide the requisite documentation issued in the country of shipment and/or origin required for importation in the destination country or transit countries.

The buyer's obligations are less onerous and include: to take delivery of the cargo and pay the requisite cost as specified in the sales contract; to fund any pre-shipment cargo inspection arrangements; to bear all the risk and expense from the time the cargo has been placed at the disposal of the buyer on board the vessel awaiting discharge at the destination port; to bear all the cost associated with the provision of documentation obtained by the seller necessary for the importation of the goods both in destination and transit countries; to obtain at the buyer's expense all licences or similar documents necessary for the importing process; to bear all customs charges and other duties and taxes incurred at the time of importation.

10.2.6 DEQ Delivered Ex Quay (duty paid) . . . (named port of destination)

Under this term the seller arranges for the goods to be made available to the buyer on the quay or wharf at the destination port detailed in the sales contract. The seller has to bear the full cost and risk involved to bring the goods to the quay.

Basically there are two Ex Quay contracts in use — delivered Ex Quay duty paid and delivered Ex Quay duties on buyer's account in which the liability to clear the goods for import is met by the buyer rather than the seller. It is important that the full description of each term is given to avoid ambiguity and subsequent dispute such as delivered Ex Quay, VAT and/or taxes unpaid, or delivered Ex Quay VAT and/or taxes paid.

The seller's obligations include: to supply the goods in accord with the contract of sale terms; to make the goods available to the buyer at the specified quay or wharf within the period given in the sales contract and to bear all the associated risk and cost; to provide and pay for any import licence and bear all charges through importation of the goods and delivery to the buyer; to provide and pay for the customary packing of the goods unless it is the custom of the trade to ship the cargo unpacked; to pay the cost of any scrutiny immediately prior to the goods being placed at the disposal of the buyer; at the seller's expense to provide the delivery order or other relevant documents necessary for the buyer to take delivery of the goods.

The buyer's task is twofold: to take delivery of the goods as specified in the contract; to bear all the expense and risk of the goods from the time the cargo has been effectively placed at the disposal of the buyer. The cost of pre-shipment cargo inspection is borne by the buyer unless when mandated by the authorities of the country of export.

This term should not be used if the seller is unable to obtain directly or indirectly the import licence.

10.2.7 FAS Free Alongside Ship (named port of shipment)

The obligations of the seller are realized when the goods have been placed alongside the ship in the quay or on lighterage at a specified port of shipment. At this stage and thereafter the buyer has to bear all the cost and risk of loss of or damage to the goods and the buyer is responsible for exportation and customs arrangements.

The salient features of FAS for the seller include: to supply the goods in accord with the contract of sale terms; to arrange delivery of the cargo by the date or within the agreed period alongside the specified vessel at the loading berth and port as named by the buyer; to help the buyer on request and at the buyer's expense to obtain the export licence or other governmental authorization necessary to export the goods; to bear all cost and risk of the goods until they have been effectively delivered alongside the specified vessel — this includes the funding of any formalities necessary to fulfil the order to deliver the goods alongside the ship; to provide and pay for the customary packing of the goods unless it is the custom of the trade to ship the cargo unpacked; to render to the buyer on request and at the buyer's expense the Certificate of Origin; to assist the buyer on request and at the buyer's expense to obtain any documents issued in the country of origin or shipment (including Bill of Lading and/or consular documents) required for importation of the goods into the destination country and their passage through transit countries.

The buyer's responsibilities include: to give the seller prompt notice of the name of the vessel, loading berth and delivery dates; to bear all the expense and risk of the goods from when they have been effectively delivered alongside the vessel as specified; to fund any additional cost and to accept the risk in the event of the vessel not arriving on time or the shipowner being unable to accept the cargo. In the event of the buyer failing to notify the seller of the name of the vessel, and port of shipment within the prescribed period, the buyer would bear all consequential cost and risk from the expiry date of the notification period, subject to the goods being duly appropriated by the seller to the contract; to meet all costs of obtaining the export licence or other governmental authorization necessary to export the goods, together with the Certificate of Origin and any documents necessary for the importation of the goods, including the Bill of Lading and consular documents. The cost of pre-shipment cargo inspection is borne by the buyer unless when mandated by the authorities of the country of export.

This term should not be used where, according to regulations of the country of export, the buyer cannot obtain directly or indirectly the export licence.

10.2.8   DAF Delivered at Frontier (named point)

Under the 'delivered at frontier' term the seller's obligations are concluded when the goods have arrived at the named frontier point place or customs examination border. It is usual, to avoid ambiguity, to quote the two countries separated by the frontier. This term is used primarily for rail- or road-borne traffic but can be used for other transport modes in varying circumstances. Its use could become more common through the development of the combined transport operation for international consignments. The term requires the seller to clear for export.

The seller's main obligations include: to supply the goods in accord with contract of sale terms at the seller's risk and expense; to place the goods at the disposal of the buyer at the specified frontier point within the stipulated period and in so doing provide him with the necessary customary documentation including consignment note, export licence, delivery order, warehouse warrant etc., to enable the buyer to take delivery of the cargo; to fund any customs charges and other expenses incurred up to the time when the goods have been placed at the buyer's disposal, and bear all the risk throughout this period; to obtain and pay for all documentation necessary for the exportation of the cargo, including transit countries needs and placing them at the disposal of the buyer as appropriate; to fund all transport costs (including incidental charges raised during the transit) up to the nominated frontier point; if no particular frontier point is quoted, the seller may choose the one which is most convenient to him provided he notifies the buyer promptly and it offers adequate customs and other facilities to enable the contract to be executed satisfactorily by both parties; to supply the buyer on request the through consignment note embracing the origin and destination place in the importing country — such a request to be executed by the seller on the condition he incurs the risk, or expense other than is customary to incur; in the event of the goods being unloaded on arrival at the frontier point, such cost to be borne by the seller, including lighterage and handling charges (this would also apply if the seller used his own transport); to notify promptly the buyer that the goods have been despatched; to provide and pay for the customary packing of the goods unless it is the custom of the trade to ship the cargo unpacked; to fund any cargo scrutiny necessary to transport the goods to the specified frontier point; to bear any additional cost incurred to place the goods at the buyers disposal; and render to the buyer on request and at the buyer's expense all reasonable assistance to obtain documents inherent in the importing process in the destination country.

The buyer's obligations include: to accept delivery of the goods at the specified frontier point and accept all transportation and handling costs therefrom; to meet the risk and custom duties and other costs incurred from the time the goods have been placed at the buyer's disposal relative to the process of importation of the cargo; to fund incidental expenses incurred to unload the cargo at the specified frontier point; in the event of the buyer not taking delivery of the cargo duly put at his disposal in accord with the sales contract, the buyer will pay all additional cost and bear all the risk resulting therefrom; to obtain at his expense any import licence and other documentation required to process the cargo through importation; to fund any additional expense incurred by the seller to obtain the consignment note for the buyer which could include documentation; and to supply the seller on request with details of the ultimate destination of the goods; to fund any expense incurred by the seller to provide the buyer with any third party certificate of conformity of the goods stipulated in the contract of sale. The cost of pre-shipment cargo inspection is borne by the buyer unless when mandated by the authorities of the country of export.

In addition to the foregoing eight cargo delivery terms which are the most popular, there are five others in Incoterms 1990. A brief commentary on them follows:

10.2.9   DDP Delivered Duty Paid (named point)

It will be recalled that under the term Ex Works, the seller has the minimum obligation in terms of despatching the cargo. Conversely the term 'delivered duty paid' places the maximum obligation on the seller regarding the cargo despatch arrangements. Under such terms the seller is responsible for the conveyance of the goods at his own risk and expense to the named destination located in the buyer's country on the contract of sale. This includes the task of processing the cargo through both exportation and importation including duties and taxes plus customs clearance, loading and unloading, together with the related documentation which the buyer usually obtains as necessary on request but at the seller's expense. The seller may use his own transport throughout the conveyance.

The buyer's role is to accept the goods at the named place of destination and he is responsible for all subsequent movement cost of the goods including handling. Any form of transport can be used. The cost of pre-shipment cargo inspection is borne by the buyer unless when mandated by the authorities of the country of export.

The term should not be used if the seller is unable to obtain directly or indirectly the import licence. If the parties wish that the buyer should clear the goods for import and pay the duty, the term DDU should be used.

Hence the seller fulfils his obligation when he has delivered the goods, cleared for export, into the charge of the carrier named by the buyer at the named place or point. If no precise point is indicated by the buyer, the seller may choose within the range stipulated where the carrier shall take the goods into his charge. When according to commercial practice the seller's assistance is required in making the contract with the carrier, (such as in rail or air transport with fixed freight rates) the seller will act at the buyer's risk and expense. This term may be used for any mode of transport.

10.2.10 DDU Delivered Duty Unpaid (named point)

The seller fulfils his obligations when the goods have arrived at the named point or place in the country of importation. The seller has to bear the full costs and risks involved in bringing the goods there to, excluding duties, taxes and other official charges payable upon importation. If the parties wish to include in the seller's obligations some of the cost or official charges payable upon import of the goods (such as value added tax (VAT)) this should be made clear by adding words to this effect (for example, 'delivered duty unpaid, VAT paid'). The term may be used irrespective of transport mode.

10.2.11 FCA Free Carrier (named place)

This term is primarily for the combined transport operation such as a container, or roll on/roll off operation involving a road trailer and sea ferry. The term is based on the FOB principle except that the seller fulfils his obligations when he delivers the goods into the custody of the carrier at the named place found in the sales contract or subsequently agreed by the parties. This is likely to be used by a freight forwarder engaged in the international road haulage business. The risk of loss of or damage to the goods is transferred from the seller to the buyer at the time the nominated carrier accepts them at the prescribed place and not at the ship's rail as with FOB. When the seller has to render to the buyer or other person prescribed the Bill of Lading, Waybill, or carrier's receipt, as evidence of the delivery acceptance of the goods, the seller's contractual obligations are fulfilled.

Hence the seller fulfils his obligation when he has delivered the goods, cleared for export, into the charge of the carrier named by the buyer at the named place or point. If no precise point is indicated by the buyer, the seller may choose within the range stipulated where the carrier shall take the goods into his charge. When according to commercial practice the seller's assistance is required in making the contract with the carrier, (such as in rail or air transport with fixed freight rates) the seller will act at the buyer's risk and expense. This term may be used for any mode of transport.

10.2.12 CPT Carriage paid to (named point of destination)

Under such a term the seller pays the freight for the carriage of the goods to the named destination. The buyer's risk commences when the goods have been delivered into the custody of the first carrier. Moreover, at this point the buyer accepts full liability for any additional cost incurred in the conveyance of the goods. On request the seller may have to provide a Bill of Lading, Waybill or carrier's receipt to the buyer or other person prescribed at which stage the seller's obligations are fulfilled. In common with the 'free carrier' term, it is ideal for the multi-modal transport operation which includes roll on/roll off and container movements.

10.2.13   CIP Freight Carriage and Insurance Paid (named point of destination)

This term is identical to the previous item except that the seller also funds the cargo insurance. Again it is ideal for the combined transport operation and the seller's liability ceases when the cargo has been accepted by the first carrier at the named place and any requested Bill of Lading, Waybill, or carrier receipt has been handed over.

Importers should fully comprehend the 13 terms described. A major feature of Incoterms 1990 is that it recognizes the electronic message (EDI). Hence the seller and buyer may communicate the document electronically.

The importance of all involved in negotiating and executing sales contracts understanding the foregoing cargo delivery terms cannot be overstressed. The following checklist may prove helpful to the buyer (importer):

1. Endeavour to do as much planning as possible for each imported consignment. Close liaison with the buyer's agent is essential.
2. Ensure the personnel concluding the export sales contract on behalf of the buyer are fully conversant with the Incoterm used, especially the impact it will have on the total price of the goods at the time of importation and the workload and responsibility imposed on the buyer regarding transportation and documentation. Substantial cost savings may be realizable if the transportation and insurance arrangements are undertaken by the buyer using his national airline or shipping line and effecting the insurance in the buyer's country.
3. Exercise great care in selecting a suitable forwarding agent both in the seller's and buyer's country (see Chapter 14).
4. Monitor closely the stages of the product being imported. It will help to identify any problem areas and, through the adoption of remedial measures, lessen the risk in the future.
5. If the distribution arrangements are unsatisfactory endeavour to establish what the competitors do − can any lessons be learnt?
6. Study closely the *Uniform Customs and Practice for Documentary Credits* (Appendix A) and dealing with commercial documentary credits operations (see pages 97-9).
7. Review distribution arrangements and cargo delivery terms regularly to ensure that they are the most suitable in the situation obtaining.

11 *Processing the import order*

An important activity of import practice is the processing of the consignment. Before examining the procedures involved, however, we must consider the contract of affreightment embraced in the terms of delivery.

11.1 CONTRACT OF AFFREIGHTMENT: TERMS OF DELIVERY

The basis of a price quotation depends on the correct interpretation of the delivery trade terms. The buyer (importer) will, through experience, accumulate information which will enable him or her to develop a good knowledge of the cargo delivery term ideal for the trade. It is important to bear in mind each delivery trade term quoted embraces three basic elements: the stage at which title to the merchandise passes from the exporter (seller) to the importer (buyer), a clear definition of the charges and expenses to be borne by the exporter and importer, and finally, the stage and location where the goods are to be passed over to the importer (buyer).

The international consignment delivery terms embrace many factors including insurance, air- or sea-freight plus surface transport costs, customs duty, port disbursements, product cost and packing costs. The importance of executing the cargo delivery in accordance with the prescribed terms cannot be overstressed and this involves a disciplined process of progressing the import order (see below). Ideally, the import order should also define the delivery terms. The import manager should devise the order in consultation with relevant colleagues within the company and outside bodies such as carriers or forwarding agents.

There must be no ambiguity in the interpretation by either party of the delivery terms quoted, particularly in the area of cost and liabilities, or costly litigation could arise. Incoterms 1990 (see Chapter 10) can be quoted, but it must be borne in mind that special provisions in individual import contracts will override anything provided in Incoterms 1990. Also, items such as breaches of contract, and their consequences, together with ownership of the goods are outside the influence of Incoterms 1990.

Given below are the four main groups:

Departure:	EXW
Main carriage unpaid:	FCA, FAS, FOB
Main carriage paid:	CFR, CIF, CPT, CIP
Arrival:	DAF, DES, DEQ, DDU, DDP

11.2 ROLE OF FREIGHT FORWARDERS

Many importers use the services of a freight forwarding agent to facilitate the transit arrangements and customs clearance. The following points are relevant:

1. The agent can advise on the most suitable cargo delivery term for the transit.
2. The agent who has contractual arrangements with the carrier can obtain guaranteed cargo space on the flight or sailing specified.
3. The agent who guarantees traffic volume to the carrier can obtain discounted rates which can be passed on to the buyer (importer).
4. Many agents provide consolidated or groupage services which are very competitive by air, container (LCL) or trailer.
5. The agent is likely to have offices at the departure and destination seaports or airports. Close liaison is thus maintained with carrier and customs which minimizes delays and speeds up customs clearance. Hence the importer should ensure that the agent's name features on the Bill of Lading, Sea Waybill, Air Waybill or CMR consignment note to ensure that the carrier notifies the agent of the goods' arrival date. This will speed up the process of assembling all the documents for customs entry and clearance and avoid cargo delays. The buyer is likely to meet the cost of demurrage in the warehouse, container, or trailer, which arises when the cargo has been detained beyond its free period.
6. The agent is experienced in the trade and/or commodity and thereby can ensure the goods have a trouble-free transit. This is especially relevant to customs procedures and documentation needs.
7. The agent is well versed in the customs arrangements and the following points are significant:
   (a) Value added tax is payable at the time of importation but not on all goods.
   (b) The customs tariff based on the 'harmonized system' (see Chapter

6) contains 15 000 headings in 97 chapters. It is the basis on which the customs duty is raised and each imported product is allocated a commodity code obtained from the customs tariff.

(c) Goods bought from an overseas supplier and used in the UK are regarded as home use and when cleared through customs are regarded as in free circulation.

(d) Three types of customs locations where clearance may take place exist as under:—

   (i) Local import and control (LIC, page 89).

   (ii) Inland clearance depot (ICD, page 72).

   (iii) A manual customs station such as a small port where there is no connection with the customs' main computer system, DEPS. In such situations the agent would prepare the relevant entry form such as SAD 88, C105, C109 and take it to the EPU (entry processing unit) at the local customs office. It would be checked by the Passing Officer against the supporting documents. If the duty offered is agreed then the entry is passed for payment. The agent can settle by cheque or the sum can be debited to his deferment account. The passed entry will then be taken to the customs landing officer at the place of arrival, who will examine the goods checking them against the entry. If he is satisfied that they conform to the entry details he will sign and stamp a document releasing them from customs control.

At ICDs and other larger customs locations, they are connected to the main DEPS computer system. Two systems exist:

   (iv) The entry is manually prepared by the forwarder and taken to the EPU. At that point it is fed into the computer by the customs staff. The computer will decide whether the goods or documents are to be examined. If no such examination is undertaken the entry details will be verified and authorization given for their release from customs control.

   (v) All major seaports and airports have now the direct trader input (DTI) system. In such circumstances the same data as specified under (iii) is required but the forwarder will be submitting the data via a VDU (visual display unit) from his own office. A hard copy entry will be printed and taken to the EPU. Hence the DTI system provides an immediate response as regards the type of customs examination which has been selected and any queries involving the entry details will be highlighted immediately. Such a VDU facility connected to the DTI network is only likely to be available to the forwarder as the importer would not be able to justify such an investment.

11.3 THE OVERSEAS TRADE CONTRACT

Negotiation of the overseas trade contract can be difficult and, accordingly, particular care should be taken in preparation of its terms. It must be recognized, however, that a significant number of import orders are secured on a commercial invoice and no formal contract is concluded.

The importer (buyer) is usually the stronger party in the negotiation of the contract, especially if it is a buyer's market, i.e. the level of trade is low and the exporter is anxious to develop new business in an attempt to sustain his company. Furthermore the importer can secure cost savings in a number of areas which can become very significant as the volume of business improves:

1. Undertake all the insurance arrangements.
2. Purchase on a FCA, EXW, DAF basis thereby undertaking all the transportation arrangements. In some situations, particularly over shorter distances, the buyer's own vehicles may be used. Usually the importer appoints a forwarding agent in the exporter's country who, on behalf of the importer, looks after all the transportation arrangements, liaising with the exporter as appropriate.
3. Ensure adequate customs planning is undertaken to minimize cost as outlined in pages 209–12.
4. Undertake adequate financial planning (see Chapter 7). This is a critical area and the buyer can usually benefit by taking advice from his international bank.
5. Ensure all the documents are in order for customs clearance and the appropriate customs clearance option is exercised (see pages 209–10).

Details contained in a typical overseas trade contract are given below, but it must be stressed that they differ by individual country:

1. The exporter's (seller's) registered name and address.
2. The importer's (buyer's) registered name and address.
3. A short title of each party quoted in items (1) and (2).
4. Purpose of the contract. For example, it should confirm the specified merchandise is sold by the party detailed in item (1) to the addressee quoted in item (2), and that the latter has bought according to the terms and conditions laid down in the contract.
5. The number and quantity of goods precisely and fully described to avoid any later misunderstanding or dispute. In particular, one must mention details of any batches and reconcile goods' description with customs tariff specification.
6. Price. This may be quoted in sterling depending on its general stability or some other currency which is not likely to vary in value significantly throughout the contract duration, such as US dollars or deutchemarks. To counter inflation, particularly in a long-term

contract, it is usual to incorporate an escalation clause, and to reduce the risk of sterling fluctuations implications, the tendency is to invoice in foreign currencies. Readers are particularly urged to read Chapter 7.

7. Terms of delivery, for example, CFR Felixstowe, CPT Bangkok or FCA Munich. The economic options of using for example EXW, FCA, CIP, CFR should be evaluated. It is important that both parties to the contract fully understand their obligations as the interpretation of the terms of delivery can sometimes vary by individual country. The ideal solution is to quote Incoterms 1990 which are generally recognized worldwide.

8. Terms of payment, for example, open account, cash with order, Letter of Credit, open account or documents against payment or acceptance. Again this requires careful consideration, particularly the relevant aspects dealt with in Chapter 7.

9. Delivery date/shipment date or period. The buyer should check with the sales or production department the delivery date is convenient and conforms with marketing needs or production schedules.

10. Methods of shipment, for example, container, train ferry, Ro/Ro or air-freight. Different transport modes offer differing transit times and rates. Each should be evaluated and the value-added benefit for each mode to the buyer determined (see pages 46-50).

11. Method of packing. It is desirable for both parties to be fully aware of and agree on the packing specification to ensure no dispute arises later.

12. Cargo insurance policy or certificate terms. This may be for the buyer's or seller's account.

13. Import or export licence details or other instructions. The period of their validity must be reconciled with the terms of payment and delivery date/shipment date or period. Import and export licences can be related to quota systems and their availability needs to be checked.

14. Shipping, freight, documentary requirements and/or instructions. This includes marking of cargo. The onus is placed on the buyer or seller regarding processing the shipment arrangements and payment of freight under the requisite Incoterm 1990.

15. Contract conditions, for example, sale, delivery, performance (quality) of goods, arbitration, etc. With regard to arbitration, this tends to speed settlement of any disputes without costly litigation. The contract may be for one year; renewal by mutual consent.

16. Signature. The contract should be signed by a responsible person at Director or Managerial level on behalf of both parties, and the date recorded.

Obviously the terms of the overseas trade contract will vary by circumstance but other areas which may feature include agency involvement, after-sales activities such as availability and supply of spares, product servicing, and so on. A copy of the contract should be retained by each party.

11.4 PROCESSING ACCORDING TO TRANSPORT MODE

Deep sea containerization

Most container operators, through their agents some 10 days before, tell the 'Notify party' named on the Bill of Lading or Waybill the scheduled arrival time of the vessel. This document provides details of the import goods, name of vessel, arrival time and date at the berth in a specified port, and the agent or shipowner handling the cargo import. It is important that the shipowner is informed of any amendments to the delivery requirements or a transfer of interest in the goods.

At this stage the importer (consignee) must inform the forwarding agent (if he is using one) of the impending arrival of his goods to enable HM Customs clearance procedure to commence. The consignee may appoint the shipowner to act as agent in preparing and lodging customs entries. This should be indicated on the Bill of Lading or Sea Waybill. All the requisite documents to enable clearance of the goods through customs should be forwarded to the forwarding agent or shipowner's office, ideally some 4 working days prior to ship arrival or other prescribed period. Customs clearance documents required for a container originating outside the EC are as follows:

1. Completed C105B Customs Declaration. Details required on customs entry include the supplier of the goods, the importer, the goods, shipment details, duty, VAT, etc. The document must be completed by the importer or his authorized agent. Customs entries can usually be presented before the expected arrival of the ship or aircraft, although they should not be earlier than 4 working days. Normally completed entry forms must be presented to customs within 14 days (7 days by air) of the ship or aircraft arrival. A specimen is shown in Figure 11.1.
2. Certificates of Origin.
3. Supplier/export invoices and packing note.
4. Health, Veterinary, Phytosanitary (Plant Health) Certificates, etc., as appropriate.

In the event of the sea-freight being paid by the importer (buyer), a freight invoice detailing charges due will be despatched to the nominated payer by the shipowner or forwarding agent. The Bill of Lading will specify the outstanding freight to be paid. Consequently the importer

(Methods other than Method 1)
DECLARATION of Particulars relating to Customs Value

HM Customs and Excise

1. Insert name and address of consignor (BLOCK LETTERS)	FOR OFFICIAL USE (No. of entry)
2. Insert name and address of consignee (BLOCK LETTERS)	
Tel. No.:	

3. Number and date of invoice(s) or other documentary evidence identifying the imported goods

4. Terms of delivery (e.g. fob New York)

5. Date and number of any previous Customs decision concerning the Method of Valuation to be used

VI .... dated .... 19 ....

Enter √ where applicable

6. The appropriate Method of Valuation applicable to the imported goods is: (ONLY ONE BOX TO BE TICKED)

(a) The transaction value of identical goods (Method 2) . . . . ☐

(b) The transaction value of similar goods (Method 3) . . . . ☐

(c) Unit price at which the *imported goods/identical goods/similar goods* are sold in the greatest aggregate quantity to unrelated customers at or about the time of importation of the goods to be valued (Method 4[a]) ☐

(d) Unit price at which the *imported goods/identical goods/similar goods* are sold to unrelated customers in the condition as imported at the earliest date after the importation of the goods to be valued (Method 4[b]) ☐

(e) The computed value (Method 5) . . . . ☐

(f) The 'fall back' method (Method 6) . . . . ☐

7. Give reasons why the value cannot be determined under the provisions of any Method preceding the one applied in Box 6 and why the Method indicated in Box 6 can be used.

8. For Method 4(b) only: Give an estimate of the Customs value which will be determined within 90 days of importation.

9. Describe either the evidence (attached) to substantiate the declared Customs value or the evidence which will be submitted within 90 days of importation.

10. Insert name and address of declarant (i.e. company, partnership etc.) if not the consignee (BLOCK LETTERS)	11. I the undersigned, declare that all particulars given in this document are true and complete.
	Signature ....
	.... Name (BLOCK LETTERS)
	Status of signatory.. (Director/Company Secretary/Partner etc.)
Telephone Number..	Date ....19 ....

B

C 105 B   *Delete as necessary   F 5049 (April 1987)   DU 4003/85 AUG AK   [CONTINUED OVERLEAF

Figure 11.1 Customs Declaration, reproduced by kind permission of HM Customs and Excise.

SPECIFICATION of Customs Value			Item	Item	Item ....
METHODS **2 or 3** **ONLY**	A. Basis of calculation	12. Transaction value of *IDENTICAL/SIMILAR goods in currency of EEC country where value was established			
		In National currency (Rate of exchange ....)			
	B. **DEDUCTIONS** Quote below previous relevant Customs decision, if any. V/	13. (a) Quantity adjustment			
		(b) Commercial level adjustment			
		(c) Cost of transport to			
		(d) Loading and handling charges			
		(e) Cost of insurance			
		14. SUB TOTAL B			
	C. **ADDITIONS** Quote below previous relevant Customs decisions, if any. V/	15. (a) Quantity adjustment			
		(b) Commercial level adjustment			
		(c) Cost of transport to			
		(d) Loading and handling charges			
		(e) Cost of insurance			
		16. SUB TOTAL C			
		17. VALUE DECLARED (A − B + C) .			
METHOD **4(a)** **ONLY**	D. Basis of calculation	18. Unit price(s) at which the *imported goods/identical goods/ similar goods are sold to customers unrelated to the seller in the greatest aggregate quantity, at or about the time of importation of the goods being valued, in currency of EEC country of sale.			
		In National currency (Rate of exchange ....)			
	E. **DEDUCTIONS** Costs in national currency included in **D** above Quote below previous relevant Customs decisions, if any. V/	19. (a) Commissions paid or to be paid			
		(b) Profit and general expenses			
		(c) Cost of transport from			
		(d) Cost of insurance			
		(e) Loading and handling charges			
		(f) Other transport costs			
		(g) Further processing costs			
		(h) Duties and taxes			
		20. SUB TOTAL E			
		21. VALUE DECLARED (D − E)			
METHODS **5 or 6** **ONLY**	F. Basis of calculation	22. *COMPUTED VALUE/VALUE of the imported goods (in National currency). Quote previous relevant Customs decision, if any, accepting the Method used to calculate the value. V/..			
	G. **ADDITIONS** Costs in national currency NOT included in **F** above	23. (a) Cost of transport to			
		(b) Loading and handling charges			
		(c) Cost of insurance			
		24. SUB TOTAL G			
		25. VALUE DECLARED (F + G)			

* Delete as necessary

DU 4003/85 AUG CL (R)

Figure 11.1 (contd).

cannot claim the merchandise until all outstanding payments have been made. It is desirable that the Bill of Lading be lodged as early as possible since any delay in receiving this document could result in additional charges accruing.

Hence there are three matters to be dealt with before the goods can be released by the shipowner to the importer (buyer).

1. The completion of the HM Customs clearance together with any other statutory restraints e.g. Port Health, Ministry of Agriculture, Fisheries and Foods.
2. Surrender of Bill of Lading/Sea Waybill.
3. Payment of outstanding charges. This may include:
   (a) sea-freight;
   (b) delivery cost;
   (c) customs clearance;
   (d) customs duty and VAT;
   (e) turn out — the process of container being destuffed (unloaded) for the purpose of customs examination to verify that the container contents conform with the cargo description submitted;
   (f) miscellaneous charges raised by the agent to cover costs of telephone, telex, etc;
   (g) warehouse/demurrage charges.

Charges will vary according to whether the consignment is FCL or LCL. It is important that the clearing agent or freight forwarder prepares and lodges the customs entry for the goods to be imported as quickly as possible. For containers being cleared through an inland clearance depot, the customs entry can be lodged in the entry processing unit (EPU). Customs will issue a removal note when the goods have been cleared. The time-scale varies from hours to days depending on the nature of the goods and the clearance procedure involved. Incorrect documentation is a major cause of customs clearance delays which emphasizes the amount of planning required by the importer and his agent.

Bulk cargo shipment
A significant volume of cargo is moved in bulk shipments. It may be a raw material, foodstuffs or manufactured goods such as cars. The vessel maybe under charter to the supplier (manufacturer). The carrier document will be a Bill of Lading or Sea Waybill. A similar procedure obtains to process cargo through customs, but usually the shipments are regular and the system well established. Customs are particularly interested in the relevant health certificates associated with the product and its quality and weight/quantity. The latter may require a weight certificate supplied by the seller.

Dangerous cargo

Shipments by sea or air classified as dangerous must comply with strict regulations regarding documentation, stowage, packaging, handling, labelling, quantities, etc., (see pages 53-4). The carrier gives priority to the handling of such cargoes which are usually placed in an isolated part of the seaport or airport. Customs clearance is accorded a priority and adequate planning and preparation by the buyer and clearance agent is paramount to ensure prompt despatch to the consignee's premises.

Livestock

Limited quantities of livestock are conveyed by air and sea. These include bloodstock, day-old chicks, pigs and sheep. Regulations are very stringent. Customs clearance involves the appropriate health and veterinary documents. Special facilities are provided at airports and seaports to handle such cargo.

Trailer cargo

A large volume of imports flow from the EC by road haulage. The great majority are customs cleared at the port of entry. The cargo can be cleared within 4—6 hours of arrival. The documents required by the clearance agent include the CMR consignment note, the Single Admin-istration Document, supplier/commercial invoice and health certificate. Most of such cargo is on open account. Trailers conveying goods from outside the EC require customs declaration form C195 rather than SAD.

Air-freight

A large volume of goods is imported by air-freight. The documentation required for goods originating from the EC include Air Waybill, SAD, supplier/commercial invoice and health certificate. Goods originating outside the EC require customs declaration form C195 rather than SAD. Customs entry can be presented before the expected arrival of the aircraft within 4 days of the arrival. However, completed entry forms must be presented to customs within 7 days of the aircraft's arrival.

It will be appreciated that the HM Customs entry procedure is computerized through the direct trader input (DTI) system described on page 195.

11.5 CHECKS BY THE BUYER

Given below are the details the buyer must check before despatching the overseas trade contract or order.

1. Clear description of the goods.
2. Specification — use metric units.

3. Quantity to be supplied, with delivery programme details.
4. Price — amount or per unit, currency and delivery terms, i.e. FOB, CFR, FCA.
5. Terms of payment including provisions for currency rate variation.
6. Transportation modes — container (LCL/FCL), air-freight, trailer, sea-freight.
7. Insurance — buyer's or seller's account.

The foregoing could be in the form of a pro forma invoice to raise funds through the bank for payment of the goods.

The following aspects must be followed up both before and after the order has been placed:

1. Goods — quality, quantity and description. Ensure they comply with the buyer's needs especially in regard to the overall specification and conform with BSI standards. Adequate storage facilities must be available within the company; otherwise alternative arrangements will be required. A large bulk overseas purchase may offer favourable price concessions but it can generate cashflow and storage problems.
2. Payment — price and method (Letter of Credit, open account, or documents against payment or acceptance). Consultation should take place with the buyer's bank to conclude the most satisfactory arrangements. Provision should be made for any currency variation and the time-scale agreed. Payment arrangements should be concluded before the order is placed.
3. Shipment — modes of transport, route, transhipment, any constraints such as weight statutory obligations, and time-scale. If the buyer is undertaking the shipment arrangements it would be prudent to make cargo reservations on the flight or ship at an early date in consultation with his freight forwarder. The freight forwarder should be told of the order and instructed to put all the necessary transportation arrangements in hand, albeit on a provisional basis initially.
4. Insurance. If the buyer is arranging for the insurance cover such as under CFR the importer must put in hand at an early date the insurance provisions. In particular, contact an insurance broker specializing in cargo insurance — details of addresses are in the British Importer's Association annual handbook.
5. Documents. Contact the HM Customs Office when in doubt. The buyer must quickly establish the documentation required at customs clearance. This must be checked out before the order is placed and in consultation with the buyer's freight forwarder. It will be necessary to instruct the seller to supply specific documents.
6. Inspection requirements. It maybe necessary to have the goods examined prior to shipment. This can be arranged through an inspection agency such as SGS (see pages 174-6).

7. Transportation arrangements from the customs clearance depot. It will be necessary to conclude the transportation arrangements from the port or airport when delivery of the cargo is accepted following conclusion of the customs clearance. Provisional arrangements need to be put in hand when an estimated date of the arrival of the goods plus customs clearance period has been established.

The import manager will need to confer closely with other departments affected by the order: the production manager to process the raw materials or assemble the component parts; the distribution manager for despatch of the goods to clients (who maybe wholesalers, retailers or the end-user); the sales manager to promote the product; the accountant to arrange funding for the order. It is likely that the buyer will work closely with the import manager. Much benefit will accrue through regular in-house discussions by all interested departments to discuss import strategy and individual suppliers portfolios. An increasing number of importers use an import data folder (Figure 11.2). It should be studied closely.

11.6 CUSTOMS PROCEDURES

As we move towards the Single Entity Market in 1992 traders will be reviewing their customs arrangements to facilitate the changeover on 1 January 1993. At this date all physical examination of imports by customs will cease for goods originating from one of the member states of the EC. Present customs arrangements will remain for the importation of goods from countries outside the EC.

As explained on page 89 local import controls (LIC) have been in existence for some time, but traders have not favoured them strongly for a variety of reasons. However in the Autumn of 1989 HM Customs and Excise launched a new LIC package, the salient features of which are given below. Importers are urged to consider using it and study the relevant HM Customs and Excise Notice No. 464A. It reflects the HM Customs and Excise strategy to move away from examinations at seaports and airports consequent on 1992 and provide a localized service to the importer. Traders opting for the LIC system will find the implications of 1992 less severe when customs clearance at the seaport or airport will no longer operate.

1. Physical examination of the goods will be more audit-based with periodic examination of the trader's records and less physical examination of the goods.
2. The trader is obliged to let customs have details of the goods by telex or fax immediately such data comes to hand.

IMPORT DATA FOLDER

	PURCHASE ORDER No. or CONTRACT No.	

OVERSEAS SUPPLIER (Consignor)

SUPPLIER'S REP./AGENT (or Confirming House)

Date Order Placed

Our Internal Ref.

Time Difference
+
−   Hrs.

Contact Name | Tel. No. | Telex

Contact Name | Tel. No. | Telex

BUYER

CONSIGNEE (and Delivery Address if different to Buyer)

Import Licence No.

Payment Terms

L/C Number & Dates

Contact Name | Tel. No. | Telex

Contact Name | Tel. No. | Telex

ARRIVAL PORT CLEARING AGENT

TERMS OF DELIVERY (Incoterms)

Loading Point	
Discharge Point	
Vessel/Flight No.	
Container No.	
B/L - AWB No.	
Est. Arrival Date	@
Act. Arrival Date	@

See also back page

INSURANCE

Seller	Tick relevant box
Buyer	
Insured Value	

FREIGHT

| Prepaid | Tick relevant box |
| Collect | |

Contact Name | Tel. No. | Telex

DETAILS OF GOODS PURCHASED

Figure 11.2 Import Data Folder, reproduced by kind permission of Formecon Services Ltd.

NOTES	
Date	Record of All Actions Taken, Telephone Conversations, Etc.

Figure 11.2 (contd).

ENCLOSURES

Retain all relevant documents in Data Folder
Note inclusion thus ✔

Supplier's Quotation	
Costing Record	
Official Order to Supplier (Copy)	
Letter of Credit (Details)	
Import Licence (Details)	
Supplier's Order Acknowledgement	
Supplier's Despatch Advice	
Instructions to Import Clearing Agent	
Supplier's Invoice (Copy)	
Bill of Lading / AWB (duplicate)	
Insurance Certificate	
Health Certificate	
Preferential Certificate	
Supplier's Certificate of Origin	
Supplier's Packing Spec. Note	

NOTES

Figure 11.2 (contd).

RECORD OF ORDER COMPRISING MORE THAN ONE IMPORTATION

Individual Consignments	Despatched from Supplier	Mode of Despatch *Sea Freight, Air Freight, Road, Rail Post (Air or Surface)*	E T A	Received at Destination
Number and Content of Packages	Date	Mode (Name / Number)	Place and Date	Date

DISTRIBUTION / RESALE OF CONSIGNMENT

Date	Delivered to	Item Ref.	Quantity	Price	Balance of Item Remaining	Remarks

RECORD OF CLAIMS

Date	Description of Item(s) Claimed for	Quantity	Value of Claim	Reason for Claim

Insurance Company		U.K. Agents		Appointed Surveyors	
Contact Name		Contact Name		Contact Name	
Tel. Number		Tel. Number		Tel. Number	

Figure 11.2 (contd).

3. Trailers moving from the seaport are not obliged to contain a customs seal from an EC state but require to do so from third countries (those outside the EC).
4. Both part and full loads can be processed through the LIC for clearance. This applies to both sea transport and air-freight.
5. Circumstances permit the trader and customs to agree on a mutually acceptable time-scale having regard to traffic patterns, resources available, physical distances involved and so on. This is a major benefit to the trader.
6. The requirement that cleared and non-cleared goods should be segregated at the traders premises no longer applies.
7. LIC facilities are granted on the basis of a maximum of 500 entries annually.
8. All health checks such as examination of beef carcasses will be examined at the LIC centre.
9. Customs entries must be via a computer system.

There are several alternative import procedures, the choice of which will depend on the consignment and the circumstances:

Temporary importations into the European Community. This involves the importer obtaining customs duty relief to particular goods temporarily imported into the European Community. It also embraces certain goods permanently imported for consumption or use at exhibitions or similar events. Additionally, the temporary importation covers the conditions and procedures for claiming relief from payment of VAT on goods temporarily imported from outside the Community for subsequent exportation from the United Kingdom.

Temporary imports from the European Community. This involves the temporary importation of goods from other Community countries. It also embraces relief from value added tax (VAT) for goods which will be re-exported unaltered.

Outward processing relief. This embraces a duty relief which applies to Community goods sent outside the Community for process and subsequent re-importation. Provided certain conditions are met, the goods, or goods produced from them can be re-imported with total or partial relief from import duties. The goods which result from the processing operations are termed 'compensating products'.

Inward processing relief — import duty relief for exports. The inward processing relief gives relief on goods coming from outside the

European Community if products made from them are exported outside the Community. It also gives relief from customs duty, agricultural charges and anti-dumping duty if prescribed conditions are met. A process can be anything from repacking or sorting of goods to the most complicated manufacturing. The system operates either through suspension or drawback. With suspension one does not pay the duty at import as long as one exports either the goods or the products you make from them. However, if one does not do either, one has to pay the duty. With drawback one pays the duty at import and claims it back if one exports the goods or the products made from them.

The following check list must be adhered to when using inward processing relief:

1. The importer must make application for inwards processing relief to the local excise officer prior to importation to obtain the requisite authority and establish the procedures.
2. The goods must be entered for inwards processing relief at the time of import. It is not possible to reclaim relief retrospectively.
3. Inwards processing relief applies only to duty relief and not to VAT.
4. In the event of the importer not knowing the percentage or proportion of goods which will be re-exported, it is possible to use the drawback system.
5. Export to a third country means an overseas territory outside the European Community.
6. To avoid misinterpretation it is desirable the importer apportions a part of the consignment one expects to re-export to inward processing relief and the residue to the home market for free circulation.
7. It is not possible for the importer to switch from inwards processing relief to free circulation when the firm decision has been taken with customs to adopt inwards processing relief.

Customs warehousing. This is a facility for the duty-free storage of imported goods; goods liable to import duty or otherwise not in free circulation in the UK can be stored free of duty and VAT in premises approved by HM Customs and Excise. Customs warehousing is ideal under the following circumstances: for the importer who wishes to delay paying duty on stocks of imported goods; for re-exportation of imported good (in which case import duty and VAT may not be payable at all); when, at the time of import, there is difficulty in meeting particular conditions such as certain import licensing requirements; where, for financial or marketing reasons, there is no immediate use for the goods, and the importer is therefore happy to allow the goods to remain warehoused after benefiting from a volume purchase at a competitive price. The facility also caters for goods originally imported into another customs regime (such as inward processing relief or free circulation) where relief from or repayment of import duty depends on the re-export of the goods. The duty and VAT becomes payable by the importer immediately the goods are withdrawn from the customs warehouse for home consumption.

Free ports/free trade zones. A free trade zone is an area where trade is based upon the unrestricted international exchange of goods with customs tariffs used only as a source of revenue and not as an impediment to trade development. Goods imported are not subjected to any duty or VAT until they actually leave the free trade zone. If their destination is another foreign country, they are permitted to leave the free trade zone without duty or VAT payment. For the home market they are subject to duty and VAT payments. Such facilities exist at main ports such as Liverpool and Southampton.

Transhipment. Goods being transhipped from one vessel to another to continue their journey are immune from duty and VAT.

Rejected imports: repayment of duty and tax. Importers can claim repayment of import duty, excise duty and VAT. This may arise because the goods are defective, damaged before being cleared by Customs, or do not comply with the terms of the international trade contract. It may also be granted on goods sent in error, which failed to get an expected relief, which were wrongly ordered or which are unsaleable, unusable or received late. The regulations regarding this facility are very severe.

Home use — entry for free circulation. This is the most common method whereby goods are imported for home use and thereby are in free circulation. In such circumstances the customs entry must be lodged up to 4 days before the arrival of the carrying vessel or aircraft. It involves the completion of C105B customs declaration (see page 199). The goods must be identified by a Tariff Trade Code Number and must be described in accordance with the tariff. This determines the duty level. The description includes their value and country of origin, the name and nationality of the carrying vessel or aircraft, the ports or airports of arrival and departure, the Bill of Lading or Air Waybill number and the marks and numbers on the cases or packages in the consignment.

Pre-entry system. The import entry generally described as the pre-entry system has to be supported by the consignment documents such as commercial invoices, packing list, Certificates of Origin, Health Certificate, etc. The customs entry declaration may involve the Single Administration Document (see page 77) or form C105. Alternative customs forms maybe required plus supporting consignment documents according to circumstances. These may include an import licence. An out of charge note issued by Customs (provided the entry is passed) will receive an official stamp and become the authority to release the goods out of customs charge into 'free circulation'. Documents which are not available or arrive late present serious problems to the importer. Facilities exist for telex information, facsimiles, and declarations to be lodged in place of certain originals but this excludes Certificates of Origin and the import licences.

Period entry scheme.   To amplify the documentation required for the import of goods HM Customs and Excise have devised the period entry imports scheme. This allows approved importers to obtain clearance on their goods by presenting a single simplified document (form C91) plus commercial invoices to cover a complete shipment. The detailed information to support the import of goods under the scheme must be processed by the importer on computer and the results submitted periodically to HM Customs on magnetic media or by data transmission. Clearance of the goods is not held up while this information is prepared by the importer or his agent. All goods imported under an Open General Licence that also qualify for deferment of duty can be imported using the period entry (imports) scheme.

12 *Import facilitation organizations*

There are an increasing number of organizations in international trade which are either allied to international distribution arrangements or provide direct help to the importer in the facilitation of international trade, product selection, and so on.

12.1 THE BALTIC EXCHANGE

A large volume of world tonnage is engaged in tramping. These vessels are employed under a document called a Charter Party wherein a shipowner agrees to the charterer engaging a vessel for a specific voyage or period of time (Details in Chapter 15 of *Elements of Shipping*, see Appendix A.)

The voyage charter relates to a stated voyage to carry a specified amount of cargo at so much per tonne. Time charters contract for the hire of a vessel for a specified period of time. There are two types of time charters (1) when the charterer hires the vessel 'all found' and (2) where the owner hires his ship for a period to the charterers to be operated by them as they wish, the charterers supplying crew and fuel, and paying all costs for one agreed rate of hire known as a 'bare-boat' or demise charter. These charter rates fluctuate almost daily in accordance with the conditions of supply and demand operating in the market. The importer with a shipload of cargo is likely to charter a vessel under non-demise voyage Charter Party terms engaging the services of a shipbroker.

A considerable amount of the world chartering is undertaken on the Baltic Exchange where the shipowners and charterers are able to arrange their business under conditions of reliability through a shipbroker. The Exchange is situated in London, and has over 600 member companies involving over 2000 individual men and women who are entitled to trade on the 'floor' of the exchange. Its work may be divided into four main classes:

1. Purchase and sale of oil seeds and vegetable oils.
2. Purchase and sale of grains.

3. Chartering of ships or space in ships for the carriage of all types of cargo to and from all ports of the world.
4. Chartering of aircraft or space in aircraft for cargo or passengers.

Chartering operations represent the most numerous transactions on the Baltic Exchange, and are mainly concerned with, although not entirely confined to, tramp ships. The dealers on the Exchange are known as chartering agents who represent charterers, that is, the merchants and other interests who charter ships to carry their cargoes (see page 221). Others known as owners' brokers, represent the shipowners. Additionally, there are many broking firms who have both charterers and shipowners among their clients, who may be in London or anywhere else in the world. Many merchants and shipowners are members of the Exchange and have their own chartering staff in the Exchange, who take the place of chartering agents and brokers but perform the same function.

A number of other activities take place on the floor of the Exchange as mentioned earlier involving commodities and futures trading. Under the umbrella of the newly formed Baltic Futures Exchange (BFE), future trades are undertaken by members of BFE in Freight (BIFFEX Dry Bulk Cargo contract), grain (wheat and barley), potatoes (main and earlies), soya bean meal (pigment and beef). BIFFEX (the Baltic International freight Futures Market) was opened in 1 May 1985 (see *Elements of Shipping*, pages 192–196). A BIFFEX futures contract is traded against the Baltic Freight Index (BFI) published daily. Each of these futures markets is conducted across a 'ring' during two trading sessions held daily, each session being opened and closed by the ringing of a bell. This 'open outcry' system means that contracts are made as a result of bids and offers across the ring so that all traders are aware of market prices, and have an equal opportunity of doing business. In active sessions hundreds of contracts can be traded in a matter of minutes.

Airbroking is another of the activities of members of the Baltic Exchange, involving aircraft operating companies from all parts of the world. The Baltic Air Charter Association (BACA) is the trade body of the airbrokers.

In August 1987 the London Corn Exchange moved to the floor of the Exchange where it holds its weekly market session on Mondays.

12.2 BRITISH IMPORTERS CONFEDERATION (BIC)

The British Importers Confederation (BIC) aims to look after the interests of parties concerned with importing into the UK. It is the flagship of the importing business and grows in influence annually. Membership is comprised of individual businesses and import trade associations. There are three types of membership:

Ordinary membership. Open to companies, firms, partnerships or sole traders in the United Kingdom principally concerned with importing or providing import services.

Association membership. Open to trade associations and similar organizations in the United Kingdom whose members are concerned with importing.

International membership. Open to foreign organizations engaged in trade or promotion of trade with the United Kingdom.

The Confederation works in close consultation with Government Departments and HM Customs and Excise when new import policies and tariffs are being negotiated, and acts as a pressure group representing the interests of importers. Its services can be summarized as follows:

1. It is the only organization in the UK representing the interests of United Kingdom importers, irrespective of the goods in which they deal.
2. It represents importers' views to the British Government, the European Commission in Brussels, and all who influence trade.
3. It is concerned both with general trade policy and with specific problems faced by members.
4. Membership provides the opportunity to influence policy and the regulations that affect import business. Members gain early and detailed knowledge of official proposals relating to trade issues.
5. The Brussels connection enables traders to put their case most effectively to the European Commission. It also provides members with early warning of future EC moves that may affect trade.
6. It has representation on a number of International Trade and Customs Committees and Associations, including Joint Customs Consultative Committees; Customs/Trade Associations Group; and EC Advisory Committee on Customs.
7. It maintains close contact with government departments such as the Department of Trade and Industry, and is consulted on matters relating to import restraints, safety regulations, shipping and other issues which influence trade.
8. It is represented on the Port Users Consultative Committees in London and Liverpool, and also has direct access to other Port Authorities, Shipping/Liner Conferences, and IATA.
9. Members receive frequent circulars on matters of concern to importers and also regular newsletters.
10. It organizes regular seminars for its members on customs, finance transportation and product liability.
11. Ministers and other prominent personalities are invited to informal discussions at luncheons organized for members.

12. It helps members to arrange meetings with potential overseas exporters and provides advice on any aspects of import practice.

The governing body of the BIC is its Council which consists of the honorary officers, elected ordinary members and representatives of each member association. The Council is advised by an Executive Committee of experienced members of the Council. The Transport Sub-Committee is concerned with all matters relating to the movement of goods. This includes customs activities.

The Trade Committees carry out valuable work on behalf of its members. For example, the Clothing and Textiles Sub-Committee performs a most important function as a liaison group between importers and the Department of Trade and Industry in the discussion of restraints on imports of textiles and garments. Sections covering footwear, hardware and electrical goods enable the Confederation to convene *ad hoc* committees on any trade issue. There are 19 member associations including Basketware Importers' Association; British Jewellery and Giftware Association; British Photographic Importers' Association; Fruit Importers' Association; Glass and Allied Trades Association; Honey Importers and Packers Association; British Sports and Allied Industries Federation; International Consumer Electronics Association; Toy and Giftware Importers Association; and Watch and Clock Importers' Association (see Appendix C).

The BIC also produces a bi-monthly magazine *Importing Today* which keeps members up-to-date on developments within the industry and opportunities. It has a high profile and contains many articles of interest to importers.

There is no doubt that BIC contribute to the development of a high professional profile of the British import industry. Companies are urged to become members of BIC and also of their Import Trade Association (see Appendix B).

12.3 BRITISH OVERSEAS TRADE BOARD

The British Overseas Trade Board (BOTB) is a government agency striving to support and stimulate the sale of UK products overseas. It receives an annual grant from the Department of Trade and Industry. The BOTB role includes promotion, development and facilitation of UK exports embracing re-exports; overseas market advice and information service; statistics and market intelligence library; export market research; inward missions; outward missions; trade fairs; overseas seminars and so on.

The importer involved in the re-export business can obtain much useful advice and data through the BOTB services or through its Regional Offices under the auspices of the Department of Trade and Industry Enterprise Scheme.

12.4 BRITISH STANDARDS INSTITUTION AND INSPECTION SERVICES

All imported manufactured goods must meet UK standards, details of which are available from the British Standards Institution. Certain goods, drugs and dangerous commodities are restricted or banned under the requirements of the 'Other Prohibitions and Restrictions' legislation. Restrictions are placed on the importation of sensitive agricultural and animal products. Some of these products are banned. The UK Government have also concluded voluntary export restraint agreements with Japan and a few other countries limiting the value or volume of goods which maybe imported into the UK. Trade arrangements with USSR and other Eastern European countries provide for quotas on some manufactured products and special import permits for these are necessary.

The potential importer, therefore, should check the import product specification with the appropriate organization – the British Standards Institution, HM Customs and Excise, Department of Trade and Industry, British Overseas Trade Board, trade association, Import Licensing Branch, etc., (see Appendix B) – before embarking on import strategy. This will indicate whether the product may be imported and whether any specification modification is required. The needs of 1992 must also be considered.

Legislation exists in the UK and in many other countries regarding the sale of goods, consumer protection, and product liability. Under the *Sale of Goods Act* retailers are required to offer for sale only goods of merchantable quality. *The Consumer Act* places a responsibility on the manufacturer or importer to place only safe goods on the market and also legislates for misleading advertising. In regard to product liability, the EC is currently drawing up new regulations which place stricter liability on the manufacturer for damage caused by defective products. The importer can usually ensure that standards and specification are met and maintained by engaging the inspection services for testing raw materials and manufactured goods dealt with on page 218.

The British Standards Institution determines the standard or specification of a product through a committee system. The best available knowledge is used and the standard defined legally defines the product. The importer may regard this standard as the norm or as a minimum standard (when choosing to import goods of superior specification). The importer should ensure that all quotations for supplies are based on this standard; if in doubt the importer should submit details and/or samples to the British Standards Institution for their guidance.

Testing of a product can also be undertaken by the British Standards Institution who work on behalf of government departments for trading standards officers; private clients; certification bodies such as the British Electrotechnical Approvals Board, and many laboratories.

Test laboratories are co-ordinated by the National Test Laboratory Accreditation Service, which is used widely by importers. There are some 300 laboratories accredited to the National Test Laboratory Scheme, including the one from the British Standards Institution. They can give the importer an assurance of competence.

The importer can ensure the manufacturer maintains continuous standards by adopting the British Standards BS 5750: Quality systems concept, published in 1979. Additionally, the British Standards Institution Quality Assurance Service provides an independent assessment of the supplier's quality system.

It is appropriate to mention the British Standards Institution Kitemark Scheme, which has been in operation many years. It covers the Wool Mark, BEAB Mark, BASEC for electric cables and so on. This enables the importer to indicate that not only has the product been produced to the BSI specification, but also it has been tested and certified by them. The Kitemark scheme requires that the product is typed tested; the manufacturer has a quality system to BS 5750, and the compliance of the product is kept under constant surveillance through visits to the manufacturer by BSI inspectors and periodic audit testing.

In 1989 HM Government recognized the importance of ensuring that certification bodies are competent, and established the National Accreditation of Certification Bodies.

There is no doubt that the practice of testing for quality under the pre-shipment aegis (pages 174-6) will be expanded as the import volume of manufactured goods rises and the consumer becomes more discerning. Companies which fulfil this role include: Bayliss Brown Ltd, The Banks, Long Buckby, Northants, NN6 7QO; Cotecna Inspection Ltd, 17 Berkeley Street, London, W1X 5AE; SGS Inspection Services Ltd, 329–331 London Road, Camberley, Surrey; Yarsley Technical Centre Ltd, Trowers Way, Redhill, Surrey, RH1 2JN.

An increasing number of importers are now adopting the pre-shipment inspection procedure which has been developed by the International Federation of Inspection Agencies (IFIA). It involves the following code of practice:

1. Activities of pre-shipment inspection companies (PIC) in the country of export may be undertaken on behalf of a foreign government, government agency, central bank, importer (buyer) or other appropriate governmental authority and may include:
   (a) physical inspection for quantity and quality of goods;
   (b) verification of export prices, including financial terms of the export transaction and currency exchange rates where appropriate;
   (c) support services to the customs authorities of the country of importation.
2. The general procedures for physical inspection of goods and the

examination of the price of exports out of any particular country will be the same in all exporting countries and the specific requirements established by the importing country will be administered by the PIC in a consistent and objective manner.

3. The PIC will provide assistance to exporters by furnishing information and guidelines necessary to enable exporters to comply with the pre-shipment inspection regulations of the importing country. This assistance on the part of the PIC is not intended to relieve exporters from the responsibility for compliance with the import regulations of the importing country.

4. Quantity and quality inspections will be performed in accordance with accepted national and/or international standards.

5. The conduct of pre-shipment activities should facilitate legitimate foreign trade and assist bona fide exporters by providing independent evidence of compliance with the laws and regulations of the importing country.

6. Pre-shipment activities will be conducted and the Clean Report of Findings, or notice of non-issuance thereof, will be sent to the exporter in a timely and convenient manner.

7. Confidential business information will not be shared by the PICs with any third party other than the appropriate government authority for which the inspection in question is being performed.

8. Adequate procedures to safeguard all information submitted by exporters will be maintained by the PIC, together with proper security for any information provided in confidence to them.

9. The PIC will not request from exporters information regarding manufacturing data related to patents (issued or pending) or licensing agreements. Nor will the PIC attempt to identify the cost of manufacture, level of profit or, except in the case of exports made through a buying agent or a confirming house, the terms of contracts between exporters and their suppliers.

10. The PIC will avoid conflicts of interest between the PIC, any related entities of the PIC or entities in which the PIC has a financial interest, and companies whose shipments the PIC is inspecting.

11. The PIC will state in writing the reason for any decision declining issuance of a Clean Report of Findings.

12. If a rejection occurs at the stage of physical inspection the PIC will, if requested by the exporter, arrange the earliest date for re-inspection.

13. Whenever so requested by the exporter, and provided no contrary instruction has been issued by the government authority, the PIC will undertake a preliminary price verification prior to receipt of the import licence on the basis of the binding contractual documents, pro forma invoice and application for import approval. An invoice price

and/or currency exchange rate that has been accepted by the PIC on the basis of such preliminary price verification will not be withdrawn, provided the goods and the previously submitted documentation conform with the information contained in the import licence. The Clean Report of Findings, however, will not be issued until appropriate final documents have been received by the PIC.

14. Price verification will be undertaken on the basis of the terms of the sales contract and it will take into consideration any generally applicable and allowable adjusting factors pertaining to the transaction.

15. Commissions due to an agent in the country of destination will be treated in strict confidence by the PIC, and will only be reported to the appropriate government authority when so requested.

16. Exporters or importers who are unable to resolve differences with the PIC may appeal in writing, stating facts of the specific transaction and the nature of the complaint, directly to a designated appeals official of the PIC. Exporters wishing to appeal the results of a pre-shipment inspection may also seek review of the decision of the PIC in the importing country.

In cases where a PIC is considered not to have observed any article of this Code of Practice, this may be reported to the Director General of IFIA.

Two types of inspection are most commonly employed: the production check and the final random inspection. Production checks are carried out both at the beginning of the manufacturing process and half-way through the production run. An inspector will draw samples at random according to modern, internationally-recognized statistical procedures such as BS 6001 and will then check them against agreed specifications and samples. Any defects or non-conformities will immediately be notified to both the buyer and the supplier so corrective action can be taken and potential delays avoided or reduced.

The final random inspection is normally undertaken when the whole consignment has been produced and at least 80% has been packed and made ready for export. Samples are again drawn according to internationally-recognized procedures, and only provided they conform to agreed quality levels, will a satisfactory certificate be provided to the supplier to enable him to obtain payment from the bank. Hence the importer is able to monitor the quality of his goods throughout the production process, and to obtain confirmation that they meet all his specifications before the exporter despatches the consignment and is paid. Payment is controlled by the insertion of a clause in the Letter of Credit or other method of payment, stating that a satisfactory certificate of inspection is required. The document involved is the pre-shipment certificate. This embraces the six-part Export Declaration Document; a five-part inspection report and a two-part inspection report and clean report of findings (*Import/Export Documentation*, pages 61—78, see Appendix A).

12.5 CHARTERED SHIPBROKERS

The basic function of the shipbroker is to bring together the two parties concerned, involving the ship and cargo owners. Following negotiations between them, a Charter Party is ultimately concluded. The brokers' income is derived from the commission payable by the shipowner on completion and fulfilment of the contract.

A further role of the shipbroker, other than fixing vessels, is acting as agent for the shipowner. As such, he is responsible for everything which may concern the vessel whilst she is in port — customs formalities, matters concerning the crew, loading and discharge of vessels, bunkering and victualling, etc.

Duties of the shipbroker can be summarized as follows:

1. Chartering agent, whereby he acts for the cargo merchant seeking a suitable vessel in which to carry the merchandise.
2. Sale and purchase broker acting on behalf of the buyer or seller of ships, and bringing the two parties together.
3. Owner's broker whereby he acts for the actual shipowner in finding cargo for the vessel.
4. Tanker broker dealing with oil tanker tonnage.
5. Coasting broker involving vessels operating around the British coast and/or in the short sea trade, e.g. UK—Continent. At the same time, he can act for the cargo merchant in this trade should circumstances so dictate. The deep-sea broker, however, will act for the shipowner or cargo merchant, but not at the same time.
6. Cabling agent, involving communication with other international markets.

12.6 CONFEDERATION OF BRITISH INDUSTRY (CBI)

The Confederation of British Industry was founded in 1965 and is an independent, non-party political body financed entirely by industry and commerce. It is the principal focal point for the British Business community's views and exists primarily to ensure that UK Governments of all political complexions understand the needs, intentions and problems of British business. The CBI represents more than 17 000 individual companies and more than 200 trade associations, employer organizations and commercial associations. It covers all sectors of business, from manufacturing to agriculture, construction to distribution, and mining to finance.

The CBI has a regional network and its prime objective is to facilitate the development of British Business and Commerce. Importers can obtain much useful data from the regional and national offices of the CBI. Regular seminars and business luncheons are held on specific topics, which give members the opportunity to exchange views and develop ideas.

12.7 FREIGHT TRANSPORT ASSOCIATION (FTA) (INCORPORATING THE BRITISH SHIPPERS' COUNCIL (BSC))

The British Shippers' Council was founded in 1955 to further the interests of importers and exporters in the United Kingdom in all matters concerning the overseas transport of their goods, whether by sea or air. The Council was the first such national body to be formed but, under the stimulus of organizations such as the International Chamber of Commerce and UNCTAD, the movement has spread rapidly in the last 35 years and there are few significant trading countries which do not now possess one. Since the early 1960s, the movement has become particularly strong in Western Europe where there are now 14 national councils, many of whose activities are co-ordinated through an International Secretariat at the Hague.

The British Shippers' Council is an independent, voluntary functional trade association whose membership comprises other trade associations, representing most of the major industries of the country (including the Confederation of British Industry and the Association of British Chambers of Commerce) as well as individual trading companies numbering some 150. It is widely recognized both in governmental and commercial circles as the representative body of the users of international freight transport.

In mid-1979, the Council was absorbed into the Freight Transport Association (FTA), the membership of which ranges from small businesses operating only one or two small vans to the largest industrial concerns in the country. Hauliers, other transport providers, local authorities, statutory boards and indeed anyone with an interest in freight transport and distribution are also to be found in the ranks of the associate members.

About 90% by value, and a much higher percentage by volume, of international trade is carried by sea. The remainder is carried by air. It is thus natural and inevitable that the main emphasis of the Council's work has been with the problems and costs of the sea carriage of our goods but, in recent years, much more attention has been given to the interests of the air shipper. It is fair to say also that the majority of our import trade is bought on CIF or similar terms, and even where goods are bought Ex Works or FOB, it is frequently the case that the seller acts as agent for the buyer in arranging the shipment. Thus, no matter what the terms of sale, the importer has a direct interest in the cost of the overseas movement of his goods and in the efficiency with which they are handled and carried, so that their delivered price may be competitive. These considerations tend to place the main emphasis of the FTA's work on import trades.

The FTA is consulted by Government when new transport laws are under consideration. In addition, with the agreement of the CBI, it represents the UK on the important transport commission of UNICE, the organization covering the whole of industrial interest in the 12 EC countries. Additionally, FTA has its own contacts with EC officials responsible for transport and with similar bodies in all other 11 EC states. It is currently involved in the 1992 Single European Market developments.

The FTA is a service-based organization offering a wide range of tangible services, including consultancy, engineering, cost and rates, and wages, education, and training and information.

12.8 INTERNATIONAL AIR TRANSPORT ASSOCIATION (IATA)

The International Air Transport Association is a voluntary, non-exclusive, non-political and democratic organization. Membership is automatically open to any operating company which has been licensed to provide scheduled air services by a government eligible for membership of the International Civil Aviation Organization (ICAO). Airlines directly engaged in international operations are active members, while domestic airlines are associate members. Some 98% of scheduled international air services are operated by IATA members. The airlines have achieved a great deal of standardization through IATA, which has contributed greatly to the development of the business. It operates through committees and is responsible for: documentation − Air Waybill; freight rates; appointment of IATA freight agents; dangerous cargo code, and a wide range of similar commercial activities in the passenger sector.

12.9 INTERNATIONAL CHAMBER OF COMMERCE (ICC)

The fundamental role of the International Chamber of Commerce is to promote an expansion in international trade and investment by encouraging national economic growth. Its objective is the integration of the business community's approach to world economic progress and problems. The ICC is represented in 101 countries where it functions through national committees and councils. Its headquarters are in Paris. It has over twenty commissions and committees dealing with multi-national enterprises; international monetary relations; international trade, industrial and commercial policy; energy; insurance; taxation; banking technique and practice; maritime transport studies, air transport etc. Their publications. *Incoterms 1990* and *Uniform Customs and Practice of Documentary Credits* (see Appendix A) closely involve the importer.

The range of these activities demonstrates the breadth of influence of the ICC today in developing world trade on the sound basis of ethical, economic and financial codes of practice. Its importance will grow as a result of the increasing integration of the world economy in the years to come. The ICC will continue to play a foremost role in preparing codes of business practices, facilitating international trade and investment through the harmonization and standardization of trade practices, and finally to provide a central forum for the discussion of policy problems faced by businessmen in communities throughout the world.

12.10   INTERNATIONAL MARITIME ORGANIZATION (IMO)

The International Maritime Organization is a specialized agency of the United Nations concerned solely with maritime affairs. Its interest lies mainly in ships used in international services. Altogether 131 states are members of IMO, including ship-owning nations, countries which use shipping services and countries in the course of development.

The objectives of IMO are to facilitate co-operation among governments on technical matters affecting shipping, particularly from the angle of life at sea, and the prevention of marine pollution from ships. This entails providing an extensive exchange of information between nations on technical maritime subjects and the concluding of international agreements. IMO is responsible for the code of practice regarding the shipment of dangerous classified cargo embracing stowage, documentation, labelling, packaging and the nine classifications (pages 53-4).

12.11   LINER CONFERENCES

The Liner conference is an organization whereby a number of shipowners offer their services in a given sea route on conditions agreed by the members. They are, in other words semi-monopolistic associations of shipping lines formed for the purpose of restricting competition between their members and protecting them from outside competition.

Conference agreements may regulate sailings and ports of call, and, in some cases, arrangements are made for the pooling of net earnings. They control prices and limit entry to the trade. Their chief policy is to establish a common tariff of freight rates and passenger fares for the trade involved, members being left free to compete for traffic by the quality and efficiency of their service. The organization of a conference varies from one trade to another. It may consist of informal regular meetings of shipowners at which rates and other matters of policy are discussed, or it may involve a formal organization with a permanent secretariat and prescribed rules for membership, together with stipulated penalties for violations of the agreement. Members are often required to deposit a cash bond to cover fines in respect of non-compliance with their obligations to such conferences, which are international in character. For example, the Far East Freight Conference, which operates in the Far East — European trade, comprises British, French, Dutch, Italian, Swedish, Danish and Japanese lines. Shipping lines often belong to several conferences and there are several inter-conference agreements. In most cases, conference policy is decided by the votes of the members. Conference rights have a market value when shipping lines are sold. An area of controversy in the liner conference system is the deferred rebate system whereby the conference retains the rebate for 6 months and payment is only made to the shipper if he remains loyal to the conference.

Overall there are some 365 liner conferences and some 75% of liner deep-sea trade is conveyed under the liner conference system.

12.12 LONDON CHAMBER OF COMMERCE AND INDUSTRY

The London Chamber of Commerce was founded in 1881. It has two main functions: to protect the domestic trade interests of commerce and industry in London and the South East, and to develop the international trade of all British companies. An examination will be made of the latter.

The Chamber has a membership of some 7000 firms covering all business sectors. Its operations are divided into departments — international, export services, home affairs, economic, press, administration, membership, finance and trade. It issues export documents and these include primarily Certificates of Origin, ATA carnets, national standard shipping notes, movement certificates, cocoa certificates and the certification of commercial invoices. The Chamber is the UK guarantor for ATA carnets which allow the temporary importation into other countries of certain types of goods. The Chamber deals with a wide range of enquiries concerning customs, legislation and regulations both in Britain and throughout the world. It also deals with tariffs and the general rules and conditions governing the movement and finance of re-export and imports.

The London Chamber of Commerce and Industry is the largest of 50 Chambers in the United Kingdom. Importers are urged to join their local Chamber and obtain the benefits of their seminars and business luncheons. It provides an opportunity to obtain new ideas and meet other importers.

12.13 SIMPLER INTERNATIONAL TRADE PROCEDURES BOARD (SITPRO)

SITPRO was set up in June 1970 to 'guide, stimulate and assist the rationalisation of international trade procedures and the information flows associated with them'. The Board's members include shippers, carriers, forwarders, bankers and government officials. The staff is small, consisting of a chief executive and secretary with directors and their assistants dealing with various areas of SITPRO activities. The Board is financed by the Department of Trade and Industry through an annual grant but is independent within its agreed terms of reference.

SITPRO work is primarily concerned with International Trade facilitation and has contributed extensively worldwide in this area since its formation. It has developed the SPEX computer facility which has proved popular and enabled many exporters and importers to computerize their international trade documentation work at low cost. Currently SITPRO is developing EDI (electronic data interchange) in consultation with banks, carriers, shippers and so on. SITPRO issues a house magazine which is available free and enables exporters and importers to keep up to date on developments and opportunities in international trade.

12.14 RESEARCH ASSOCIATION FOR THE PAPER AND BOARD, PRINTING AND PACKAGING INDUSTRIES (PIRA)

PIRA, located at Leatherhead, Surrey, is the UK national technical centre for paper and board, printing and packaging, carrying out research work for the benefits of its members. It also undertakes multi-client research projects for groups of members and confidential sponsored work for individual firms. Other services for management include consultancy, technical enquiry, testing, information, training, and techno-economic studies.

Given below is a summary of PIRA services of particular interest to importers and re-exporters:

1. Courses available for packaging staff at all levels. These can be arranged either at PIRA premises or in the shipper's own works.
2. Supply of information on packaging suppliers' regulations and appropriate standards.
3. Measurement, testing or analysis of the properties of packaging materials to enable shippers to prepare adequate specifications; to check that the materials conform to packaging requirements or recognized standards; to assess their ability to withstand transit conditions; and finally, to detect and prevent anything harmful in a specific packaging material.
4. To evaluate in laboratory conditions at PIRA the performance of filled packages under simulated international transit conditions.
5. To arrange consultancy facilities in, for example, (a) the development of packaging for new products, (b) techniques to reduce packaging costs and to improve the protection provided by existing packs, and (c) how best to organize the packaging activity in the exporter's company.
6. The Association library provides members with English translations of selected articles on packaging extracted from overseas publications. It also undertakes literature searches and the compilation of bibliographies.

Each month PIRA produces three technical journals: *Paper and Board Abstracts, Printing Abstracts* and *Packing Abstracts*. A fourth publication, also issued monthly, is called *PIRA Management and Marketing Abstracts*.

PIRA is a useful organization to contact when the importer wishes to improve the packaging specification and techniques to lessen the risk of damage, pilferage, improve stowage, aid handling and ensure the goods arrive in a marketable condition.

12.15 ROAD HAULAGE ASSOCIATION (RHA)

The assistance given by the RHA to its members in relation to international movement of goods is threefold: the provision of certain customs documents; general information on the regulations and conditions in Europe and the Middle East; representing the British international hauliers' point of view to the Government, EC and other transport associations in Europe.

The RHA is a member of the International Road Transport Union (IRU) in Geneva, which is the guaranteeing body for the issue of TIR carnets. The TIR carnet is a very important document which allows vehicles, when properly approved, to pass through foreign frontiers, usually without inspection of the goods, and it also acts as a bond. The RHA is able to make this document available to those of its members who have provided the appropriate indemnity, enabling them to participate in international haulage to countries outside the EC. Within the EC, the guarantee voucher provided by the RHA acts as a guarantee to the customs authorities in the European Community, Austria and Switzerland.

The RHA has prepared information sheets on all the countries in Europe and many in the Middle East, providing basic information on the need for transport authorizations and where they may be obtained, the regulations governing weights and dimensions of vehicles, traffic restrictions, taxes and other relevant matters. These sheets are regularly revised to take account of changes in different countries. The Association also publishes, from time to time, through circulars, its journal *Road Way* and its new electronic information dissemination and network system 'Cargo fax', and additional information that it is able to acquire through its close contacts with the Department of Transport in this country and through other transport associations in Europe. Comprehensive information on all aspects of international haulage is, therefore, available to members both through documents and through consultation with officials.

The RHA represents the views of international members to the Department of Transport on all legislation affecting this type of operation. Moreover, through its connection with IRU, it is able to make its views known to the European Commission in Brussels; this is increasingly important with the introduction of more EC legislation on road transport. In addition, the RHA represents the views of its members to other associations in this country, including the Confederation of British Industry.

The RHA can assist the importer on the range of international road haulage services available, its regulations, the tariff structure, the operators and other useful market information.

12.16   UNITED KINGDOM TRADE AGENCY FOR DEVELOPING COUNTRIES (UKTA)

This is an organization established by the British Government Overseas Development Administration to provide assistance to developing countries planning to expand and diversify their export trade. Whilst helping exporters from overseas, they also assist UK businesses who import goods from developing countries. They act as the UK planning organization for trade missions from overseas and mount major international exhibitions where overseas companies exhibit their products. They also inform UK businesses of the latest international conventions relating to trade with developing countries and supply overseas companies with details of UK firms wishing to import goods.

12.17 WATCH AND CLOCK IMPORTERS' ASSOCIATION

This trade association was formed in 1948; its prime objective is to protect and promote its members' interests. Many of the members are either the UK subsidiaries of overseas manufacturers (Swiss and German in particular), or are tied by exclusive contracts to a large foreign manufacturer. Their function is, therefore, principally wholesale distribution. Trade associations represent the importers in national negotiations such as at Government and HM Customs and Excise level. Moreover they provide advice in importing techniques and a number run seminars/ training courses on import facilitation. The role of the trade association is becoming more important and particularly in working closely with the British Importers Confederation.

13 *Overseas business trips*

13.1 OBJECT OF OVERSEAS VISIT

The successful importer works closely with his/her manufacturer, a relationship which can benefit from regular overseas visits in the following ways:

1. A good professional relationship is built up and the importer can see at first hand the products being manufactured and meet the workforce and company executives.
2. The importer can keep up-to-date on the latest product developments and manufacturing technology. The importer can also quickly identify new business opportunities by attending demonstrations of new products within the exporter's environs.
3. The importer has the opportunity to review the overall efficiency of the distribution arrangements and resolve any inadequacies.
4. The importer and exporter can review their contractual arrangements and effect any desirable changes.
5. The importer can look at any competition.
6. The importer can conduct an audit of the exporter to establish their profile; position in the market; calibre of management and workforce; degree of technology used in manufacturing process; quality control and future investment plans.
7. Any dispute with the exporter can be resolved.

Other reasons for overseas visits include:

1. Attendance at a trade exhibition to identify a suitable exporter for a specified product, keep up-to-date with market and technological trends and review the competition.
2. Participation in a trade mission.
3. Attendance at an international trade convention to view exporters' exhibits for potential importers.
4. Selection of a suitable exporter from a shortlist, including an 'on the spot' investigation into the exporter's profile and visit to the manufacturing premises.

5. Selection of a suitable forwarding agent to handle all the imports from a specific buyer.

13.2   PLANNING THE OVERSEAS VISIT

Maximum benefit is achieved if an overseas trip is well planned. The following points are relevant.

1. Contact the importers' trade association (see pages 257-60) or the Chamber of Commerce of the country one is planning to visit to obtain details of prospective exporters. The importer's bank may be able to assist by contacting branch offices in the country to be visited.
2. Time the visit to ensure one does not arrive during any holiday period as most business personnel are likely to be away. Check out the normal working hours and any cultural differences.
3. Plan the itinerary to allow adequate time for travel and for seeing the various people with whom contact has to be made. A joint meeting involving the exporter and freight forwarder can resolve a distribution problem. Allow a modest time for any journey delays. An increasing number of travel agents provide a Travel Management Centre and Fares Advisory Unit to help business clients with routeing, fares, and schedules to meet their individual needs on a cost-effective basis. Such travel advice can prove very advantageous. All necessary visas must be obtained before leaving including 'transit visas' when merely stopping *en route*. If in doubt about the requirements for visas, seek advice from the Passport Office (Clive House, Petty France, London, SW14 9HD) or the local Trade Council Chamber of Commerce. All journeys should be booked in advance through an airline, ship or ferry operator, or an accredited travel agency. Ensure onward flight reservations are concluded as many carriers are often fully booked. Membership of a travel agents', airline, ferry operators' business club may prove beneficial in terms of discounted travel and hotel accommodation and regular issue of the business travellers' house magazine.
4. Ensure you are adequately briefed to meet your exporter. This would include (on a first visit to select an exporter) information on: the product specification in detail; the price range, the terms of sale, payment arrangements, warranty conditions; annual volume, method of shipment, spares availability and so on. Other items of significance will emerge from the series of 'in-house' meetings conducted with other departments prior to the departure date. It may be advantageous, for example, for an engineer to accompany the buyer on a visit to buy capital goods. Product samples and/or specification plans should be sought, evaluated and compared with those from other sources before arriving at a decision.

5. Ensure adequate personal insurance is arranged in all relevant areas. Baggage should be of modest proportions and clothes should be compatible with the climate and circumstances. Always appear smartly dressed when on business. If you cannot speak the language competently, an interpreter should be present at the meetings. The visit should allow adequate time for relaxation and the usual health precautions should be adopted, including any vaccinations prior to departure.

6. Ensure all the clients on your itinerary are aware of your visit and its purpose so that they are adequately prepared and senior staff are available. It maybe desirable to have a lawyer present in any complex contractual negotiations.

7. Details of your intinerary, including transport schedules, hotels and companies to be visited, should be prepared and deposited with a senior person 'in house' and next of kin so that you can be contacted quickly in an emergency. The hotel should have telephone, telex and fax facilities.

8. The country or countries to be visited should be adequately researched, especially within the context of the purpose of the visit and the product involved. Risk areas should be evaluated, especially attitudes towards external trade development, political situation, need for any export licences, any trade quota system in being, experience of previous UK importers, trading relations with UK; physical distribution resources, infrastructure and culture of the country. Above all, the importer should not rush into making a decision regarding a specific exporter but carefully evaluate the situation with his colleagues when he has returned home and conducted further 'in house' discussions. The price and product specification might be available from the exporter based on an Ex Works quotation, but other costs must be considered including distribution and customs duty (pages 202-4). Evaluation should also include the process of ensuring the imported product conforms with the UK Standards as specified by the British Standards Institute or other authorized body.

13.3 OVERSEAS BUSINESS TRIP – CHECK LIST ON IMPORT CONTROLS

The business person conducting/planning his/her overseas trip requires to be well informed/advised on import duties, exchange control regulations, taxes, and any other legislation affecting UK imports. A check list is given below:

1. Import regulations/tariffs of the specific product;

2. Acceptance of the commodity specification as specified by the British Standards Institute or other authorized body;
3. Customs duty on the product;
4. Nature of the packaging and marking;
5. Documentation requirements;
6. Payment arrangements;
7. Insurance and Incoterms 1990.

This area of preparation for the business trip requires close attention, and if necessary, consultation with the importers bank, freight forwarder, customs carrier etc. Adequate planning, strategy determination and costing are required. Data on other supply/product sources would be useful to enable comparisons to be made and the most competitive purchases realized. Such preparation will ensure the most meaningful/productive discussion/negotiations are concluded in the overseas market. A discussion plan would be useful.

14 *Transport distribution analysis*

14.1 THE SIGNIFICANCE OF SPEED, FREQUENCY, RELIABILITY, QUALITY, AND COST OF TRANSPORT FOR THE IMPORTER

During the past 20 years there has been extensive modernization in all forms of transport. This has resulted in quicker transits,more reliable schedules, more capital-intensive system, development of the most advanced technology, greater integration between modes of transport, permitting more intermodal transport systems, and so on. The importer now has a wider choice of transport systems to suit individual needs in a more competitive environment. Overall the modernization of transport systems worldwide encourages trade and develops new markets, especially in the areas of air-freight, international road haulage and containerization; countries and markets which are not served by modern transport systems internationally are at a major disadvantage in the development of their trade.

The five transport factors of particular relevance to the importer are detailed below:

Speed
Goods which shippers need to receive quickly include fashionable garments, perishable goods such as foodstuffs which are influenced by market prices, spares for cars and other manufactured items, etc. Speed of delivery reduces the lead-time between payment for the goods by the importer and the sale to the customer, who may be a retailer; it is particularly important to importers of consumer goods, avoiding the risk and expense of obsolescence if large stocks are carried. Clothes which are influenced by fashion and retail in a very sensitive market, are a good example here. Reduced stocks result in less warehouse space required, less working capital needed to run the company, and overall a better cashflow situation as the turnover is quicker. These factors strongly favour air-freight, which features very prominently in the distribution of fashionable clothes in certain trade routes, particularly the North Atlantic.

Commodities such as fresh fruit, and semi-frozen products, must have a regular and fast delivery, constraining the development of trade in these items to areas within a defined transit time-band. These factors are very relevant to the large volume of fruit imported from European countries to the UK by sea transport, TIR road vehicles and (sometimes) containers. Chilled or frozen products have less constraints upon them now with the enormous advancement in recent years in the techniques of despatching them in refrigerated containers, road vehicle units, and train ferry wagons.

Transit times have been most reduced by air-freight on the long distance routes, giving great benefit to the importer both in existing trades and in opening up new markets. Deep-sea container schedules have, too, revolutionized transit times in recent years and have made the liner service more competitive than air-freight in certain trades because of the 'cost of speed'. For the liner operator, speed is expensive both in terms of initial expenditure in the marine engines and the actual fuel cost; the aim is to provide a vessel with the maximum speed at optimum expense which will meet importers' needs. Speed is likewise very costly to the air-freight operator, however. Indeed, economically more so bearing in mind the limited capacity of the aircraft (averaging 30 tonnes) compared with the container vessel (with 2500 containers with a total of 40 000 tonnes of cargo), the economics of speed can put the air-freighter at a disadvantage. On the North Atlantic service, air-freighters have a capacity of up to 93 tonnes However, on an increasing number of routes (particularly across the North Atlantic) the wide-bodied air-freighter is being introduced such as the Boeing 747 permitting bulkier and heavier loads to be conveyed, with a capacity up to 93 tonnes. Consolidation involving numerous consignments conveyed in ULDs (small containers) under agent sponsorship has also contributed to the market expansion.

Further improvements will be achieved in transit times by development of the combined transport system probably of unitized cargo consignments and cargo being processed at an inland clearance depot or container freight station close to the importer's premises.

Speed is not so important when cargoes with relatively low values are being carried, as in the world tramp trades and where many trades are moving under programmed stockpiled arrangements. In this category are coal, minerals, ores, etc. These cargoes incur low transport costs. Oil transportation deserves particular mention: with over-production in the market in recent years there has been a tendency for oil tankers to operate at reduced speeds to sustain a larger operational fleet rather than resort to a number of tankers being laid up.

Frequency
Frequency of service is most important when goods can only be sold in small quantities at frequent intervals, but many importers prefer the

frequent service with the smaller shipment rather than a less frequent service with the larger shipment. Overall, it produces an improved cashflow for the importer, with less lead-time from payment for the goods until sale to the retailer or consumer. Other benefits include reduced risk of stock deterioration and less tie-up of capital in stock with its attendant warehouse risk. To offset such benefits the importer must bear in mind that the smaller consignment tends to be more expensive in cost per tonne shipped.

Frequency of service is a very strong point in favour of the air-freight operator, particularly in the long-distance markets. Frequent schedules coupled with fast transits enable stocks to be quickly replenished, thereby avoiding excessive stockpiling. The Ro/Ro services fulfil these criteria in the UK—Continental trade. Over 50 routes exist, the great majority offering daily services. On the more popular routes such as those to and from Dover there are up to ten sailings daily. The overnight services are the most practical to the international road haulier as the driver can have a good night's rest in preparation for the next day's driving. Both the frequency of service and night sailings enable the importer of perishable goods, to obtain maximum benefit in the market place by retailing quality goods at favourable prices. An increasing number of marketing boards representing the producers of perishable goods are storing their products in large refrigerated computer-controlled storage plants. This not only preserves the goods in a quality condition, but also enables the producer to ship the goods throughout the year at the most favourable prices and not flood the market in the production season at relatively lower prices. Deep-sea container services offer frequent schedules, often at regular time intervals such as every week or fortnight from specified ports.

To the tramp charterer frequency of sailings is not of paramount importance. He must not of course allow his stocks to run down too fast, but he will have a margin within which he can safely operate, and the importer will come in to buy and ship when market conditions suit him.

Reliability

Reliability is essential to the importer whose goods are shipped against an import licence expiry date and who must receive merchandise in a good condition. Failure to fulfil these criteria can result in lost markets, reduced market values, and much loss of good will. To the importer, therefore, reliability infers that the ship, air-freighter, international road haulage vehicle etc., will depart and arrive at the advertised time; the ship or air-freight operator will look after the cargo during pre-shipment throughout the voyage (road, rail or air transit) and after discharge; and finally, the operator can be relied upon to give adequate facilities at the

docks or airport and his offices to enable the appropriate documents and
other formalities to be satisfactorily completed.

Cost
Transport costing of individual services has become an important aspect
in transport management today. It is a commodity difficult to cost,
particularly when a multifarious service or joint supply is offered, for
example, a vehicular ferry conveying passengers, motorist, cars, coaches,
lorries and/or trailers. The position is more complex when on one sailing
the vessel conveys motorists with cars, whilst on another it is simply
lorries and trailers with drivers. The same applies to an aircraft which
may be exclusively used for passengers on one flight and for a mixture
of passengers and cargo on another.

The importer marketing goods of relatively low value must seek the
lowest possible transport charge, as the freight percentage of the total
value may have a direct bearing on the saleability of the commodity. The
tramp vessel is most suitable for this market. The importer has, thus, a
prime interest in the availability of tramp shipping space at any particular
time because freight and chartering rates will vary, reflecting the
economic forces of supply and demand. In a market situation where there
are plenty of vessels the importer will be able to charter at a fixture rate
level which will be only marginally above the operating cost of the
vessel. Conversely, when available shipping capacity is scarce the fixture
rate rises which places a limiting factor on the competitive price of the
commodity at the point of sale. Hence the importer must reconcile the
freight cost (by sea or air) under chartered conditions with the product
selling price in the market place.

In the liner trade and scheduled air-freight services the tariffs are more
stable and controlled primarily under the aegis of the liner conference
system or IATA. Both the ship and air operator are able to hold their
rates at a fair level to show a very modest profit margin based on a fairly
high load factor. In both the liner and air-freight markets the freight
forwarder and container operator are tending to play a greater role in
rate-making by offering not only the trunk haul (the maritime or flight
element), but also the feeder service (collection and delivery) to and from
the seaport, ICD, or airport, in their tariff structure. The rates are usually
based on W/M (weight/measurement) option.

Moreover, the freight forwarder, container operator and TIR road
haulier in the liner cargo trades and scheduled air-freight markets offer
facilities for consolidated consignments at very competitive rates and
transit times. This allows the importer to receive the goods quickly and
at a competitive rate which will aid marketing the commodity at a
favourable price. The importer is well advised to contact a number of
freight forwarders or IATA agents to obtain the best deal in rates, transit

times, service frequency, and so on.

A facility which is in its early stages of development is the international express air-freight network. TNT, for example, operates its own air-freighters worldwide and is served by its own fleet of road vehicles to and from the airports. The rates are very competitive and outside IATA control. TNT have their own consignment note covering the door-to-door transit and depots in all the countries they serve.

To conclude, it is evident that service standards will continue to improve to the benefit of the importer and international trade development.

14.2 SELECTION OF THE MOST SUITABLE MODE OF TRANSPORTING AN INTERNATIONAL CONSIGNMENT

With the continuing expansion of international trade in many markets coupled with the increase in the range and extent of transport services available, the importer must evaluate the options available and decide on the most acceptable. The importer may decide to use a number of services or routes between two countries to meet varying situations — air-freight for urgent goods, trailers for another movement, and containers as the regular core transit. The ultimate selection can vary by season and by quantity.

In a world where nations are trying to improve continuously their overall trade balance, an increasing number of buyers (importers) are insisting on shipment by their own national airline or shipping service, irrespective of the commercial advantages of using competitors. This involves flag discrimination and cargo preference laws which are fully explained in *Economics of Shipping Practice and Management*, Chapter 18 (see Appendix A). Such a policy enables the buyer's country to have control over the cost of such transportation and ensures the payment of freight is in a local currency and not in a foreign currency which adversely affects the trade balance of the buyer's nation.

Today more and more importers are setting up their own shipping departments to undertake all the distribution arrangements of their imported product. Many buy EXW, DAF, or FOB and conduct their arrangements through a forwarding agent in the seller's country. This policy is especially common to the buyer situated in an Eastern Bloc territory, less developed countries (LDCs), and newly industrialized countries (NICs.) In situations of bulk commodities imported in complete shiploads the buyer will provide the vessel which usually is chartered tonnage.

The following are the more important aspects for the importer to consider in the evaluation of international transport arrangements.

The nature of the commodity. Dimensions, weight and whether any special facilities are required for it during the transit (for example livestock requires special facilities and meat requires refrigerated accommodation). This is a major consideration and the importer must liaise closely with the exporter and carrier to determine the most acceptable method of transportation on a cost-effective basis. The product must be made or packaged with a view to attaining the most productive use of available shipping capacity and lessening the risk of broken stowage. For example, for full container load shipments, careful and skilful stowage planning might increase the number of units in a container by 10%, and also result in less broken stowage. A 10% improvement in container capacity utilization lowers the unit distribution cost of the commodity shipped and thereby improves the buyer's market penetration through more competitive pricing and favourable profit levels.

The degree of packing and cost thereof. This requires constant evaluation by the importer in liaison with the seller and carrier. Test transits should be conducted to ensure the best packing, taking into account continuing improvements in packing technology and improved quality distribution systems. The buyer must strike a balance between effective packing aiding stowage, handling and protection of the goods, and an acceptable minimum risk of damage and pilferage to produce a competitive insurance premium. Overall, packing cost can form a very significant proportion of the overall distribution expense varying from 2 to 6% of the market value of the product. The longer the transit distance the higher the percentage. Air-freight requires very limited packing especially when the goods are affixed to a pallet with the cargo enveloped in a plastic cover to protect it from scratching, dust, moisture, etc. Containerization and trailer movement cargo, such as found in the European markets under consolidation arrangements, requires limited packing. However, for cargo shipped under break-bulk conditions involving 'tween deck tonnage, extensive packing is required to afford adequate protection. The importer may find it advantageous to appoint, in the seller's country, a forwarding agent who also specialises in packing.

Ease of handling in a particular transport mode. For example, palletized cargo facilitates handling by fork-lift truck whilst cartons are ideal for containers and facilitate stowage or stacking. Conversely, the awkwardly-shaped cargo may require special handling arrangements and may be subject to a freight surcharge; such consignments encourage broken stowage and tend to be more prone to damage which increases their insurance premium level. Ideally, the consignment should be easy to handle from the time it leaves the factory premises until it reaches the retailer. Importers must liaise closely with the carrier, seller and their overseas agent to ensure the handling needs in the buyer's country reflect the type of packing adopted.

Any statutory obligations imposed relative to the transit.   Certain products need special facilities, both in transport mode and terminal. This in itself restricts choice of route and transport mode. For example, the movement of meat and offal requires special shipping facilities and inspection facilities at the terminal. Additionally, most countries have weight and length restrictions on road vehicles. This is particularly relevant to weight of containers. Likewise there are restrictions on lorry driver's hours and some EC countries restrict road haulage movement at weekends. Statutory obligations also influence the type of packaging, for example, as found in the Australian trade in the use of straw/wood (where such material has to be fumigated) and marking of cargo.

Transport systems available in countries in question.   The nature of the transportation systems in both the seller's and buyer's country, including the collection and delivery arrangements, are basic to choice of arrangements. Generally speaking, in most Western economies the transport infrastructure is well organized and uses much advanced technology to integrate with seaports and airports. In LDCs the transport network tends to be primitive in parts, with limited rail and road networks. In many situations the containers, for example, rarely go beyond the port environs and are stuffed and unstuffed within the port authority domain. Security and work practices tend to be outmoded and sluggish. The importer must aim for the most modern transport system which will aid trade development.

The overall market image of the company or importer.   There is a strong tendency for the buyer's company to select a transport mode in keeping with its market image. For example, a multinational company tends to select a reliable modern service rather than one prone to delays, disputes and damage which may offer cheaper rates.

Distribution factors.   In an increasing number of LDCs, the tendency is to market their commodity products through marketing boards. At the same time, agricultural husbandry storage techniques and quality control continue to improve. This might make possible all-the-year-round, rather than seasonal, distribution from the producer's country. This aids the international distribution of the product.

Dangerous cargo.   Stringent rules apply regarding packaging, stowage and mixture with other cargoes during stowage. This can restrict routeing, service and schedules. Close liaison must be maintained between the buyer, seller, carrier and buyer's overseas agent to ensure that arrangements are satisfactory. Regulations are becoming more stringent (see pages 53-4).

Suitability of available transport services. For example, air-freighters have limited capacity in terms of both weight and dimensions, and the cargo may require extensive collection and delivery arrangements. On the other hand, it offers fast transits and reduced packaging needs. In contrast, a deep-sea container service will have a much slower transit, probably less collection and delivery expense (if it is a consolidated consignment), slightly more packing expense, less frequent service, but lower freight rates. The Ro/Ro operation will have similar features to the containerized consolidated consignment, except that in the UK–Continent trade the transit time is likely to be more competitive with air.

This aspect requires very careful consideration. Importers may be able to use their own vehicles to distribute their products in the Continent–UK trade. In exceptional circumstances the importer may resort to chartering an aircraft or vessel if sufficient cargo is available; alternatively, the importer may find it more convenient to ship the cargo over a prescribed period rather than on a single chartered shipment.

The transit time and related urgency of consignment. To determine the overall transit time one must bear in mind the periods of collection and delivery of the cargo. Air-freight services offer the fastest schedules and are particularly suited to the urgent consignment. The importer is frequently placed in a situation where goods are required urgently and in such circumstances full use should be made of an IATA agent in liaison with the seller.

Quantity of cargo and period over which shipment is to be made. In broad terms, the greater the quantity available for shipment, the lower the overall distribution cost per unit weight. For example, if the importer can originate a full container or trailer load, the overall freight will be much cheaper than despatching the cargo under consolidation arrangements. Furthermore, a guaranteed substantial quantity of cargo conveyed over a period of time under contractual arrangements could attract a concessionary tariff. Again, if the circumstances are favourable, it may be advantageous to charter an aircraft or ship. There may be a case for centralizing all the imported products in one country and operating a distribution centre therefrom to neighbouring countries. This will encourage full-load containers or trailers which will lower distribution cost compared with despatching the goods direct to the various countries concerned under consolidated arrangements.

Insurance of cargo. An increasing number of importers undertake their own insurance arrangements in their own country, thereby saving hard currency, and facilitating the insurance arrangements and the processing of any cargo claims. The level of premium is determined by numerous factors but it is primarily the nature of the cargo, the mode of transport, the type of packaging and finally the case history of hand-ling such business by the underwriter. Air-freight cargo insurance with its quick transits and low risk of damage and pilferage tends to have the most favourable premium rates. Container shipments and trailer movements offering door-to-door or warehouse-to-warehouse shipments with no transhipment of cargo in transit countries offer very competitive premiums.

Terms of export sales contract. The importer (buyer) is the party who has the final say regarding the terms under which the goods are bought. Obviously the buyer will take many factors into account, especially market conditions and the range of export contract options offered by seller. Ultimately, the export terms usually reflect the custom of the trade and previous experience between the seller and buyer in regard to the sale of the goods. In recent years the importer has tended to exercise more dominance in the negotiations and become more involved in the distribution arrangements. There are 13 Incoterms 1990 (see pages 178-82) and the importer must decide which is the most suitable. Substantial savings of hard currency can be achieved by importers carrying the goods on their national shipping lines or airlines, and concluding the insurance cover in their own country.

Freight and documentation. In broad terms, the actual cost of sea-freight tends to be very much lower than air-freight, in terms of freight. However, such costs cannot be considered in isolation as one must bear in mind the total distribution costs — packing, insurance, etc., — to obtain a fair assessment. Air-freight tariffs, compared with road and rail, tend to be high, but the margins lessen significantly the longer the transit. Documentation cost between various transport modes do not vary a great deal but with the development of the combined transport concept in recent years (particularly involving road) and the through ISO container, documentation has tended to become simpler because of through-rates and consignment notes with no intermediate customs examination in transit countries.

Postal systems. If the commodity is a package of up 20 kg, it can be despatched through the parcel post system. The weight limitation varies by surface and air. Courier services may also be suitable for distribution of samples and documentation.

Thus, the importer, in consultation with the overseas agent and seller, must produce an overall distribution cost based on evaluation of realistic alternatives. The four most decisive factors are the terms of the export sales contract, commodity specification, freight and overall transit time, including service quality. Other factors embrace cost of packaging (very significant in air freight); convenience and reliability of service; charges for insurance, documentation and warehousing, — frequent service requires less storage in warehouse, reduced risk of product obsolescence, less working capital, facilitation of smoother production flow and better customer relations that emerge through a regular reliable service. Low risk of pilferage and damage, and the arrival of the goods in a quality condition are also significant factors.

14.3 TYPES OF AGENTS AND CRITERIA FOR APPOINTMENT

The great majority of importers conduct their business through an agent. The agent may be in the seller's country, arranging transportation and documentation of the goods; at the destination airport, seaport or ICD, arranging clearance of the goods through customs and despatch to the consignee's premises; a clearance agent at the airport or seaport undertaking the customs clearance and notifying the consignee of their arrival to collect, and so on.

14.3.1 Types of agents

The agent represents a principal (the buyer or seller); a brief description follows of the types of agents which can be employed by importers:

Freight forwarder. This is a company or person responsible for undertaking export and import arrangements on a client's behalf at a seaport, airport or ICD. At a seaport duties would include collection of freight; collection and issuing of Bills of Lading; notification of arrival and loading of goods; customs, import and export documentation; payment of duties and levies as necessary; issuing of landing accounts and certificates of shipment; and arranging sorting of cargo, cold-storage, warehousing and transport to destination. At an airport the role would be similar but involve the Air Waybill instead of the Bill of Lading. Some larger freight forwarders also offer a packaging service. In some countries the title given is 'shipping and forwarding agent'.

Port agent. An agent at a particular port is primarily involved with looking after the needs of his principal, usually a shipowner. In such a situation this would involve the provision of berth resources, cargo handling equipment, dock labour; transport distribution, customs clearance and so on. The port agent must ensure the prompt turn-round of the principal's vessels and the efficient processing of cargo including liaison between customer, consignor and consignee, and cargo collection and distribution. An importer can become involved with a port agent directly or through another agent.

Ship's agent.   The ship's agent represents the shipowner or master at a particular seaport. The agent's role is to give notification of the arrival and departure of the vessel; acceptance of vessel for loading; discharge, repairs, storing and victualling; arranging berths, tugs, ordering stevedores, cranes, equipment and so on. Port requirements include the needs of the master including stores, bunkers, provisions, crew mail and wages, engine and deck repairs; completion of customs, immigration, and port health formalities, collection of freight and issuing of Bills of Lading and so on. Sometimes the ship's agent represents the shipper, cargo owner or importer as well, for example when a vessel is under charter conveying a complete shipment of a bulk commodity such as rice, timber or grain. The agent then looks after the interest of both the shipowner and the cargo owner (the importer). This can create a conflict of interest, especially when a dispute arises, and it is advisable to have separate agents — a ship's agent for the shipowner and possibly a clearance agent for the cargo merchant (the importer).

Clearance agent.   One who represents a principal (the importer) and in so doing undertakes all the requisite documentation work and associated items to process a consignment through customs, thereby enabling the goods to be released and continue on their transit. Usually the clearance agent is situated at a seaport, airport or ICD and deals with imported cargo.

Receiver's agent.   One who represents a principal (the importer/receiver) and in so doing looks after the processing and facilitation of customs cargo clearance at a seaport or airport. At a seaport the receiver's agent may undertake the clearance of the cargo through customs or engage a clearance agent to do this work. The prime consideration is to ensure the merchandise is promptly processed through customs and discharged in an efficient, cost-effective manner following arrival of the ship in the port or its environs.

It will be appreciated that the range and description of agencies varies by country. In particular, the receiver's agent is widely used in many countries.

14.3.2. Criteria for selection of agents

In examining the criteria for appointing an agent one must bear in mind that individual circumstances will vary and the emphasis of some factors in the selection process can change as the importer's business develops. A commentary on the salient factors is given below:

1. The qualifications and calibre of the directors and senior managers of the agency. This requires careful evaluation of their previous experience in other companies and their loyalty and service to the agency. In some countries agency staff at all levels can experience a high turnover of personnel; usually one finds only the more able and ambitious person moves from one agency company to another.

2. The general market image of the importer. An up-market importer would tend to select an up-market agency to maintain the desired image in the market place.

3. The nature of the importer's business. Agents tend to specialize in handling particular products or a range of products. Accordingly, the importer should target those agents compatible with the company's products.

4. Emerging from the previous item, the experience of the agency in handling the type of business or product in question. For example, an importer who is a wholesale fruit merchant would require the agency to be aware of the best distribution methods and the importance of quick customs clearance to ensure the commodities arrived on schedule to catch the market. A late arrival could result in an inferior product and substantial financial loss.

5. The agent's tariff structure and general competitiveness in the market place. Price is a dominant factor in the agency evaluation but it must be reconciled with the quality of service, general reliability and the overall efficiency. An agent offering particularly cheap services can prove to be unreliable and provide a poor quality service. A significant proportion of most agency tariffs are determined by their trade association.

6. Any association with a legal dispute or fraud. This could have an adverse effect on the importer's market image.

7. Relationship with other organizations. The agent may be part of a large company which is competitive to the importer's business.

8. Conclusions of any market research exercise undertaken to find suitable receiver or agent. Shortlisted candidates should be researched further and discussions held with them before final selection. Trade associations offer valuable help and guidance in research.

9. Legal constraints in agency appointment and whether this reflects local conditions.

10. Age of company and its experience and contacts in the market. A

long-established company tends to have particular traditions and usually, market creditability. A younger company could project a modern image with high technology. The two have to be reconciled with the importer's needs.

11. Degree to which the agent projects a modern outlook and encourages staff training and adoption of modern techniques and technology. Usually the larger the agency the more financial resources they have available to modernize their infrastructure. Conversely, the smaller agency can offer a more personal service, with high technology in specific areas. Such information can be obtained by probing the company structure, activities and management style.

12. Membership of any trade association(s). This adds much creditability to the agency and can aid the selection process.

13. The last 3 years' annual published accounts. This will reveal the financial performance, the extent of any growth, and investment and profitability levels.

14. The agency agreement terms, which should have a termination clause. Some agency agreements are renewed annually, others are for a specific period, whilst others are used on an *ad hoc* basis. Legal advice should be sought to ensure the agreement is adequate with an arbitration clause to quicken the settlement of any disputes.

15 *Import planning and import strategy*

During the past 10 years, more and more companies have become involved in the importation of goods. In many situations such involvement has arisen due to force of circumstances and not resulted from any preconceived policy. The end result is sometimes that the company resources are not always used cost-effectively, nor the strategies well conceived. Hence senior management must devote adequate time and energy to effective planning and the evolvement of sound strategies.

When a company is committed to a policy of product importation it must earmark adequate resources in terms of personnel, finance, and accommodation for production, assembly and storage. Such figures should be incorporated in the company's annual budget. Import personnel should be professionally qualified in the area of processing the imported product and, where appropriate, should be linguists. The importer should take a keen interest in the supplier's product and technical development to ensure it is competitive in the market place and cost-effective to buy. Regular visits should be exchanged with the exporter. Company policy towards importation should be continuously reviewed with regard to cost-effectiveness and consumer needs, bearing technical and legal considerations in mind. Market research techniques should be employed to determine consumer needs and monitor the adequacy of the product or service. Both these factors can change quickly, so should be subject to frequent review.

15.1 IMPORT PLANNING

Import planning is the process whereby the company must decide which strategy to adopt in relation to its products or services and the options available and the resources which will need to be allocated in order to put the strategy into effect. It is the establishment of objectives and the formulation, evaluation and selection of the policies, strategies, tactics and action required to achieve these objectives. It will reflect the company's strategy both in the short and long term and the aim will be to execute the strategy cost-effectively and to realize a zero failure rate. It is a corporate function involving the company's resources of personnel, production and assembly, marketing in devising a strategy which will optimize the company's results in the market place.

1. Assessment of current situation

To execute the first stage it is usual to adopt the 'SWOT' analysis technique whereby the importer establishes the Strengths, Weaknesses, Opportunities and Threats of the present situation. Overall, this is an analysis of the pros and cons of developing an import-based strategy, including the following: specification and quality of product, components and materials; import controls and customs tariffs; technology; political stability of overseas territory; profitability; competitiveness of present strategy; experience with existing importing method of distribution and effectiveness and so on. It is called a situation analysis and involves seven stages. Each stage requires a close evaluation of the importer's company strategy and resources. This involves an explanation of the company objectives/business plan, budgetary formulation/control systems; level of profitability; company resources and their adequacy. A further aspect is the decision making process and how it will reflect any corporate policy inherent in a large multi-national company. In the smaller company with less resources in finance, personnel, production or assembly, etc., the planning procedure will be on a smaller scale but with the same objectives and disciplines.

The critical area is the objective analysis of the rationale for product or service importation. It may be a need for essential raw materials, that component parts are not available in the home market, or importation of a product for resale. The circumstances surrounding the decision to import will vary by company, and the options and risk in terms of cost and market demand will vary. Hence the need to have effective budgetary control techniques and continuous monitoring of the market situation.

2. The way forward

This results in a statement of objectives correlated to company resources (finance, personnel, production, research and development, etc.) For example, a company's product may lack advanced technology in one of its component parts so the company may resort to importation of the desired part to sustain the competitiveness of the product in the market place. The objectives must be realistic and profit-motivated within a time-scale. Contingency options must be evaluated and processed.

3. Methodology

The methodology is an important area and especially involves analysis of imported products, components, raw materials and services, and the overall impact on profit level and consumer acceptance. It also involves review of product specification to meet consumer needs in the home market, pricing strategy and its relationship with the importation costs and exchange rate fluctuation. Typical inputs comprise the following:

1. Independent review and analysis of importer's customer portfolio and how such clients' aspirations and goals are being matched relative to the current imported products. This involves market research techniques.
2. Screening of available products, components, raw materials and services with a view to choosing the best options ('best fit') in terms of cost, profitability, adequate home market share, competition, market development and so on. Any imported product or service profile in terms of price, quality, etc., should match up to the importer's company profile and its product and service projection.
3. In depth study of 'best fit' market to establish a product and service source strategy.

4. *Time-scale and schedule*
These require careful consideration. It is most important that the schedule is realistic and personnel in all departments are aware of their commitments. This involves detailed analysis of products, service and finances to decide the best option. It may involve the importation of a new product and consideration of the available overseas supply sources including quality, delivery terms and price. Alternatively, the importer may be reviewing the overseas supply sources of raw materials and looking for more reliable and improved quality suppliers. Overall, it includes the imposition of adequate control and monitoring techniques and the establishment of priorities within the agreed strategy of the business plan and the part import-led products and services play in such a situation.

5. *Monitoring the plan*
This requires detailed financial presentation incorporating all the elements of the plan. It involves optimization of the use of the company's resources and an appreciation of the logistics of the plan. One must bear in mind that the import manager is responsible for processing the imported products from the time the contract has been placed until the goods arrive on the importer's premises. This involves cost-effective funding of the product and distribution arrangements. Contingency plans should be drawn up to counter problem areas and shortcomings.

6. *Cost and method of funding*
The cost of executing the import plan and which members of the team will execute it must be determined. It will be appreciated the imported

product may involve a production or assembly process and marketing the product. All these areas involve various departments within the company and require effective co-ordination. Finally, an overview of the plan especially in the area of resource commitment. This embraces a financial appreciation especially in the risk areas and feasible options/alternatives both in the short and long term. A discounted cash flow analysis should be undertaken.

It will be appreciated any analysis is conducted against a background of available data and one cannot stress too strongly the need to have access to reliable information. Market research will play a part in such a situation.

15.1.1 Benefits of effective import planning

1. Resources are used to maximum advantage and a minimum unit cost criteria is developed, thereby facilitating the generation of a positive cashflow.
2. Competitiveness is maximized.
3. The best value for money is attained as the most favourable options are adopted.
4. The concept of 'management by objectives' is developed as personnel work towards an attainable goal and the formulation of the business plan and budget is facilitated.
5. Time-scale and work disciplines are developed within a company, which help to measure individual performance. Overall, they develop motivation at all levels within a company.
6. The risk of wrong decisions, negative attitudes and policies is minimized.
7. Available resources within a company are balanced against the market opportunities and alternatives, both overseas and at home.
8. The company resources are co-ordinated and personnel who have a commitment to the plan are better able to realize its objectives and the implications of any variation. Communication *esprit de corps* is developed within the company.

15.2 IMPORT STRATEGY

Import strategy and import planning are interrelated in their evaluation and objectives, namely to aid the development of a viable business plan for a company featuring imported products and services in a consumer-led and market-orientated competitive environment. Given below are the factors involved in the formulation of an import strategy.

Piggy-back concept. This is the process of importing product(s) with another importer, thereby lowering distribution costs. It can be co-ordinated by a freight forwarder and enable importers fresh to the business to gain experience and knowledge from an established importer operating in the same overseas supply source.

Centralized distribution. A number of importers situated in neighbouring countries may be importing a common product from the same buyer or exporter. The importation can be centralized to one country and distribution services operated to neighbouring territories to serve the individual exporters. The exporter can negotiate lower freight charges on a higher volume shipment basis: for example, exporter selling citrus fruit from the Far East to buyers in Germany Belgium, France, UK and Holland can centralize all the distribution on Belgium and operate distribution services to the other four countries.

Transport distribution analysis.   This is fully explained in Chapter 14. The importer evaluates the various transportation options and decides the most favourable one on the basis of cost, reliability, product quality on arrival, etc. This factor should be reviewed regularly in the light of changing transportation schedules, routes, tariffs and facilities, and volume of cargo shipped by the importer.

Joint venture.   This involves two trading companies from different countries (at least one being local such as the importer) forming an agree-ment to manufacture goods on a joint basis. Usually the importer provides the expertise on the local market needs and the workforce, whilst the exporter supplies the product specification, technology and management. The capital involvement is 50/50 or 51/49 in favour of the importer. The directors could be similarly apportioned. Other financial variations exist.

This option lessens the cost of importation and enables the joint venture company to export the product to neighbouring territories. Such joint ventures are on the increase in the UK and could well be set up in depressed industrial areas thereby enabling the company to obtain a government grant.

Licensing agreement.   A licence agreement can be negotiated between the importer and exporter, permitting the importer who is also the manufacturer to produce the commodity on a royalty payment basis. The name of the licensee or exporter and exporter brand name can be used. It is a low-cost method of importation and permits the importer to serve the home market and other neighbouring markets. The arrangements are monitored by the exporter by regular visits. The licence agreement is valid for 1—2 years and maybe subject to renewal conditions. All the manufacturing costs are met by the importer who controls the cost and price.

Import finance.   Payment for the imported product is a critical area of strategy and importers fresh to the business should take advice from an international bank. Various options exist including; open account (cheque, banker's draft, telegraphic transfer, international payment order, or international money order); documentary Bill of Exchange; Documentary Letter of Credit (confirmed, unconfirmed, irrevocable credit, or revocable credit). Foreign exchange has attendant risks. Three ways by which the importer can guard against exchange rate fluctuations are: forward foreign exchange contracts, foreign currency deposits and foreign currency accounts. Funding imports presents a number of options; sterling loan, foreign currency loan, product loans, and acceptance credit finance. All these require the most careful evaluation to determine strategy on a continuing basis and are fully explained in Chapter 7.

Counter trade.   This involves the sale of goods or services to a country which is linked contractually to an obligation to buy goods or services from that country. It is practised by over 100 countries and is usually master-minded by international banks to whom the importer is advised to contact for advice. It is unlikely to arise on a deal involving the direct importation of goods to UK, but could arise through switch trading involving a third party. Counter trade is fully explained in pages 189–191 of *Economics of Shipping Practice and Management* (see Appendix A)

Factoring.   It can help the importer who is involved in buying and selling aspects of the business at the expense of administration. International banks can give adequate advice to the importer. This involves the factoring company administrating the sales ledger and collecting payments on behalf of an Exporter once the goods have been shipped in accordance with the export sales contract.

Free trade zone.   An area usually associated with a seaport or airport which is treated as being outside the customs territory. It permits the unrestricted international exchange of goods. Duty is payable only when goods move into the host country. It is intended to attract foreign goods and investment; the importer can set up a business in such an area with many advantages, including investment grants. The subject is fully examined in *Elements of Port Operation and Management*.

Incoterms 1990.   Some 13 Incoterms exist, as explained in Chapter 10, for the importer to choose which is the most cost-effective for individual circumstances. FCA, Free carrier or FOB terms of sale enable the importer to decide the carrier and control physical distribution cost. Use of the importer's national carrier can save hard currency by dealing in the importer's own currency.

Administration of importation.   The importer of large volumes of cargo is likely to have an extensive organization under the import manager to process the cargo from the time the order has been accepted until the goods arrive — booking cargo space, negotiating rates with the carrier, processing documentation, and arranging payment. The extent to which the importer becomes involved is dependent on the cargo delivery terms such as EXW, FCA, FOB etc. A further factor is the amount of work entrusted to the freight forwarder and the cost-effectiveness of such an operation. The import manager's staff will become highly professional in their task as they deal in specialized markets on a regular basis.

Choice of supplier.   A good exporter will liaise continuously with the importer to retain his custom and develop a good business relationship. Nevertheless the importer must continuously review the supply source to determine its adequacy and competitiveness. The importer fresh to the business, endeavouring to obtain a suitable supplier, should seek advice from the British Importers Confederation, the relevant importers' trade association or local Chamber of Commerce. Full details are found in Appendix C. At the same time the home market option must be reconsidered regularly.

Government attitudes.   Government attitudes towards importers vary by country. The UK is regarded as a free open market with no significant controls or protectionist policies. There is a high volume of imported products which are imported and later re-exported with some value added benefit, such as importing component parts and re-exporting the completed product. The strategy of relying on imported products and services requires continuous review by any importer in the light of changing government attitudes and impositions of controls and fiscal measures.

Market research.   This must continuously aid the importer in his strategy to ensure the goods meet the consumer needs in a competitive environment. It can be undertaken in consultation with the exporter and thereby gain the latter experience in other markets.

Market development and promotion.   This can prove costly to the importer. The exporter can make a contribution to such needs if appropriate.

The business plan.   The role imports play in the company business and the strategy behind such commitment should be reviewed continuously on a corporate basis.

15.3 THE FUTURE

The 1990s will undoubtedly be a period of great change, but they will also present opportunities that importers (overseas buyer) must grasp if they are to succeed.

Import practice techniques will continue to improve in all areas as the consumer and industrial markets become more competitive (not only in price, but also in acceptable product specification and after-sales service); greater emphasis on pre-shipment quality control; more emphasis on planning and import strategy; development of more strategic payment techniques; extension of the electronic data interchange (EDI) system; provision of more cost-effective distribution systems involving the continuing development of the combined transport operation; improved efficiency in customs clearance and processing; further expansion of the tendency for the importer to undertake control of all the transit distribution and cargo insurance arrangements; improved financial resourcing strategy; and so on. The culmination of the foregoing factors is the development of a viable import strategy which ensures that the best quality goods are secured at the lowest possible prices.

High professional standards are essential if the import and re-export industries are to develop on an efficient basis and thereby raise living standards throughout the world. It is hoped this book will make a modest contribution towards attainment of that objective, forming the basis for further study (see Appendix A) and becoming the *aide-mémoire* to the importer and overseas buyer.

Appendix A

RECOMMENDED READING

Branch, A.E. (1989) *Elements of Shipping*, 6th edn, Chapman and Hall, London.

Branch, A.E. (1988) *Economics of Shipping Practice and Management*, 2nd edn, Chapman and Hall, London.

Branch, A.E. (1986) *A Dictionary of Shipping/International Trade Terms and Abbreviations* (9000 entries), 3rd edn, Witherby, London.

Branch, A.E. (1984) *A Dictionary of Commercial Terms and Abbreviations* (6000 entries), Witherby, London.

Branch, A.E. (1989) *Import/Export Documentation*, 1st edn, Chapman and Hall, London.

Branch, A.E. (1990) *Multilingual Dictionary of Commercial International Trade and Shipping Terms* — English–French–Spanish–German (12000 entries), 1st edn, Witherby, London.

Branch, A.E. (1988) *Dictionary of English–Arabic Commercial, International Trade and Shipping Terms* (4500 entries), 1st edn, Witherby, London.

Mitchelhill, A. (1989) *Bills of Lading – Law and Practice*, 2nd edn, Chapman and Hall, London.

Schmitthoff, C.M. (1980) *The Export Trade*, 8th edn, Sweet and Maxwell, London.

Watson, A. (1990) *Finance of International Trade*, 4th edn, London Institute of Bankers.

Incoterms 1990, International rules for the interpretation of trade terms, International Chamber of Commerce publication No. 350.

Uniform Customs and Practice of Documentary Credits, International Chamber of Commerce publication No. 400.

Appendix B

INTERNATIONAL TRADE ORGANIZATIONS

Baltic and International Maritime
  Conference
19 Kristianiagrade
DK-2100
Copenhagen
Denmark

Baltic Mercantile and Shipping
  Exchange
St Mary Axe
London EC3 8BU
UK

International Air Transport
  Association (IATA)
26 Chemin de Joinville
1216 Contrin
Geneva
Switzerland

International Chamber of
  Commerce (ICC)
38 Cours Albert ler
75008 Paris
France

International Maritime
  Organization (IMO)
101–104 Piccadilly
London W1V OAE
UK

Organization for Economic Co-
  operation and Development
  (OECD)
2 Rue Andre Pascal
75775 Paris Cedex 16
France

Simpler Trade Procedures Board
  (SITPRO)
Venture House
29 Glasshouse Street
London W1R 5RG
UK

United Nations Commission on
  International Trade Law
  (UKCITRAL)
United Nations
New York
NY10017
USA

United Nations Conference on
  Trade and Development
  (UNCTAD)
Palais des Nations
CH – 1211 Geneve 10
Switzerland

Appendix C

IMPORTERS' FACILITATION ORGANIZATIONS

American Chamber of Commerce
75 Brook Street
London W1Y 2EB
UK

Anglo—Israel Chamber of
    Commerce
126—134 Baker Street
London W1M
UK

Arab—British Chamber of
    Commerce
42 Berkeley Square
London W1A 4BL
UK

Association of British Chambers of
    Commerce
212 Shaftesbury Avenue
London WC2
UK

Association of Oriental Carpet
    Traders of London
8 Baker Street
London W1M 1DA
UK

Australian—British Trade
    Association
6th Floor Dorland House
18—20 Lower Regent Street
London SW1
UK

Basketware Importers' Association
86—87 Westbourne Park Road
London W2
UK

Belgian Chamber of Commerce
36—37 Piccadilly
London W1V OPL
UK

Brazilian Chamber of Commerce
35 Dover Street
London W1X 3RA
UK

Britanny Chamber of Commerce
54 Conduit Street
London W1
UK

British Association of Canned and
    Preserved Food Importers &
    Distributors
15 Dufferin Street
London EC1Y 8NB
UK

British Chemical Distributors' and
  Traders' Association
126 Westminster Palace Gardens
Artillery Row
London SW1
UK

British Importers Confederation
69 Cannon Street
London EC4N 5AB
UK

British Jewellery and Giftware
  Association
27 Frederick Street
Birmingham B1 3HJ
UK

British Overseas Trade Board
  (BOTB)
1 Victoria Street
London SW1H OET
UK

British Photographic Importers'
  Association
c/o Binder Hamlyn
7—15 Lansdowne Road
Croydon
Surrey CR9 2PL
UK

British—Soviet Chamber of
  Commerce
2 Lowndes Street
London SW1
UK

British Sports and Allied Industries
  Federation
Prudential House
10th Floor (East Wing)
Wellesley Road
Croydon
Surrey CR1 9XY
UK

British Standards Institution (BSI)
Linford Wood
Milton Keynes MK14 6LE
UK

Canada—United Kingdom
  Chamber of Commerce
British Columbia House
1—3 Lower Regent Street
London SW1Y 4NZ
UK

Confederation of British Industry
  (CBI)
Centre Point
103 New Oxford Street
London WC1A 1DU
UK

Department of Trade and Industry
1 Victoria Street
London SW1H OET
UK

Freight Transport Association
  (British Shippers Council)
Hermes House
St Johns Road
Tumbridge Wells
Kent TN4 9UZ
UK

Fruit Importers Association
114—115 Fruit and Vegetable
  Market
New Covent Garden
London SW8 6LP
UK

German Chamber of Industry and
  Commerce
12—13 Suffolk Street
London SW1Y 4HG
UK

Glass and Allied Trades
  Association
69 Cannon Street
London EC4N 5AB
UK

Grain and Feed Trade Association
Baltic Exchange Chambers
24-28 St Mary Axe
London EC3 8EP
UK

HM Customs and Excise
Kings Beam House
Mark Lane
London EC4
UK

Honey Importers and Packers
  Association
6 Catherine Street
London WC2B 5JJ
UK

Imported Tobacco Products
  Advisory Council
2 Queensway
Redhill
Surrey RN1 1QS
UK

India Chamber of Commerce
20 Saville Row
London W1X 2DQ
UK

Institute of Bankers
10 Lombard Street
London EC3
UK

Institute of Chartered Shipbrokers
25 Bury Street
London EC3A 5BA
UK

Institute of Export
Export House
64 Clifton Street
London EC2A 4NB
UK

Institute of Freight Forwarders
Redfern House
Browells Lane
Feltham
Middlesex TW13 7EP
UK

International Chamber of
  Commerce (ICC)
ICC (United Kingdom)
Centre Point
New Oxford Street
London WC1A 1QB
UK

International Consumer Electronics
  Association
16a The Broadway
London SW19 1RF
UK

International Federation of Freight
  Forwarders Association (FIATA)
CH 8050
Zurich
Switzerland

Japanese Chamber of Commerce
  and Industry
Temple Court
11 Queen Victoria Street
London EC4
UK

Netherlands—British Chamber of
  Commerce
The Dutch House
307—308 High Holborn
London WC1V 7LS
UK

New Zealand—UK Chamber of
  Commerce Industry
6th Floor
Derland House
18—20 Lower Regent Street
London SW1Y 4PW
UK

Nigerian British Chamber of
  Commerce
75 Cannon Street
London EC4W 5AB
UK

Norwegian Chamber of
  Commerce
Norway House
21—24 Cockspur Street
London SW1Y 5BN
UK

Research Association for the Paper
  and Board Printing & Packaging
  Industries (PIRA)
Randalls Road
Leatherhead
Surrey KT22
UK

Simpler Trade Procedures Board
  (SITPRO)
Venture House
29 Glasshouse Street
London WIR 5RG
UK

Spanish Chamber of Commerce
5 Cavendish Square
London W1M ODP
UK

Swedish Chamber of Commerce
17 Charles Street
Mayfair
London W1X 7HB
UK

Toy and Giftware Importers
  Association
Trade Association Management
  Services Ltd.
Tamesis House
9 Wapping Lane,
London E1 9DA
UK

United Kingdom Trade Agency
  for Developing Countries
69 Cannon Street
London EC4N 5AB
UK

Watch and Clock Importers
  Association
278 Lymington Avenue
Wood Green
London N22 6JN
UK

British International Freight
  Association (BIFA)
Redfern House
Browells Lane
Feltham
Middx TW13 7EP
UK

Appendix D

PUBLICATIONS AVAILABLE TO HELP THE IMPORTER

ABC Air Cargo Guide
Business News — published by Department of Trade and Industry
Chambers of Commerce Journals and Newsletters
Croners reference book for Exporters
Exporter and Forwarder — annual publication
Export Direction ⎫
Export Times ⎬ contains data on import and re-exporting
Export Today ⎭
Freight Management
Freight News
Handy Shipping Guide
HM Customs and Excise Notices — available free from Information Officer, HM Customs and Excise, Kings Beam House, Mark Lane, London EC2 (see page 92)
Importers Handbook — annual publication of British Importers Association
Importing Today — bimonthly publication
Institute of Freight Forwarders Journal
Institute of Marketing Journal
International Chamber of Commerce
International Freighting Weekly
Lloyds List and Shipping Gazette
National newspapers including *Financial Times, Guardian, Independent, The Times, Sunday Times* and the *Observer* feature, from time to time, surveys on international trade and profiles on overseas markets which contain useful data for the importer.
The Economist
Transport — bimonthly journal of Chartered Institute of Transport. Various publications and handbooks (usually free) on import practice and import finance are available from the international major banks.
World Freight — BIFA magazine

Appendix E

INTERNATIONAL TRADE AND SHIPPING TERMS

A/C. Account current

Accepting bank. The bank which is to accept a Bill of Exchange under a credit

Accepting house. Finance house (often a merchant banker) specializing in financing foreign trade

Act of God. Any fortuitous act which could not have been prevented by any amount of human care and forethought

ADR. European agreement on the international carriage of dangerous goods by road

Advising bank. The bank through which the issuing bank advises its credit. It may be in the beneficiary's country or in another country

***Ad valorem* freight**. Freight rate based on percentage value of goods shipped

Affreightment. A contract for the carriage of goods by sea expressed in a Bill of Lading or Charter Party.

Agent. One who represents a principal, or buys or sells for another

Air Waybill. Air-freight consignment note

Amendment. An alteration to the credit. Advice of any alteration comes from the issuing bank only and must be advised to the beneficiary through the advising bank if there is one. Irrevocable credits cannot be altered without the consent of all parties to the credit. An International Finance definition

Applicant. The person, usually the buyer, on whose behalf the credit is issued. Sometimes known as the 'opener'. An International Finance definition

Arbitration. Method of settling disputes which is usually binding on the parties concerned

ATA Carnet. International customs document to cover the temporary export of certain goods (commercial samples and exhibits for international trade fairs and professional equipment) to countries which are parties to the ATA convention

AWB. Air Waybill

Back freight. Freight (additional) incurred through cargo being returned from destination port, usually because its acceptance was refused

BAF. Bunker adjustment factor — freight adjustment factor to reflect current cost of bunkers

Balance of trade. Financial statement of balance of a country's visible trade exports and imports

Beneficiary. The person to whom a credit is addressed and who may benefit from it.

BIFA. British International Freight Association — organization representing freight forwarders, express couriers, and intermodal transport operators

Bilateralism. Trade between two countries.

Bill of Exchange. Written request from a creditor to a debtor ordering the debtor to pay a specified sum to a specified person or bearer at a certain date

Bill of Lading (B/L). Receipt for goods shipped on board a ship signed by the person (or his agent) who contracts to carry them, and stating the terms on which the goods are carried.

B/L Tonne. Bill of Lading ton. The greater of weight or measurement of goods where one tonne is either 1000 kilograms or one cubic metre (freight tonne)

Bond. Guarantee to customs of specified amount of duty to be paid

BOTB. British Overseas Trade Board

B/P. Bills payable

Broken stowage. Space wasted in a ship's hold or container by stowage of uneven or irregularly-shaped cargo.

BSC. British Shippers Council

BSS. British Standards Specification

Blue book. Carriage of dangerous goods in ships. The Department of Trade and Industry's requirements for shipping dangerous goods on British vessels or any vessel in British ports

Box. ISO container.

Box rates. Container rates.

Break-bulk cargo. Goods shipped loose in the vessels hold and not in a container.

Bulk unitization. Means to consolidate multiple packages or items into a single load device.

CABAF. Currency and bunker adjustment factor — a combination of CAF and BAF

Cabotage. Leasing of containers to other operators to reposition them.

CAD. Cash against documents

CAF. Currency adjustment factor. Freight adjustment factor to reflect currency exchange fluctuations

C & D. Collected and delivered
Cargo manifest. Inventory of cargo shipped
Carr fwd. Carriage forward
CAP. Common Agricultural Policy
CB. Container base
CBR. Commodity box rates
CC/O. Certificate of Consignment/Origin
CENSA. Council of European and Japanese National Shipowners Association
Certificate of Origin (C/O). Document certifying the country of origin of goods which is normally issued or signed by a Chamber of Commerce or Embassy.
CFR. Cost and freight (named point of destination) – Incoterm 1990
CFS. Container freight station – place for packing and unpacking LCL consignments
CHIEF. Customs handling of import and export freight – to replace DEPS in the 1990s
CI. Consular invoice
CIF. Cost insurance freight (named point of destination) – Incoterm 1990
CIM. Convention Internationale concernant le transport des Marchandises par chemin de fer. International convention on carriage of goods by rail
CIP. Freight carriage and insurance paid (named point of destination) – Incoterm 1990
Clean Bill of Lading. A Bill of Lading which has no superimposed clause(s) expressly declaring a defective condition of the packaging or goods
Closing date. Latest date cargo accepted for shipment by (liner) shipment for specified sailing
CMI. Comite Maritime International – international committee of maritime lawyers
CMR. Convention relative 'au contract de transport international des Marchandises par vois de Route'. International convention on carriage of goods by road
C/N. Consignment Note
C/OC. Certificate of Origin and Consignment
COD. Cash on delivery
COGSA. *Carriage of Goods by Sea Act*
COI. Central Office of Information
Com/I. Commercial Invoice
COMPROS. The forum in which EC trade facilitation organizations meet
Conference. Organization whereby number of shipowners, often of different nationality, offer their services on a given sea route on conditions agreed by members.

Confirming bank. A bank other than the issuing bank which undertakes on its own responsibility to pay, accept, or negotiate under credit.

Consignee. Name of agent, company or person receiving consignment and to whom goods are addressed.

Consignor. Name of agent, company or person sending the consignment (the shipper)

Consolidation. Process of grouping together combatible cargo for despatch as one consignment by air, sea or road

Consul. Commercial representative of one country residing officially in another whose duties are to facilitate business and represent the merchants of his nation

COT. Customers own transport

COU. Clip-on unit. Portable refrigeration units

CP. Charter Party

CPT. Carriage Paid to (named point of destination) Incoterms 1990

CRN. Customs Registered Number. A number allocated by Customs and Excise to an exporter or agent (freight forwarder) for use when exports are to be entered under the Simplified Customs Procedure

CSC. Container safety convention — international convention for safe containers

CT. Combined transport — carriage by more than one mode of transport under one contract of carriage or Community Transit (EC)

CTD. Combined Transport Document as found in the Combined Transport Operators Bill of Lading

CTL. Constructive total loss — cargo insurance term

CTO. Combined transport operator — a carrier who contracts as a principal to perform a combined transport operation

Customs examination. Process of clearing import or export cargo through customs examination

CV. Certificate of Value

C/VO. Certificate of Value and Origin

CWE. Clearance without examination — cleared by customs without inspection

CY. Container yard — collection and distribution point for FCL containers

D/A. Documents against acceptance or deposit account

DAF. Delivered at frontier (named point) — Incoterms 1990

DES. Delivered Ex ship (named point of destination) — Incoterms 1990

DEQ. Delivered Ex Quay (named point of destination) — Incoterms 1990

DDP. Delivered duty paid (named point) — Incoterms 1990

DDU. Delivered duty unpaid (named point) — Incoterms 1990

Dead freight. Space booked by shipper or charterer on a vessel but not used

Deferred rebate. System whereby shippers are granted a rebate on freight for consistent exclusive patronage over a given period.

Del credere. Agent/broker guarantee to principal for solvency of person to whom he/she sells goods

Delivery order. A document authorizing delivery to a nominated party of goods in care of a third party. It can be issued by a carrier on surrender of a Bill of Lading and then used by a merchant to transfer title by endorsement

Demurrage. Charge raised for detention of cargo or ship (under charter) or transport unit for longer period than agreed. For example a vessel under charter when layday period is exceeded, or for detaining FCL container/trailer at CFS for longer period than specified in the tariff

Depot. A CFS or place where cargo is assembled, loaded or discharged

DEPS. Departmental Entry Processing System. Current computerized Customs entry processing system to be replaced by CHIEF in early 1990s

Detention. A charge raised for detaining a container or trailer at customer's premises for longer period than specified in tariff

Dis. Discount.

Discount. The purchase by a bank or finance house of a Bill of Exchange at its face value less interest

Discount Market. Process of selling and buying Bills of Exchange and Treasury Bills, and providing a market for short bonds

DISH. Data Interchange in Shipping. A system for exchanging data between carriers and merchants electronically

D/N. Debit note

D/O. Delivery order

Doc credit. Documentary credit

D/P. Documents against payment

Draft. A written order for payment as found in a Bill of Exchange

Drawback. Repayment of duty upon re-exportation of goods previously imported

Drawer. The person who issues a Bill of Exchange

D/S. Days after sight

DTI. Direct trader input

Dunnage. Wood mats etc. used to facilitate stowage of cargo

Dutiable cargo. Cargo which attracts some form of duty, that is, Customs and Excise, or VAT

DWT. Dead weight tonnage

EGGD. Export Credit Guarantee Department. HM Government-sponsored insurance on goods shipped against non-payment by reason of commercial and/or political risks as arranged

EC. European Community — often referred to as European Common Market

ECSI. Export cargo shipping instruction − shipping instructions from shipper to carrier

EDI. Electronic data interchange − computer processing of data.

EHA. Equipment handover agreement. Agreement acknowledging condition signed when taking over carrier's equipment and when returning it, incorporating terms of contract under which hirer takes over the equipment.

EPU. Entry procesing unit

ESC. European National Shippers Councils

ETA. Estimated time of arrival of a ship, flight or consignment

ETD. Estimated time of departure of a ship, flight or consignment

Exchange rate price. Price of one currency in terms of another.

EXW. Ex Works (named point) − Incoterms 1990

FAK. Freight all kinds. System where freight is charged per container, irrespective of nature of goods and not according to a commodity code tariff

FAS. Free alongside ship (named point of shipment) − Incoterms 1990

FCA. Free carrier (named place) − Incoterms 1990

FCO. Franco (free to named point) − Incoterms 1990

FCR. Forwarders Certificate of Receipt

FCL. Full container load. Arrangement whereby shipper utilizes all the space in a container which he packs himself

Feeder vessel. A short sea vessel used to fetch and carry goods to and from deep sea vessels.

FFI. For further instructions − used where final destination uncertain at time of shipment.

FIATA. International Federation of Freight Forwarders Association

FIO. Free in and out − charterer pays for cost of loading and discharging

FIO stowed. Free in and out and stowed − charterer pays for cost of loading and discharging cargo including stowage

FIO trimmed. Free in and out and trimmed − charterer pays for cost of loading and discharging cargo including trimming

Fixture. Conclusion of shipbroker's negotiations to charter a ship

Floating exchange rate. Currency rate which varies according to world trade distortions and is not subject to exchange control

Floating policy. Cargo policy which underwrites series of consignments declared FLT. Fork-lift truck

FOB. Free on board (named point of shipment) − Incoterms 1990

Forwarders Delivery Order. A document issued by a freight forwarder authorizing the entitled party to deliver the goods to a party other than the consignee shown on the consignment note.

FPA. Free of particular average − a cargo insurance term

Franco pour (French). Sender undertakes to pay fixed amount in carriage charges

Freely negotiable credit. A credit under which drafts or documents may be negotiated by a bank

Freight. The amount payable for the carriage of goods and sometimes used to describe the goods themselves

Freight ton. The tonnage on which freight is charged

G/A. General average — cargo insurance term

GATT. General Agreement on Tariffs and Trade

Groupage. Consolidation of several LCL consignments into a container or by road onto a trailer or by air as one overall consignment under agent sponsorship

Groupage agent. A freight forwarder who consolidates consignments such as LCL consignments to offer to a carrier as an FCL

GSP. Generalized Scheme of Preference

Guarantee. A bond usually issued by a bank in warranty of its customers performance, e.g. under a contract

Hague Rules. The 1924 International Convention on Carriage of Goods by Sea

Hague-Visby Rules. The 1968 revision of the Hague Rules

Hamburg Rules. The 1978 UNCTAD revision of the Hague Rules

H/H. Half height Container with a height of 4 feet

H/L. Heavy lift

High stowage factor. Cargo which has a high-bulk to low-weight relationship, e.g. hay

HMC. Her Majesty's Customs

Honour. To pay or accept a Bill of Exchange. International Finance definition

IATA. International Air Transport Association

ICAO. International Civil Aviation Organization

ICB. International Container Bureau

ICC. International Chamber of Commerce

ICD. Inland clearance depot. A place where import and export cargo is cleared through customs which may also be a CFS

ICS. International Chamber of Shipping

ICHCA. International Cargo Handling Co-ordination Association

IFIA. International Federation of Inspection Agencies

I/L. Import Licence

IMB. International Maritime Bureau — organization responsible for the prevention and detection of maritime fraud

IMDG code. International Maritime Dangerous Goods code. The IMO recommendations for the carriage of dangerous classified cargo by sea.

IMO. International Maritime Organization

Incoterms 1990. International rules for the interpretation of trade terms

Indemnity. Compensation for loss damage or injury

Inherent vice. A defect or inherent quality of the goods or their packing which of itself may contribute to their deterioration, injury, wastage and final destruction without any negligence or other contributing causes

IPR. Inwards Processing Relief

Irrevocable. Cannot be revoked or cancelled without the agreement of all parties to the transaction.

IRU. International Road Transport Union. Based in Geneva, its role is to develop national and international transport

ISO. International Standards Organization. Organization responsible *inter alia* for setting standards for container construction

Issuing bank. The bank which opens the credit initially and acts for the applicant

L/C. Letter of Credit — the document in which the terms of a Documentary Credit transactions are set out.

LCL. Less than container load. A parcel of goods too small to fill a container which is grouped by the carrier at the CFS with other compatible goods for the same destination.

LDC. Less developed country

LI. Letter of Indemnity — sometimes used to allow consignee to take delivery of the goods without surrendering the Bill of Lading which has been delayed or become lost.

LIC. Local Import Control

Liner. Vessel plying a regular trade route

Liner terms. Freight includes the cost of loading onto and discharging from the vessel

Loading broker. Person who acts on behalf of liner shipping company at a sea port

LO/LO. Lift on — Lift off. A container ship onto which and from which containers are lifted by crane

Low stowage factor. Cargo which has low-bulk to high-weight relationship, e.g. steel rails.

Lump sum freight. Remuneration paid to shipowner for charter of a ship or portion of it, irrespective of quantity of cargo loaded

MAFI. A six axle trailer used for Ro/Ro tonnage

Manifest. List of goods conveyed on a vessel

Market rate. Rate charged by brokers, discount houses, joint stock banks and other market members for the discounting of first class bills

Mates receipt. Document issued to the shipper for the ships cargo loaded from lighterage and later exchanged for Bill of Lading

Maturity. The date on which a usance bill of exchange becomes due for payment.

Measurement tonne. Freight rate cubic assessment measurement based on 1000 kilograms equals one cubic metre. A criteria used to calculate a freight rate W/M

MT. Mail transfer — a remittance purchased by the debtor from his banker in international trade

NCV. No commercial vaule

Negotiable Bill of Lading. A Bill of Lading capable of being negotiated by transfer or endorsement.

Negotiating bank. The bank which negotiates under credit. It may be a bank nominated by the issuing bank or any other authorized under credit

Negotiation. The purchase of a Bill of Exchange or documents (often misused by bank abroad to describe any method of settlement under credits)

Notify party. Most contracts involving transport overseas specify a party who is to be advised of the arrival of the goods. This may be the consignee himself or an agent, and his name and address must appear on the transport document such as Air Waybill, Bill of Lading, CMR note, CIM note, etc.

NSSN. National Standard Shipping Note

NVO(C)C. Non-vessel owning/operating (Common) Carrier. A carrier issuing Bills of Lading for carriage of goods on vessels which he neither owns nor operates

OBO. Oil bulk ore carriers — multi-purpose bulk carriers

O/C. Overcharge

OECD. Organization for European Co-operation and Development

OGL. Open General Licence

OOG. Out of gauge. Goods whose total weight or overall dimension for example exceed those of the container in which they are packed.

Open cover. A cargo insurance agreement covering all shipments of the assured for a period of time subject to a cancellation clause and a limit to the amount insured in any one ship

Over-valued currency. Currency whose rate of exchange is persistently below the parity rate

Paying bank. The bank which is to pay under the credit. It can be the issuing bank itself or a bank nominated by it, usually the advising confirming bank.

Per pro. On behalf of

PHA. Port Health Authority

P and I Club. Protection and Indemnity association. Carriers mutual liability carrier.

PIRA. Research Association for the Paper and Board, Printing and Packaging Industries

P/L. Partial loss — cargo insurance term

POA. Place of acceptance. Place where goods are received for transit and carrier's liability commences. Often called place of receipt.

POD. Place of delivery — where goods are delivered and carrier's liability ceases; proof of delivery — a signed receipt showing time and date of delivery of goods.

POR. Place of receipt — see POA entry

P to P. Port-to-Port — maritime carriage only as opposed to combined transport

Principal carrier. The carrier issuing a combined transport document regardless of whether or not goods are carried on his own or a consortium member's vessel

Recourse. The right to claim back a payment made. International banking term

Reefer. Refrigerated

Removal Note. Confirmation of goods cleared by customs

Revocable Credit. May be amended or cancelled at any time without prior notice to the beneficiary

RHA. Road Haulage Association

Ro/Ro. Roll on—Roll off. A large or small ferry type vessel onto which goods and containers can be shipped. Transhipment is usually via a ramp permitting the cargo to be driven on and off the vessel

SAD. Single Administrative Document. Customs declaration form for both import and export cargoes and transit document introduced in 1988

SCP. Simplified Clearance Procedure. A simplified procedure for the exportation of goods not liable to duty or restraint (export licences). Available to shippers who have an allocated CRN, whereby the customs export declaration may be lodged after shipment and only limited details need to be supplied beforehand, per copy of the shipping note

Settlement. The giving of consideration i.e. payment of money or acceptance of a Bill of Exchange in return for documents presented under a credit. International banking definition

SGS. Societe Generale de Surveillance

Shipper. The person tendering goods for carriage

Shipping invoice. Document giving details of merchandise shipped

Shut out. Cargo refused shipment because it arrived after closing date

Sight. The time when a draft is presented to the drawee for payment or acceptance. Under a sight credit the bank should settle immediately it is satisfied with the documents (unless the sight terms of the credit are in some way modified by its contents). Banks are allowed a reasonable time to check documents

Sine die. Indefinitely — without a day being appointed

SITC. Standard International Trade Classification. Method of classifying all types of goods used in customs tariff

SITPRO. Simpler Trade Procedures Board

SOB. Shipped on board. Endorsement on a Bill of Lading confirming loading of goods on a vessel

SSN. Standard Shipping Note

SST. Supplementary Service Tariff — tariff for services other than freight
Stale Bill of Lading. In banking practice, a Bill of Lading presented so late that consignee could be involved in difficulties
Straddle carrier. Vehicle for lifting and moving containers at a terminal or CFS
Straight Bill of Lading. An American term for a Sea Waybill
Stripping. Unpacking a container
Stuffing. Packing a container
Subrogation. Process of substituting one person for another in marine insurance matters in which the latter inherits the formers rights and liabilities
STVP. Short-term vehicle park
TAN. Transit Advice Note
Tariff. Terms, conditions and scale of charges
Terminal. Airport or seaport, for example, at which containers are loaded or unloaded from container vessels
Tenor. The period of time to maturity of a Bill of Exchange. Terms usually describe the conditions of the credit and the despatch of goods and the basis on which the payment amount is fixed. An international banking definition
TEU. Twenty foot equivalent unit, i.e. 1×20 ft = 1 TEU; 1×40 ft = 2 TEU
TIR. Transport International Routier. A set of rules following a customs convention to facilitate in particular international European transport with minimal customs interference. Overall it is a customs bond operative in about 90 countries
TL. Total loss
Tramp. Vessel engaged in bulk cargo or time charter business, i.e. not a liner vessel
Transferable credit. A credit issued by a bank in one country and advised or confirmed by a bank in a second country to a beneficiary in a third country, sometimes through a third bank in the beneficiary's country
Transport documents. Documents issued by the carrier such as Bill of Lading, Air Waybill, CMR and CIM consignment notes
Transhipment. Transfer of goods during their conveyance
Transhipment entry. Customs entry for cargo imported for immediate re-exportation
Trunking. Movement of containers or trucks between terminals or CFS
TT. Telegraphic transfer — a remittance purchased by the debtor from his banker in international trade
UCP. Uniform Customs and Practice of Documentary Credits — publication No. 400 issued by International Chamber of Commerce
ULCC. Ultra large crude carrier

ULD. Unit load device

UN. United Nations

UNCITRAL. United Nations Commission on International Trade and Law

UNCON. Uncontainable goods. Cargo which because of its dimensions cannot be containerized and which is conveyed other than in a container

UNCTAD. United Nations Conference on Trade and Development

UNCTAD MMO. UNCTAD Multimodal Transport of Goods Convention

Under-valued currency. Currency whose rate of exchange is persistently above the parity rate

Unit loads. Containerized or palletized cargo

Usance. The period of time to maturity of a Bill of Exchange (see also Tenor)

VAT. Value added tax

VDU. Visual display unit

VLCC. Very large crude carrier

WA. With average — cargo insurance term

Warranty. An implied condition, express guarantee or negotiation contained in a marine insurance policy

W/M. Weight/measurement option based on evaluation of weight and volume

WPA. With particular average — cargo insurance term

Waybill. A receipt for the cargo and evidence of the maritime terms of the contract of carriage; not a document of title

Note Readers are also recommended to study the *Dictionary of Shipping/ International Trade Terms and Abbreviations* — 9000 entries (see Appendix A).

Appendix F

WORLD CURRENCIES

Country	Currency
Afgahanistan	One Afghani = 100 Puls
Albania	One Lek = 100 Qindarka
Algeria (Republic of)	One Algerian Dinar = 100 Centimes
Andorra	Spanish Pesetas and French Francs
Angola	One Kwanza = 100 Lwei
Argentina	One Argentina Peso = 100 Centavos
Australia	One Australian Dollar = 100 Cents
Austria	One Schilling = 100 Groschen
Bahamas	One Bahamian Dollar = 100 Cents
Bahrain	One Bahrain Dinar = 100 Fils
Bangladesh	One Taka = 100 Paisa
Barbados	One Barbados Dollar = 100 Cents
Belgium	One Belgian Franc = 100 Centimes
Belize	One Belize Dollar = 100 Cents
Benin (Republic of)	Communauté Financière Africaine (CFA) Franc
Bermuda	One Bermuda Dollar = 100 Cents
Bolivia	One Bolivian Peso = 100 Centavos
Botswana	One Pula = 100 Thebe
Brazil	One Cruzeiro = 100 Centavos
Brunei	One Brunei Dollar = 100 Cents
Bulgaria	One Lev = 100 Stotinki

Country	Currency
Burma (Socialist Republic of the Union of)	One Kyat = 100 Pyas
Burundi (Republic of)	One Burundi Franc = 100 Centimes
Cameroon (United Republic of)	Communauté Financière Africaine (CFA) Franc
Canada	One Canadian Dollar = 100 Cents
Cape Verde Islands	One Cape Verde Escudo = 100 Centavos
Cayman Islands	One Cayman Dollar = 100 Cents
Central African Republic	Communauté Financière Africaine (CFA) Franc
Chad (Republic of)	Communauté Financière Africaine (CFA) Franc
Chile	One New Peso = 1000 Escudos
China (People's Republic of)	One Yuan (Renminbi) = 10 Jiao and 1 Jiao = 10 Fen
Colombia	One Peso = 100 Centavos
Comoros (Republic of the)	Communauté Financière Africaine (CFA) Franc
Congo (People's Republic of)	Communauté Financière Africaine (CFA) Franc
Costa Rica	One Costa Rica Colon = 100 Centimos
Cuba	One Cuban Peso = 100 Centavos
Cyprus (Republic of)	One Cyprus Pound = 1000 Mils
Czechoslovakia	One Czech Crown (Koruna) = 100 Hellers
Denmark (including the Faroe Islands and Greenland)	One Danish Crown (Krone) = 100 Oere
Djibouti (Republic of)	Djibouti Francs (related to the USA Dollar)
Dominican Republic	One Domincan Peso Oro = 100 Centavos
Ecuador	One Sucre = 100 Centavos
Egypt (Arab Republic of)	One Egyptian Pound = 100 Piastres = 1000 Millièmes
Equatorial Guinea (Rio Muni and Fernando Poo)	One Ekuele = 100 Centimos
Ethiopia	One Birr = 100 Cents
Falkland Islands and Dependencies	One Falkland Islands Pound = 100 Pence
Fiji Islands	One Fiji Dollar = 100 Cents

Country	Currency
Finland	One Markka (Finnmark) = 100 Pennia (Pennies)
France (including Monaco)	One French Franc = 100 Centimes
French Guiana and French Antilles	French Franc
French Polynesia and New Caledonia and Dependencies	Communauté Française du Pacifique (CFP)
Gabon (Republic of)	Communauté Financière Africaine (CFA) Franc
Gambia	One Dalasi = 100 Bututs
German Democratic Republic	One Deutschemark = 100 Pfennig
Germany (Federal Republic of)	One Deutsche Mark = 100 Pfennig
Ghana (Republic of)	One Cedi = 100 Pesewas
Gibraltar	One Gibraltar Pound = 100 Pence
Greece	One Drachma = 100 Lepta
Grenada	One East Caribbean Dollar = 100 Cents
Guatemala	One Quetzel = 100 Centavos
Guinea (Republic of)	One Syli = 100 Couris (Cauris, Cory)
Guinea Bissau	One Escudo = 100 Centavos
Guyana	One Guyanan Dollar = 100 Cents
Haiti	One Gourde = 100 Centimes
Honduras (Republic of)	One Lempira = 100 Centavos
Hong Kong	One Hong Kong Dollar = 100 Cents
Hungary	One Forint = 100 Fillér
Iceland	One Icelandic Crown (Krona) = 100 Aurar (Eyrir)
India	One Indian Rupee = 100 Paise (singular — Paisa)
Indonesia (Repulic of)	One Rupiah = 100 Sen
Iran	One Rial = 100 Dinars
Iraq	One Dinar = 1000 Fils
Ireland (Republic of)	One Irish Pound = 100 Pence
Israel	One Shekel = 100 New Agorot (singular — Agora)
Italy	One Lira = 100 Centesimi
Ivory Coast (Republic of)	Communauté Financière Africaine (CFA) Franc

Country	Currency
Jamaica	One Jamaican Dollar = 100 Cents
Japan	Yen
Jordan	One Jordan Dinar = 1000 Fils
Kampuchea (Democratic People's) Republic of)	One Riel = 100 Sen
Kenya	One Kenya Shilling = 100 Cents
Kiribati (Republic of) (formerly Gilbert Islands)	Australian Dollar
Korea (Democratic People's Republic of)	One Won = 100 Chon
Korea (Republic of)	One Won = 10 Chon
Kuwait	One Kuwati Dinar = 1000 Fils
Laos (People's Democratic Republic of)	One Kip = 100 Ats
Lebanon	One Lebanese Pound = 100 Piastres
Lesotho	One Loti = 100 Lisente
Liberia (Republic of)	One Liberian Dollar = 100 Cents
Libya (Libyan Arab Republic)	One Libyan Dinar = 1000 Dirhams
Liechtenstein (Principality of)	One Swiss Franc = 100 Centimes (Rappen)
Luxembourg (Grand-Duchy of)	One Luxembourg Franc = 100 Centimes
Macao	One Pataca = 100 Avos
Malagasy Republic (Madagascar)	Madagascar Francs (MG.Frs)
Malawi	One Kwacha = 100 Tambala
Malaysia	One Malaysian Ringgitt = 100 Sen
Maldives (Republic of)	One Maldivian Rupee = 100 Larees
Mali (Republic of)	Mali Franc (M.Frs)
Malta	One Maltese Pound = 1000 Mils
Mauritania (Islamic Republic of Mauritania)	One Ouguiya = 5 Khoums
Mauritius	One Mauritius Rupee = 100 Cents
Mexico	One Mexican Peso = 100 Centavos
Mongolia (People's Republic of)	One Tugrik = 100 Mongo
Morocco (Kingdom of)	One Dirham = 100 Centimes
Mozambique	One Metical = 100 Centavos
Nauru (Republic of)	One Australian Dollar = 100 Cents

Country	Currency
Nepal (Kingdom of)	One Nepalese Rupee = 100 Pice
Netherlands (Holland)	One Guilder (Florin) = 100 Cents
Netherlands Antilles (Netherlands West Indies)	One Antillian Guilder (Florin) or (Netherlands Antilles Florin-NAF) = 100 Cents
New Zealand (including Ross Dependency)	One New Zealand Dollar = 100 Cents
Nicaragua	One Cordoba = 10 Centavos
Niger (Republic of)	Communauté Financière Africaine (CFA) Franc
Nigeria (Federation of)	One Naira = 100 Kobo
Norway	One Krone = 100 Oere
Oman	One Rial Omani = 1000 Baiza
Pakistan	One Pakistan Rupee = 100 Paisa
Panama	One Balboa = 100 Centesimos
Papua New Guinea	One Kina = 100 Toea
Paraguay	One Guarani = 100 Centimos
Peru	One Sol = 100 Centavos
Philippines (Republic of)	One Philippine Peso = 100 Centavos
Poland	One Zloty = 100 Groszy
Portugal (including Azores and Madere)	One Escudo = 100 Centavos
Puerto Rico (Commonwealth of)	One US Dollar = 100 Cents
Qatar	One Qatar Riyal = 10 Dirhams
Reunion Island	One French Franc = 100 Centimes
Romania	One Leu = 100 Bani
Rwanda (Republic of)	One Rwanda Franc = 100 Centimes
St. Helena Island (including Ascension Islands)	Currency rates issued by St. Helena Currency Board (with Sterling parity)
El Salvador	One Colon = 100 Centavos
Sao Tome and Principe	One Dobra = 100 Centimos
Saudi Arabia	One Riyal = 100 Halalas
Senegal (Republic of)	Communauté Financière Africaine (CFA) Franc
Seychelles	One Seychelles Rupee = 100 Cents
Sierra Leone	One Leone = 100 Cents
Singapore (Republic of)	One Singapore Dollar = 100 Cents

Country	Currency
Solomon Islands	One Solomon Islands Dollar = 100 Cents
South Africa (Republic of)	One Rand = 100 Cents
Spain (including the Canary Islands, Ceuta and Melilla)	One Peseta = 100 Centimos
Sri Lanka	One Rupee = 100 Cents
Sudan (Republic of the)	One Sudanese Pound = 100 Piastres = 1000 Millièmes
Surinam	One Surinam Guilder (Florin) = 100 Cents
Swaziland	One Lilangeni = 100 Cents
Sweden	One Krona = 100 Oere
Switzerland	One Swiss Franc = 100 Centimes (Rappen)
Syria (Syrian Arab Republic)	One Syrian Pound = 100 Piastres
Taiwan (Republic of China)	One New Taiwan Dollar = 100 Cents
Tanzania (United Republic of Tanganyika, Zanzibar and Pemba)	One Tanzanian Shilling = 100 Cents
Thailand	One Baht = 100 Satang
Togo (Republic of)	Communauté Financière Africaine (CFA) Franc
Tonga (Kingdom of) (Friendly Islands)	One Tonga Dollar (Pa'anga) = 100 Seniti
Trinidad and Tobago	One Trinidad Dollar = 100 Cents
Tunisia (Republic of)	One Tunisian Dinar = 1000 Millimes
Turkey	One Turkish Pound (Lira) = 100 Kurus
Tuvalu	Australian Dollar
Uganda (Republic of)	One Uganda Shilling = 100 Cents
United Arab Emirates	One Dirham = 100 Fils
United Kingdom	One Pound (Sterling) = 100 Pence
United States of America (including Virgin Islands of the USA, Guam, American Samoa and Panama Canal Zone)	One US Dollar = 100 Cents
Upper Volta (Voltaic Republic)	Communauté Financière Africaine (CFA) Franc

Country	Currency
Uruguay	1000 Uruguayan Pesos = One New Uruguayan Peso = 100 Centesimos
USSR	One Rouble = 100 Kopecks
Vatican City State	One Lira = 100 Centesimi
Venezuela	One Bolivar = 100 Centimos
Vietnam (Socialist Republic of)	One Dong = 100 Xu
Virgin Islands (British)	One US Dollar = 100 Cents
West Indies (East Caribbean Area)	One East Caribbean Dollar = 100 Cents
Western Samoa	One Tala = 100 Senes
Yemen Arab Republic	One Riyal = 100 Fils
Yemen (People's Democratic Republic of)	One South Yemen Dinar = 1000 Fils
Yugoslavia	One Dinar = 100 Paras
Zaire (Republic of)	One Zaire = 100 Makuta = 10 000 Sengi
Zambia	One Kwacha = 100 Ngwee
Zimbabwe	One Zimbabwe Dollar = 100 Cents

Index